Sex in the Head
◆
Visions of Femininity and Film in D.H. Lawrence

Linda Ruth Williams

University of Liverpool

**HARVESTER
WHEATSHEAF**

New York   London   Toronto   Sydney   Tokyo   Singapore

First published 1993 by
Harvester Wheatsheaf
Campus 400, Maylands Avenue
Hemel Hempstead
Hertfordshire, HP2 7EZ
A division of
Simon & Schuster International Group

Typeset in 10/12pt Sabon
by Hands Fotoset, Leicester

Printed and bound in Great Britain by
BPCC Wheatons Ltd, Exeter

British Library Cataloguing in Publication Data

A catalogue record for this book is available from
the British Library

ISBN 0-7450-1330-9 (hbk)
ISBN 0-7450-1331-7

1 2 3 4 5 97 96 95 94 93

For Mark Kermode
and in memory of Allon White

'Then it became an orgy, making pictures'
– D.H. Lawrence, 'Making Pictures'

◆
Contents

◆
Preface and acknowledgements

The autumn of 1992 was an eventful time in the colourful posthumous career of D.H. Lawrence. Four incidents in particular ensure that his controversial profile remains high, and demonstrate the sublime and the ridiculous ways in which his influence is still felt. Most importantly, the new uncensored Cambridge University Press edition of *Sons and Lovers* appeared in September, including scenes, phrases, and words which could not be included for reasons of obscenity when the novel was originally published. In tandem with this, three televisual events used Lawrence more and less faithfully: Ken Russell completed filming his television adaptation of *Lady Chatterley's Lover*, and in the Channel 4 arts slot 'Without Walls' came a discussion of surreptitious homoeroticism in Lawrence's work ('Dark Horses', 27 October 1992). Finally, riding on the discovery by the pornography industry that women like porn too, Simitar Entertainment released in England an erotic video for women called 'Dream Dates', which features two fantasy scenarios, one of which is called 'The Game Keeper'. On the sleeve we are invited to 'Be Lady Chatterley as the rugged game keeper takes you nude picnicking, takes you skinny dipping, and then just takes you'. Whilst the literary Mellors only ever does the last of these, it is testament to the notoriety and force of *Lady Chatterley's Lover* that over sixty years after the book was written and over thirty years after its famous trial, the marketers of sex videos for women in the 1990s consider Mellors a potent enough fantasy figure to merit a large financial investment in the ghost of his image.

As this book will demonstrate, Lawrence would have despised each of these visual events, yet his texts continue to lend themselves to such popular reworkings. Against the grain of his polemic against cinema, 'deviant' or 'inauthentic' (as he characterised it) sexuality, and the pornographic gaze of women, another Lawrence lurks who embraces all of the things he fears and loathes. Lawrence is not simply the dark masculine soul he would persuade us of, he is also the eager feminine voyeur he disavows; more sexually divided than heterosexual prophet, the Lawrence who would close the eyes of his culture is also the orgiastic picture-maker. The tension between these two Lawrences is the subject of this book.

Throughout this book I have wherever possible used recent Penguin editions of Lawrence's works, referring across to the Cambridge editions where necessary. I am grateful to Laurence Pollinger Ltd and the Estate of Frieda Lawrence Ravagli for granting me permission to quote from Lawrence's works. I would also like to thank Josie Dixon at Cambridge University Press for giving me access to the new Cambridge version of *Sons and Lovers* ahead of publication in 1992.

I must first of all thank Jacqueline Rose, who supervised this study at its origin as a doctoral thesis, for her generous support, astute advice and unfailing encouragement. This book would not have been written without the inspiration I gained from her teaching. My teachers at Sussex University, but in particular Allon White, helped me to gather together confidence and intellectual courage, and I owe them a great debt. Allon is much missed, but it is not only his writing which continues to have an influence; he was a superb teacher and that work also continues.

Isobel Armstrong, Homi Bhabha, and Briar Wood read and commented on this work in its early stages and encouraged me in its development. I would also like to thank Jackie Jones at Harvester Wheatsheaf for her continuing faith and interest in this project, and Louise Wilson for seeing the book through production. In my tour of temporary academic jobs at British universities I have encountered many colleagues who have also offered strong advice. As Lees Fellow at Manchester University I was given the space to develop some of this work, and I am extremely grateful to colleagues at Exeter University, in particular to members of the Michael Wood's Theory and Text group, who have commented enthusiastically on versions of two of these chapters. Richard Maltby's advice about the uses of Nirex has stayed with me through the writing of this book.

I would also like to thank students taking the 'Visions of Excess' course at Liverpool University in 1991–2, and my colleague on that course, Geoff Ward, for providing me with a fine context within which to work through the relationship between film and literary transgression. Robert Fawcett, Janice Hoadley, Paul Simpson, Marion Wynne-Davis and Nigel Floyd have responded with indulgence and good-humour when I have forced my obsessions upon them; in particular I would like to thank Nigel for giving me access to his dissertation on voyeurism, and for his general argumentativeness and energetic devil's advocacy.

Finally, I must thank Mark Kermode, for his love and practical support, his meticulous and imaginative comments on this book, and for his spectacular commitment to the visual.

◆
Introduction
Lawrence, cinema and female spectatorship

The importance of the word 'Darkness' in the work of D.H. Lawrence cannot be underestimated. More than simply the absence of light, darkness is a state of being, a blind virtue, the true goal of authentic masculinity. The word is repeated to the point of nonsense and laboured at key spiritual moments in Lawrence's fictional texts to signify positive sexual and unconscious states. And just as the dark, 'blind' self is central and positively valued, so the conscious, visually fixated modern soul is denigrated. Lawrence's philosophy of life and sexual identity rests upon the tension between the two, and so darkness and light, blind sex and what he called 'sex in the head' are consequently gendered. Sex in the head is sex made visible, sex in the wrong place and aroused to visual pleasures. Darkness is the realm of the valorised macho superhero, whilst women too often prefer the illuminated world of conscious control, sexual inauthenticity, visual engagement (the qualities of Lawrence's so-called 'Cocksure woman'[1]):

> Teach a woman to act from an idea, and you destroy her womanhood for ever. Make a woman self-conscious, and her soul is barren as a sandbag. Why were we driven out of paradise? . . . Not because we sinned. Ah, no. All the animals in Paradise enjoyed the sensual passion of coition. Not because we sinned, but because we got our sex into our head.
>
> When Eve ate that particular apple, she became aware of her own womanhood, mentally. And mentally she began to experiment with it. She has been experimenting ever since. So has man. To the rage and horror of both of them.[2]

D.H. Lawrence had little to say about cinema, the new cultural form which was growing up around him, but what he did write was negative. He had much more to say about modern femininity, and the vision of women, and rather a lot of that was negative too. How Lawrence articulates and

1

'genderises' his visual vices and dark virtues is the subject of this book. To see or not to see, that is Lawrence's question. It is a question which has implications for the whole organisation of sexual difference and power. Far from celebrating the darkness, this book concentrates on the convergence of these antipathies towards women and vision, and the anxious disavowal which accompanies that convergence. It discusses how, despite his negative pronouncements, Lawrence contradicts himself, enjoying the visual, experimenting with forms of narrative which are cross-fertilised by cinema technique, looking with the eyes of femininity.

From the perspective of Lawrence the cine-phobe and macho misogynist, this conclusion might yet seem a long way off. Since his misogyny is perhaps more famous than his film phobia, here is a brief précis of his sporadic diatribe against the new form, which remained remarkably consistent throughout Lawrence's changeable writing career. In *The Lost Girl*, the novel which contains his most sustained critique of cinema, a music hall performer sets up an opposition between her own live – but dying – art, and the burgeoning form of film, prioritising live speech over celluloid words:

> 'The pictures are cheap, and they are easy, and they cost the audience nothing, no feeling of the heart, no appreciation of the spirit, cost them nothing of these. And so they like them, and they don't like us, because they must *feel* the things we do, from the heart, and appreciate them from the spirit. . . . They want it all through the eye and finished – so!'[3]

A character in a novel speaks here, but this is a message which is borne out in a number of other places. In the poem 'When I went to the film' from the *Pansies* collection, what the 'I' sees is not the film itself but 'all the black-and-white feelings that nobody felt'.[4] Cinema is only there to divide viewers from themselves, and so the audience sighs and sobs 'with all the emotions they none of them felt', couples cuddle 'with rising passions they none of them for a moment felt', they moan 'from close-up kisses, black-and-white kisses that could not be felt'. Cinematic pleasure is 'flat ecstasy, supremely unfelt', experienced by 'shadows of people, pure personalities/. . . cast in black and white'.

But Lawrence wrote plays, which might seem to take him too close to the spectacle industry for comfort. In his non-fictional discussions of entertainment Lawrence often pits the merits of theatre – live spectacle, with its roots in a primitive but divine form of 'entertainment' – against the debased scene of cinema. Indeed, several times in his travel writings full discussions of live spectacles – theatrical productions, or Indian dances – are offered, but never does he go into details about a film he saw. Writing in 1913, well before the arrival of the talkies, cinema, for Lawrence, only appears and appeals to one sense (vision), and it is fast taking over from organised religion as the focal point of the community and the week:

> The theatre is an old church. Since that triumph of the deaf and dumb, the cinematograph, has come to give us the nervous excitement of speed – grimace agitation, and speed, as of flying atoms, chaos – many an old church in Italy has taken a new lease of life.[5]

In its fascination with the movement-image[6] cinema captures only the futuristic quality of 'nervous excitment', an emotional state consistently aligned across Lawrence's work with modern feminine sexuality. Cinema is conscious, frenetic, neurotic; its appeal is only to the eye, rather than to the whole self, its excitements are only mental. Its dubious sexuality is consequently situated, replayed and enjoyed, in the head of the viewer. Cinema is sex in the head made flesh, made film. In representing its world as the world-in-movement, it privileges a tendency to chaos, its movements throw fragments outwards. It cannot gather images into organic wholes, it cannot offer to centre the subjects in its audience.

Whilst this seems to add up to a discrimination between live and dead looking, theatre and cinema, a positive form of audience empathy set against a negative form of cinematic, uninvolved (and therefore irresponsible) spectatorship, what Lawrence does throughout his travel-writing discussions of entertainment is scrutinise the audience. He is often far more interested in looking at how his fellow spectators are looking than in watching the spectacle itself. For instance in 'The Theatre' (the third essay of *Twilight in Italy*) the theatrical spectacle is the theatre itself, its framing boxes and exposed seats below, not what goes on on the stage: 'I loved the theatre, I loved to look down on the peasants, who were so absorbed' (Italy, 82). His primary view is of the audience, even of himself and his reactions as a member of the audience, manipulated into identifying with the figures on the stage, and as one of those seated above, who 'have all self-consciously posed in the front of their boxes, like framed photographs of themselves' (Italy, 86). Indeed, in the same essay Lawrence posits a version of T.S. Eliot's notion of 'dissociation of sensibility', and it is significant that it is a visual work – a play – which exposes the metaphysical splitting of the modern subject. *Hamlet* is 'the statement of the most significant philosophic position of the Renaissance. . . . The whole drama is the tragedy of the convulsed reaction of the mind from the flesh, the spirit from the self' (Italy, 76). By Lawrence's time, however, contemporary theatre no longer represents this anti-sensual extreme for Lawrence – cinema takes over that role as soon as it is born, freeing Lawrence himself to write more integrated plays. Although I will not look at Lawrence's dramatic writing in this book, its existence rests upon this important distinction. In all of his comparisons of cinema and theatre, the proximity of live bodies on a stage is privileged over the displacement of human contact in time and space which cinema relies upon. Cinema emerges from another space, filmed in the past; as Christian Metz puts it, 'theatre really does "give" this given . . . : it is physically present, in the same space as the spectator. The cinema only gives it in effigy, inaccessible from the outset, in a primordial *elsewhere* . . .'.[7]

Elsewhere in Lawrence, cinema is a much dirtier subject. Cinema and sex have been intimately connected for as long as the former has existed: sex and vision are old partners. The cinematic scene, from the audience's point of view, is highly charged. Elizabeth Bowen's evocative essay, 'Why I go to the Cinema' (written not long after Lawrence's death), cuts sharply across the predominant mid-1930s highbrow position on film, unashamedly celebrating this sense of cinema as a site of secretly indulged sensual pleasures:

> like a chocolate-box lid, the entrance is still voluptuously promising: sensation of some sort seems to be guaranteed. How happily I tread the pneumatic carpet, traverse anterooms with their exciting muted vibration, and walk down the spotlit aisle with its eager tilt to the screen. I climb over those knees to the sticky velvet seat, and fumble my cigarettes out.[8]

The dark closeness, a darkness which is compromised by the fixation on the intense light of the screen, the imposition of erotically charged powerful images, the irresponsibility of one's immobility in the dark, all pump up the pressure, and also contribute to Christian Metz's analysis of the spectator's position in *Psychoanalysis and Cinema*, at which I will look in some detail in this book. Not for nothing is cinema the site of secret sex. Not for nothing, then, does Lawrence despise it as the foster ground of the 'dirty little secret.' In Lawrence's essay 'Pornography and Obscenity' the very form and function of cinema is given to be essentially pornographic (whatever the content of the films); characterised by those telling little words which usually refer to disreputable women, it is, as the music-hall artist says, cheap and easy:[9]

> One might easily say that half the love novels and half the love films today depend entirely for their success on the secret rubbing of the dirty little secret. . . . So the cheap and popular love novel and love film flourishes . . . because you get the sneaking thrill fumbling under all the purity of dainty underclothes.[10]

In '*A Propos* of *Lady Chatterley's Lover*', cinema is the arena within which pure sexuality is furtively twisted into false, second-hand emotionalism: 'The radio and the film are mere counterfeit emotion all the time . . . people wallow in emotion: counterfeit emotion. They lap it up: they live in it and on it. They ooze with it.'[11] The repetition here is significant: Lawrence's fear is that this is going on *everywhere* – this is a fear of the popular. It also speaks a diffuse anxiety concerning the infusion of the cinematic into all aspects of that culture to which writing had hitherto been central – the rapid growth of the movie industry, and its invasion and possession of our emotional life. The possibility is being confronted that perhaps life cannot now be lived except within the emotional dictates of cinema, as if cinema itself were irradiating the cultural moment of modernism, an inescapable atmosphere, or something more abject than atmosphere: 'they *ooze* with it'.

So much for cinema. But as I have already indicated, this is not the end of the visual story. Not only does Lawrence despise cinema, the experience of looking *per se* is also deeply problematic. A wealth of novelistic and critical energy is spent denigrating the act of seeing in favour of the darkness of touch. Lawrence wants to close the eyes of our culture – at the risk, perhaps, of stopping us from reading his words and from beholding his paintings, for despite his visual antipathy, Lawrence was also a painter. Philosophically suspicious of looking, he also spent most of his time professionally engaged in artistic acts of looking, for his fiction is animated by visual scenes, dramas in which the gaze is focused and exchanged. Mary Ann Caws writes in connection with E.H. Gombrich's essay 'How to Read a Painting', that literary criticism is partly concerned with 'How to See a Text'.[12] Whilst this is certainly the form of criticism to which Lawrence's work is most strongly resistant, he is nevertheless the director of a body of dramas which show characters engaging in complex and revealing acts of vision, dramas which the reader would not 'see' if it were not for a spectator-in-the-text who shows us how we should see them whilst denying he or she is doing so. Even as a painter, Lawrence practically denied that vision was necessary; painting comes, it seems, from somewhere *beyond* vision, and ideally the viewer should respond to it in the same spirit: 'I disappeared into that canvas. . . . The knowing eye watches sharp as a needle; but the picture comes clean out of instinct, intuition and sheer physical action.'[13] In place of the visual cultural forms which rely on 'the knowing eye', Lawrence would substitute, as he puts it in *Women in Love*, a 'Pure culture in sensation, culture in physical consciousness, really ultimate *physical* consciousness, mindless, utterly sensual'.[14]

It is strange, then, that Lawrence should ever be called a 'seer', given his avowed suspicion of the act of seeing. The word is of course used in its more mystical visionary sense, to connote an intense perception or view of the heart, mind or emotions, or our future possibilities. Jane Davis's claim for his radical contemporary qualities, for example, allows her to term him a 'prophet and seer' in her essay in *Rethinking Lawrence*.[15] Critics have been reluctant to explore the irony involved in deploying this word, but it is a word which I want to take seriously. Later in 'Making

Pictures', Lawrence writes that 'The only thing one can look into, stare into, and see only vision, is the vision itself: the visionary image.'[16] This is a kind of visionary version of that strange knowledge convolution which is advocated in *Women in Love*, 'the knowledge which is the death of knowledge' (WL, 402). Here vision is disavowed by the act of transcendence; elsewhere it is bypassed as Lawrence's more prosaic and often feminine visionaries are metaphorically (and sometimes actually) blinded. Cultural and personal submission to a pre-visual sensuality is bound up inevitably with a celebration of darkness. Here are two quotations, the first concerned only with looking, the second with the *femininity* of looking, the truest form of 'visual vice':

> We see too much, we attend too much. The dark, glancing sightlessness of the intent savage, the narrowed vision of the cat, the single point of vision of the hawk – these we do not know any more. . . . we live far, far too much from the *upper* sympathetic centre and voluntary centre, in an endless objective curiosity. Sight is the least sensual of all the senses. And we strain ourselves to see, see, see – everything, everything through the eye, in one mode of objective curiosity. There is nothing inside us, we stare endlessly at the outside. (from *Fantasia of the Unconscious*, 65)

> 'Ah!' she said to herself. 'Let me close my eyes to him, and open my soul. Let me close my prying, *seeing* eyes, and sit in dark stillness along with these two men. . . . They have got rid of that itching of the eye, and the desire that works through the eye. The itching, prurient, *knowing* imagining eye, I am cursed with it, I am hampered up in it. It is my curse of curses, the curse of Eve. The curse of Eve is upon me, my eyes are like hooks, my knowledge is like a fish-hook through my gills, pulling me in spasmodic desire . . . Daughter of Eve, of greedy vision, why don't these men save me from the sharpness of my own eyes!' (from *The Plumed Serpent*[17])

Lawrence's Daughters of Eve thus inherit one crucial burden, and so they are keepers of the curse of our culture: visual fixation and its heady but unhealthy powers. It is *visual* knowledge which took our sex out of paradise and into our heads, and which now keeps hooking sadistically into the flesh of men. The female gaze is at the root of modern mental fixation, and so the burden is on women to close their eyes and cease to know if paradise is to be regained.

Also collected in *Pansies*, where 'When I Went to the Film' appeared, is another, nastier, poem, concerning the mass female fan-following of Rudolph Valentino, the first major male star to be specifically marketed for a female audience. The link between easy viewing and easy virtue was clear enough in the texts I discussed earlier, but it is here that Lawrence picks on a specifically female audience. In this poem, the female gaze is described as a 'luscious filmy imagination [which] loathes the male substance / with deadly loathing':

All the women who adored the shadow of the man on the screen
helped to kill him in the flesh.
Such adoration pierces the loins and perishes the man
worse than the evil eye.

(*Poems*, 538)

Cinema, then, facilitates female visual violence: Valentino is victim of women's unwholesome 'piercing' desire, so that translating his body from flesh into celluloid becomes an act of cultural castration, as the 'fish-hook eyes' of Kate in *The Plumed Serpent* (quoted above) are multiplied on a massive scale. It is important to note that this panic about the female gaze was felt in many quarters (as Hilton Tims puts it), 'Through the era of silent movies', but particularly during the early 1920s, when 'the female audience increasingly became a prime marketing target. Male stars like Valentino, Ramon Novarro and John Gilbert commanded phenomenal hero worship, greater and farther-flung than any man had ever received previously'.[18] Thus the cinema marketing industry conveniently offers the body of the innocent Rudolph as fodder to a mass female gaze which can only look at him with worse-than-evil eyes.

There are a number of reasons for Lawrence's hostility here. As Chapter 3 will demonstrate, he was no fan of Valentino, so this implicit support is surprising. The brief discussion of him which takes place across a few of Lawrence's works concludes that real men 'aren't Rudolph Valentino' (as Hester puts it in the short story 'In Love', written two years before *Pansies* and a year after Valentino's death), and neither is that 'luscious filmy image' of Valentino a 'real man'. Lawrence (again, in Hester's words) 'loathed him really'.[19] But although Valentino is 'dead, poor dear', the female gaze is still very much alive, and it is this, rather than its object, which worries Lawrence most: the way in which the Valentino phenomenon explicitly linked female spectatorship 'to the discourse of female desire'.[20] We might ask what is wrong with vision, with taking pleasure at the movies, and one simple answer would be that everyone was doing it, but particularly women. Audiences in America and Europe were waking up to cinematic visions in unprecedented numbers and with a passion which had certainly not been inspired by older visual forms such as painting and photography. We are discussing a moment at which male anxiety about 'the flapper vote' (Lawrence also wrote a poem about *that*[21]), the instituted power of the New Woman, meets a double anxiety about the growth of cinema and its promotion of women looking on a mass scale.

Rewriting Virginia Woolf's famous phrase 'in or about December, 1910, human character changed', Stephen Heath begins his essay 'On Screen, in Frame: Film and Ideology', 'Something changes between 22 March and 28 December 1895'.[22] For Heath this tilting of cultural

emphasis was signalled by the birth of cinema, Lumière's first demonstra-
tion of the *cinématographe* and the first public film performance. For
Woolf, it is also a visual event which changes the subject – the opening of
the post-impressionism exhibition in London. Modernism is being formed
and twisted by primarily *visual* events, and it is these which are to take
the lead from writing. In reaction, literary practice grew closer to the
image, with, for example, the poetic movement of imagism itself
(Lawrence's poetry was anthologised in *Some Imagist Poets* in 1915 and
1916), and with interdisciplinary movements such as vorticism or the
loose alliances of the Bloomsbury group, which combined writing with
painting and sculpture. The new visual emphases of writing indicate the
influence of the new artistic possibilities of images in movement and
images represented through the relative gaze of the seer. However, despite
his sometime-label of imagist, Lawrence's career, with its conscious anti-
visual emphasis, seems to be a protracted act of swimming against the tide.
This book will argue, however, that Lawrence manages to swim in both
directions at once, looking yet arguing for not-looking, sometimes at the
same time and in the same text. Lawrence is, unwittingly, what Rachel
Bowlby calls a 'spectator of spectatorship',[23] but his fictions are also
shaped by an experimental 'camera-eye'[24] which looks less self-
consciously. Alan Spiegel sees the effects of this literary camera eye as
beginning with Flaubert; whilst Robert Richardson[25] argues that the
written camera eye can first be seen in the Bible. I confine my study to the
more historically demonstrable anxiety about cinema, which was fully
born ten years after Lawrence was, but grew to mass-cultural adulthood
and acceptance whilst Lawrence's work was still being censored and
burnt. Lawrence is an exemplary voice of the highbrow literary prejudice
against the new form, but he also feeds upon its developing ways of seeing.

My work on Lawrence began as an exploration of his literary
disavowal, a disavowal centring on the identification of women with
language and culture. If he reviles women, he reviles them because of their
adherence to conscious life, to 'pinning things down' to language, to having
their sex in their heads, and 'what a vice it is for a woman to get herself
and her sex into her head' (*F*, 124). In Lawrence's cultural theory modern
literary and visual forms sanitise, subjugate or spiritualise sexual and
natural reality, as a result of Western culture becoming 'feminised'. It is
women who think, look, educate, and it is cultural representations which
belong to the realm of the conscious. And since writing and speech are
part of the 'inauthentic' world of the ideal, Lawrence's heroes can only lapse
into strong silence once they have reached 'Darkness', a darkness which
therefore slips off the page. Yet as a writer, Lawrence is himself denied
access to this ideal. On his own terms, he is feminised by his profession.
Lawrence is a writer who polemicises against writing through writing, a

masculine subject who is anxiously implicated in the conscious femininity he reviles, one who writes of sex rather than doing it.

Whilst critics have recently argued for the materiality and bodily forms of language, its extricability from the 'head' (sex in a book is consequently perhaps even more corporeal, more incorporated – sexier – than 'real sex'), what I am keen to show is that Lawrence breaks his own rules. It is Lawrence who argues that sex and language, like darkness and light, do not mix. Thus in terms of the philosophy of language and culture with which he is himself working, bookish sex is 'sex in the head', and could not be further from sex in a bed. How, then, do we read a text which obsessively asserts that its textuality is inherently 'inauthentic'? My examination of the motif of the woman who is victimised for her affirmative relationship to visual and conscious (rather than 'blood-') knowledge, partly concludes that Lawrence allegorises through the predicament of his female protagonist-victims his thwarted relationship to truth-telling and the gaze. The conflict between affirmation and denial of femininity, writing, and the visual, is that which animates Lawrence's text.

Consequently Lawrence's charge that his culture was dominated by the practice and experience of sex in the head is also a self-accusation. This discussion – of vision, gender, seeing and sexuality – is also a discussion of knowledges, of what men and women can and cannot know, whether they can know the same things, and whether one sex has a stronger visual relationship with the world than the other. But it is also about how a culture 'knows itself' through its representations at any one moment. The coming of cinema altered the way that subjectivity was thought, affecting and infecting the visual shape of the world. It reformed and shifted perceptions of the self so dramatically that even discourses (like Lawrence's) which would prefer to remain pure of its influence are clearly implicated.

Lawrence the writer does not produce strictly visual objects (although we use our eyes to read), but written fictions of vision. This book analyses a set of visual theories in their intersection with other theories of vision coming from psychoanalysis and film criticism, which also discuss the sexuality of the gaze, the power of spectacle, and the philosophy and psychology of light and darkness. Lawrence did not make movies – he disliked them. He did, however, dramatise the desire of seeing in a remarkable variety of ways. In a sense, on the subject of vision he protests too much; he sees too well for one who claims to prefer darkness. The final vision might be of a world not defined by scopophilic desire, a world of darker connections, but it is still a world seen clearly and with a 'spectacular' passion. His critique of the common life of visual relationships, lived by the daylight self, is too accurately scrutinised to stand up as simple negation. His corpus as a whole, then, offers itself as a case history in visual disavowal.

The double knot which binds attitudes to writing and knowledge so intimately with attitudes to gender in Lawrence's work, was what I initially termed the Lawrentian paradox. This book acknowledges that the knot is far more intricate: still holding woman as the central thread, Lawrence's work tightly weaves female (cultural) attitudes to conscious knowledge together with a negative discourse on the gaze. Women know and see, and must be punished for it, but books also 'know', and this book will show that they also 'see'. D.H. Lawrence's relationship to modernism has never been an easy one. In his own words (and in the words of Lawrentian critics) his position is set up as a closed rejection of the experimental 'thousands and thousands of pages [through which] Mr Joyce and Miss Richardson tear themselves to pieces' which form 'the dismal, long-drawn-out comedy of the death-bed of the serious novel' ('Surgery for the Novel – or a Bomb', Px, 190). Without contradicting the specificity of this criticism, Lawrence also experimented in a number of ways – with narrative structure, with visual perception, and with sexual and character innovations. Whilst criticising many of his contemporaries, he nevertheless saw the possibilities which modernism threw up as an 'apocalyptic' (the word is Frank Kermode's[26]) opportunity for change. This book is an attempt to identify a number of contradictions at the heart of Lawrence's work: contradictions between what he says he is doing and what he actually does, between his celebration of the writing of darkness and his practice of setting up pleasurable scenes of looking, within which the female gaze facilitates the staging of a series of images of male beauty. Lawrence said no, and yes, to modernism and its visual possibilities, at the same time. This active disavowal must be fully addressed if we are to understand the crisis at the heart of his work. It is a disavowal which affects several key areas on which I will concentrate: his attitude to femininity and vision, his pleasure in the spectacle of male bodies, his fetishism and his anxious replaying of the cinematic scene itself.

Looking at Lawrence: critical scrutinies

The population of Britain and America had greatly increased by the end of the nineteenth century, and with this came an increase in literacy and buying power. Rachel Bowlby's analysis of the development of retail and shopping as activities of leisure and spectacle is important in this respect.[27] Cinema, the spectacle industry, and the popular press which also rapidly expanded around the turn of the century, cashed in on the potential of large popular audiences, but the vanguard of the intelligentsia were quick to criticise this growth and shift. Lawrence's attitude to cinema is typical of the argument made by his 'high culture' contemporaries regarding various 'low' cultural forms, and his influence was felt more strongly a little after his death, as it fed into the work of *Scrutiny* and the Leavises. On the question of popular culture, Lawrence was profoundly influential upon Q.D. Leavis's *Fiction and the Reading Public* in its prioritisation of 'difficult' writing over visual and popular fantasies, the latter of which are, for her, brim-full of stock responses, artificial emotion and substitute living (just as film is for Lawrence). As well as offering a history of the reading public's relationship to popular fiction, Leavis simultaneously traces the decline and fall of that public from highbrow to lowbrow. Her debased modern civilisation is one in which, thanks to 'Big Business', the workers can only 'have recourse to substitute living'.[28] To counter this Leavis prescribes a 'conscious and directed [critical] effort'[29] which refuses to rest in 'the consistent use of clichés (stock phrases to evoke stock responses)'.[30] To this end, Lawrence has been enlisted as saviour of man's taste; as F.R. Leavis wrote in an early edition of *Scrutiny*, 'It is difficult to believe that his influence can be anything but wholesome, and it is exhilarating to think that in a world of suburbanism, book societies and Marie Stopes he imposed himself.'[31]

'Americanisation' was in full swing at this time, introducing, for the Lawrences and the Leavises, yet more devices to sap the critical abilities of the people. *Scrutiny*'s adherents form Lawrence's direct descendants in their contradictory attitude to the United States. Both for Lawrence, and, in Francis Mulhern's words, for *Scrutiny*, 'the U.S.A. was both the homeland of modern "machine" civilization and the advance post of opposition to it'.[32] Lawrence's complex attitude to the United States is essentially a reversal of cultural history: the new burgeoning form of cinema is symptomatic of an ailing decadent culture which still existed side by side with the spirit of hope represented by the American Indian and his authentic relationship with the American Spirit of Place.[33] Cinema, as a prime agent of the Americanising process, not only represented for *Scrutiny* and Lawrence yet another attempt to pacify, and render passive, the thinking man or woman's naturally active faculties, but further threatened the hegemony of the intellectual.

As Mr May, the cinema entrepreneur of *The Lost Girl* puts it, 'England's not America – more's the pity!' (LG, 116), but his villainous role in the text is to push forward this popular 'Americanisation'. It is the immediate visual pleasure of cinematic popular culture, here perceived as an American invasion (despite its French origins), which constitutes the problem. Mr May is confused on the question of its final impact, however; responsible himself for the building of the town's cinema (which he ironically refers to as 'an erection' (LG, 115–16), for nothing could be less of a Lawrentian erection), he still stands by the power of live performance:

> 'I can't believe they want nothing but pictures. I can't believe they want everything in the flat,' he said, coaxing and miserable. He himself was not interested in the film. His interest was still the human interest of living performers and their living feats. (LG, 143)

Nevertheless, cinematic pleasure is 'cheap and easy', and Lawrence uses a telling popular phrase to convey James Houghton's glee on the opening day of 'Houghton's Pleasure Palace': 'But James, to use the vulgar expression, was in his eye-holes. . . . it merely meant that James was having the time of his life' (LG, 132). The pleasure could not be more literally visual, or more immediately popular. Cinema packs in the crowds (or rather it did in those days), and the 'living' power of theatre or 'difficult' culture is feared dying or dead.

The stock response of the reading – or viewing – public has none of the spontaneity which Lawrence and both Leavises prescribe, and so all efforts must be made to resist the tastes of the mob: Egbert in *England, My England*

> recoiled inevitably from having his feelings dictated to him by the mass feeling. His feelings were his own, his understanding was his own, and he would never go back on either, willingly. Shall a man become inferior to his own true knowledge and self, just because the mob expects it of him?[34]

In its early days *Scrutiny* bitterly attacked cinema on terms which come directly from Lawrence. Even more than Q.D. Leavis's reviled popular fiction, cinema imposes the dictates of 'mass feeling.' Just as for Lawrence cinematic emotion is 'cheap and easy', so for F.R. Leavis, '[Films] provide now the main form of recreation in the civilised world; and they involve surrender, under conditions of hypnotic receptivity, to the cheapest of emotional appeals.'[35]

This quotation comes from F.R. Leavis's *Mass Civilisation and Minority Culture* (1930), which rests upon a critique of popularism which is itself a strong component of Lawrence's critique of film. Whereas the above quote from *England, My England* attacks 'the mob', Lawrence later adopts Leavis's other role, that of champion of minority taste, here against the obscenity of close-up cinematic kisses. In *The Lost Girl*, 'The lamps go out: gurglings and kissings' (LG, 138), but by the time of 'Pornography and Obscenity', the close-up kiss has become 'pornographical':

> the minority public knows full well that the most obscene painting on a Greek vase – *Thou still unravished bride of quietness* – is not as pornographical as the close-up kisses on the film, which excite men and women to secret and separate masturbation. (Px, 326)

The close-up kiss was such a problem for Lawrence that he even painted a rather nasty picture of it called *Close-up (Kiss)*, which is reproduced in the Mandrake edition of *The Paintings of D.H. Lawrence*. Robert W. Millett interprets the painting as a critique of contemporary cinema,[36] drawing a connection with a textual 'close-up kiss' in the much earlier novel *The Trespasser*. But whereas the painting is equally critical of the man and the woman, in the novel it is only Helena who falls for the filmic gloss; like the Valentino of Lawrence's poem, Siegmund can only be felt if he is turned, in Helena's fantasy, into an image of himself:

> With her the dream was always more than the actuality. Her dream of Siegmund was always more to her than Siegmund himself. . . . For centuries a certain type of woman has been rejecting the 'animal' in humanity, till now her dreams are abstract, and full of fantasy, and her blood runs in bondage.[37]

Whilst Lawrence is not concerned with the predicament of women in bondage here, he *is* concerned with the possibility that cinema offers a more powerful substitute truth, a fantasy of masculinity which might be preferable to the real thing. In tandem with this disturbing image of a fantasy choice which escapist culture ostensibly offers, and against which real live men might seem deficient, is the Leavisian concern that cinema atrophies one's critical faculties. As Alvina puts it, again in *The Lost Girl*, 'The film is only pictures, like pictures in the *Daily Mirror*. And pictures don't have feelings apart from their own feelings. I mean the feelings of the people who watch them' (LG, 144). But another of Lawrence's female cinematic subjects speaks positively later in the novel of this same uncritical experience. In cinema,

> you see it all and take it all in at once; you know everything at a glance. . . . I like to go to the cinema once a week. It's instruction, you take it all in at a glance, all you need to know, and it lasts you for a week. You can get to know everything about people's actual lives from the cinema. (LG, 176, Lawrence's emphasis)

This is a point which Virginia Woolf also makes in her 1926 essay, 'The Cinema': 'The eye licks it up instantaneously, and the brain, agreeably titillated, settles down to watch things happening without bestirring itself to think.'[38] And whilst this essay concludes with the possibility that cinema might turn into a complex and worthwhile art form, Woolf also objects to the close-up kiss, and to the reduction of emotion into a thin range of impoverished symbols: 'So we spell them out in words of one syllable, written, too, in the scrawl of an illiterate schoolboy. A kiss is love. A broken cup is jealousy. A grin is happiness. Death is a hearse.'

This is reversed by W.H. Mellers in a later edition of *Scrutiny*. For the spectator in *The Lost Girl*, and for Woolf, Hollywood imposes a monolithic world-view on the passive subject; for Mellers, the buying public take the lead, and Hollywood is only cashing-in on the emotional needs of a public which is already demanding of it certain pleasures:

> It is often said that Hollywood emotion is essentially synthetic but this, though true, is not the whole truth. . . . it is wrong to put all the blame on Hollywood for tapping those glycerine vats in people's hearts and none on people for possessing those vats waiting to be tapped at.[39]

Mellers is perhaps kinder than both Leavises, however, in allowing that film might have *some* relationship with 'real emotion', and might finally be admitted to have some artistic worth,[40] but then by the end of the 1930s cinema was beginning to be admitted as a more respectable form, and even *Scrutiny* was beginning to take it seriously.

Lawrence's relationship to this cultural perspective is complex; his influence on *Scrutiny* and the work of both Q.D. and F.R. Leavis was powerful, and this influence has created a kind of positive feedback loop in critical history this century. So when David Boadella, as late as 1978, makes the same point about popular culture and emotional forgery, he is writing as much about and from the ideology of *Scrutiny* as about and from Lawrence himself. For Boadella, Lawrence, 'is aware of the extent to which, since genuine feelings so often do not exist, they have to be faked and are faked on a mass scale, as well as in individual lives'.[41] Lawrence's values of 'life', authenticity and spontaneity fed into Cambridge criticism, which then used those values to enshrine Lawrence as one of its prime twentieth-century literary objects.[42] It is no wonder that Leavis valued Lawrence so highly, since Lawrence was co-author of the Leavisite rule-book, contributing a range of values to the ideology of Cambridge criticism – which would then find Lawrence its vindicating object. This is particularly clear in the early essays on Lawrence in *Scrutiny* itself: saturated with Lawrentian terms, essays like 'Reminiscences of D.H. Lawrence' or 'The Literary Mind' (both 1932) function to reflect those Lawrentian values back onto Lawrence's work.

Because of this Leavisian legacy, when reading Lawrence critics have often suffered from a critical form of what Freud calls the 'blindness of the seeing eye'.[43] Reading everything on the surface – believing that he says what he means and means what he says – has meant that the other, affirmative positions Lawrence takes on visual perception and enjoyment have been ignored. Lawrence clearly does not like women who look too hard, women who believe that they possess the world and their men when they look at them, and he prefers his men to be dark, blind and actively unknowing – men whose sex is where it ought to be, 'down there' beyond the scope of the pornographic gaze. But seeing this clearly has prevented criticism from fully understanding what is at stake in Lawrence's obsession with looking at men, with looking intimately at women's clothing and forms, with looking at the women which the narrative denigrates, but particularly, with using their eyes and enjoying them. Lawrence criticism has largely been blind to this Lawrence, the pleasure-taking seer who lurks behind the polemic against seeing. For Sheila MacLeod in her feminist reading of Lawrence, 'the novelist knows better than the propagandist';[44] in this study, there is no single Lawrence who knows best, or is most representative.

Lawrence criticism has also characteristically identified Lawrence with his men, collapsing 'the Lawrence character' of the novels, often those characters which most vocally denigrate women, into the author himself. From this point of view, the narrative thrust of the texts is finally on the side of masculine, unconscious, darkly sexualised experience, and never on the side of feminine, conscious, cocksure culture. On what terms do we challenge this, in order to see Lawrence in his degraded women as well as in his men, enjoying those feminine traits he also reviles? How, moreover, can we subvert Lawrence-the-misogynist by showing a quite different Lawrence, who looks at men with enjoyment from the perspective of a feminine voyeur, a Lawrence who writes with all the conscious precision of the cocksure woman he censures? Through a series of close readings and wider discussions of sexual identity and the gaze, I hope to demonstrate how Lawrence's work subverts itself, turns itself inside out — 'itself', at least, as a monolithically misogynistic polemic. Lawrence is less consistent, less wholesomely sexually-integrated, rather *more* perverse and therefore rather *less* straightforwardly sexist, than both he and traditional criticism of him would have us believe. This is not to say that in those glimpses of perversity on which I shall concentrate in later chapters, Lawrence is being essentially radical or non-sexist. He breaks his own rules of sexual and visual propriety so glaringly (the two becoming dangerously merged at these moments) that the whole desperate edifice begins to crack, capitulating under the pressure of those pleasures which he rarely admits to partaking in.

The evil eye

Lawrence has continued to be a prime site upon which the priorities of criticism have been fought over, the debate over the status of his work exemplifying the twists of critical history since his death, but it is only relatively recently that the Leavis approach to Lawrence has begun to lose power. Feminism has always been the strongest voice to counter the now-fading Lawrence–Leavis pact, but Kate Millett's famous critique in *Sexual Politics* tackled Lawrence on very different terms than those of this book.

There is a perverse complicity in the relationship between the angry feminism of the 1970s and early 80s, and the anger at women *in* Lawrence's texts which provoked that feminist reaction in the first place. Lawrence, perhaps more than any other writer, is feminism's *bête noire*, the monster it loves to hate. But he gave as good as he got: even before the self-consciously feminist criticism of Virginia Woolf's writing on women was a glimmer in her critical eye, Lawrence was having it out in print with his female readers, who, he anticipated (with an uncanny mixture of prescience and paranoia) were there only to tear his text apart, to pin it down to distinct meanings, but most of all, to psychoanalyse it. And if, as I shall explore in Chapter 2, Lawrence's rude relationship with this imaginary devouring reader is not so simple, then neither is feminism's relationship with Lawrence. Every culture needs its monsters, and feminism is no exception. Just as Lawrence needed his hated, intellectual, cocksure woman – for a whole variety of reasons which this book will explore – so 1970s feminism needed its wolf (as well as its Woolf). But this book will not replicate the 'Trial of D.H. Lawrence' which has animated the critical debate focusing on his work in a dialogue of prosecution and defence.[45] Instead it will discuss the ambivalence of Lawrence's work as it focuses on femininity, particularly when Lawrence analyses those women he loves to hate. It is here that he is most divided: the moment at which he pours scorn upon her is also the moment at which her conscious, visual powers are most used by the text as its prime points of organisation and focus.

But there is more to this complicity between Lawrence and feminism; indeed, on the issue of the gaze there is some strong agreement. The possessive and aggressive gaze of Lawrence's cocksure woman can be easily mapped onto the violating and objectifying *male* gaze identified by feminism, specifically the feminisms emerging from two directions in the 1970s: that which takes Laura Mulvey's 'Visual Pleasure and Narrative Cinema' as its lead, and the cultural feminist critique of pornography which focused the male pornographic gaze. This book will also explore this unexpected convergence, calling a truce between Lawrence and (some) feminists over the question of 'perverse' forms of visual sexuality and the desirability of visual repression. Ironically, the decade within which feminism seemed largely to be reaching an agreement with Lawrence on the evils of the gaze was also the decade within which, after *Sexual Politics*, feminism was criticising him most bitterly for his misogyny.

There is also a long spiritual tradition which links visual knowledge to inauthentic sensibility and blindness with insight: the blind seer is a classic figure. Lawrence picks up this old chestnut and reworks it throughout his writing in a way which exposes many of the anxieties of literary modernism. What makes his discomfort about visuality more acute, and what also makes his valorisation of darkness more desperate, is the dominance of the visual priorities of his cultural moment, particularly the growth of cinema. Understandable as this is, neither Lawrence on women nor Lawrence on the look can be separated from each other. A range of theories of sexual difference which emerge from contemporary feminism and film theory relate to the work on looking, knowing, blindness and unknowing which can be found across Lawrence's corpus. Feminism has similarly read the gaze as intrinsically male, emphasising its crucial role in the construction of sexual difference and the maintenance of power relations. This book is not only a critique of Lawrence's discourse on the femininity of the look, it is also an engagement with a feminism which has continued to work with terms which situate the gaze in a particular fixed and powerful gender position.

These contradictions in Lawrence are not important simply in the context of (and for a fresh understanding of) his work. We live in a culture which is fixated upon the visual, but which also manifests a puritanical anti-ocularism. The Foucauldian critique of ocular-logocentrism,[46] the feminist critique of pornography, the holistic plea for a 'return' to more authentic non-visual sexuality, are all symptoms of a cultural strain which is fixated upon the visual even in its repudiation of it. The claim of sexual authenticity in Lawrence needs to be read in terms of the other, less authentic currents which demonstrate a fascination with the imagery and fetishism of visual sexuality. If this book has a governing position, it is that the relationship of guilty disavowal and nefarious fascination which exists between, on the one hand, the celebration of authentic dark sex, and on the other, the vilification of visual vice, urgently requires attention. This book is, then, a dehabilitation of Lawrence. Lawrence is many things to many people – the font of truth for the Leavisites, spokesman of sanitised healthy sex for a generation of 1960s swingers, darling of prime-time quality television – but he is rarely read now as an intriguing and contradictory 'deviant'. If the present analysis of Lawrence's visual pleasures is a success, then it testifies to the possibilities of interdisciplinary writing which reads against the grain, more than to the specific power of the subject under scrutiny: if one can read Lawrence-the-cinephobe in terms of perspectives on perception – Lawrence viewed, as it were, through a cinematic filter – one can do it with anyone. Lawrence is nothing if not a recalcitrant object.

This is both a 'literary' reading of Lawrence (in the sense that it engages in close readings of a wide range of Lawrence's literary texts), and a reading of the fantasy of the literary and of culture in Lawrence, and what this has come to signify culturally. Both Lawrence's phallocentric argument and my own feminist one take place within the frame of sexuality, situating the cultural practices of modernism in a bigger argument about identity. For reasons of economy, I have referred to the subject of this book as 'Lawrence', although I am drawing on a range of positions and texts which show 'him' to be divided, more like the split subject of fantasy in psychoanalysis who is able to occupy several different viewing positions at once (I will return to this in Chapter 5). It is easy to slip into unthinking psychobiography with Lawrence's work because he is such a polemicist, writing from a central 'I' subject position despite the glaring contradictions of that 'I', and despite its own famous protestation, 'Never trust the artist, trust the tale'.[47] There is something exemplary about Lawrence's positions on cinema, vision and women which characterises the attitudes of his cultural moment. Tania Modleski's reading of femininity in Alfred Hitchcock's films has a similar emphasis: 'time and again in Hitchcock's films, the strong fascination and identification with femininity revealed in them subverts the claims to mastery and authority not only of the male characters but of the director himself.'[48] As with Modleski's Hitchcock, the feminist trial of Lawrence which has taken place over the last twenty years was partly so forcefully articulated because Lawrence gives evidence to both sides – prosecution and defence can plausibly draw on him for support. This is not to say that his body of writing is a corpus of plenitude, with all sexual-political life being liberally present, but that it is deeply self-contradictory, and self-defensive. In the left corner, the chief prosecuting counsel is Millett, followed by a number of feminist readers who have reiterated her position. In the right, defending Lawrence for feminism, have come Lydia Blanchard, Sheila MacLeod (to some extent), even Carol Dix, for whom Lawrence's attacks on women constitute a bizarre kind of self-defence. But as Harold Bloom writes: '"Defence" is an odd notion, particularly in psychoanalysis, where it always tends to mean a rather active and aggressive process. In psychic life, as in international affairs, "defence" is frequently murderous.'[49] I will take this further: those 'self-defences' which are so often posed as an attack on women need to be read as self-defences which are also defences against the self. In ruling the whole subject out of court, I want to demonstrate that no crime has been committed against women and their eyes in Lawrence's texts which is not also inflicted by the text against itself.

Chapter One

◆

The blindness of the seeing eye

Visual vices and dark virtues
in Lawrence

Sitting 'between the toes of a tree, forgetting myself against the great ankle of the trunk', Lawrence writes *Fantasia of the Unconscious*, his 'tree-book' (F, 43), and perhaps his clearest polemic against visual consciousness. The forest Lawrence conjures up is one in which the open spirit cannot fail to get involved. In it there is no question of dispassionate perception: it is monstrous, 'profoundly indifferent', immediately faceless, and yet entering it also opens the door to it. Like Nietzsche's abyss, into which one looks only to find that the abyss looks back,[1] entering his forest is tantamount to extending an invitation, asking *it* to enter *you*. For a moment the 'I' panics, paranoid; it cannot surround itself in a defensive gaze which protects all horizons, it cannot look in all directions at once: 'I think there are too many trees. They seem to crowd round and stare at me, and I feel as if they nudged one another when I'm not looking. I can *feel* them standing there' (F, 42). This fear is uncharacteristic, especially in a book which advocates the loss of this fearful ego, the abandonment of defensive looking. And so he submits – 'I seem to feel them moving and thinking and prowling, and they overwhelm me. Ah, well, the only thing is to give way to them.' What this means is that in encountering the other (the forest) one allows the possibility that the forest will reach back and touch or expose something in the self which is made of the same 'substance'. This is what Nietzsche means when he writes 'And when you look long into an abyss, the abyss also looks into you.' The mutuality of this is right, but the perceptual metaphor could not be further from the spirit of *Fantasia*. Lawrence doesn't *want* to look long at anything, just to get lost in the trees and find out through their eyeless contact that once you submit to the body-without-organs of the forest, you find out how irrelevant your own organs are. For what is the point of making eye contact with something which has no eyes?

Suppose you want to look a tree in the face? You can't. It hasn't got a face.
You look at the strong body of a trunk; you look above you into the matted
body-hair of twigs and boughs; you see the soft green tips. But there are no
eyes to look into, you can't meet its gaze. You keep on looking at it part
and parcel.
    It's no good looking at a tree to know it. (F, 43)

Look long at a tree, and it deprives you of the ability to see – *that* is how
the forest looks back.

'I come so well to understand tree-worship' continues Lawrence, for
what the trees have done to him, and what an openness to the unseeing
forest of 'blood consciousness' (which trees stand for and grow from) can
do, is engender a religious state of positive unseeing. This mutual invasion
causes a radical dissolution of the self; when he writes, 'I lose myself
among the trees' (F, 44), he means it quite literally: 'They have taken some
of my soul', but moreover they have taken away the need for familiar,
visual recognition, for the motifs of ideal individuality: 'They have no
skulls, no minds nor faces, they can't make eyes of love at you. Their vast
life dispenses with all this. But they will live you down' (F, 46).

For Lawrence the seeing eye is always blind. Better to have no eyes than
to use them in 'making eyes of love' – better to find, instead, a 'vast life.'
The seeing eye can take in only the surface of things, a surface which
deflects and misdirects our concentration, so that we don't even know
something deeper exists – all this, for Lawrence, means that we are blind
to the fact that we are blind. The seeing eye cannot see the wood for the
trees: it knows their type and form, it categorises, photographs, films and
names them, but it does not come near to a true, Lawrentian contact with
the unconscious substance of wood. The seeing eye is fixated on conscious
perception and forgets 'darker' connection – it assumes that everything
that is, is visual.

In *Studies on Hysteria* Freud refers to a form of vision which disavows
the seen at moments of crisis, which he calls the 'blindness of the seeing
eye'. For Lawrence, the seeing eye is specifically blind to the darkness of
the self, unable to make sense of the creeping unconscious ones which
emerge from the forest to merge with other parts of the self when the eyes,
the agents of consciousness, are closed. His dualism is clear and familiar:
in order to see 'truly' one must give up one's reliance on visual verification,
one must become blindly sexualised. Sight is the most inauthentic sense
for Lawrence, indeed, it is hardly a sense at all – it is the sense which cuts
consciousness off from sensual life. Lawrence wants us to be invaded by
the forest, losing the emphasis of two-dimensional perception in full
baptismal immersion.

Seeing in the dark

For Lawrence, the fact that human eyes cannot see in the dark is not a problem. We must abandon the priorities of human visual perception, and embrace other ways of knowing and touching the world. What *is* the problem is the primacy of visual perception, in a culture which is systematically turning the lights on in every sphere. Because we cannot see in the dark we colonise it with the values of light:

> We have too much light in the night, and too much sleep in the day. It is an evil thing for us to prolong as we do the mental, visual, ideal consciousness far into the night when the hour has come for this upper consciousness to fade, for the blood alone to know and act. (F, 175–6)

In Lawrence's world-turned-upside-down, the decadent modern self thinks its way into the night and makes sexuality the slave of cerebration. We light up the night in order to scrutinise our sex. And the pay-off, the flip-side of this perverse nocturnal vision – the power of seeing in the dark, and thus *forgetting* that the dark *is* dark, the need to scrutinise unconsciousness – is not a newly sexualised day, the opposite of a sexually depleted night, but an exhausted culture which oversleeps: 'we protract our day-consciousness on into the night . . . and we tell ourselves we must sleep, sleep, sleep in the morning and the daytime' (F, 177). The evil of becoming nocturnal for Lawrence lies in the way it inverts the natural order of things – like going to the cinema in the afternoon. The prime act of transgression is thus to actually *look* at sexuality, to scrutinise it (this is at the root of his critique of psychoanalysis). To look *within* the sexual act – to embrace scopophilic 'perversions' – is even worse. The most decadent form which modern sensibility takes is to lead one's eyes beyond the natural realm of daylight to which they are appropriate, entering the darkness with them open, and looking hard at life as a range of images to be scrutinised. Just as there is something transgressive about leaving the sunshine to enter a dark cinema auditorium and watch 'artificial' projections – the point has been made before, but this is cinema as a latter-day Plato's cave – so taking one's eyes into Lawrentian darkness and then illuminating its secrets is a major critical problem. We fail to use our eyes where they are appropriate – to aid wholesome manual labour in the sunshine – and instead open them in the realm of 'night' where we project our mental fantasies onto our subjugated sexuality, and exhaust ourselves mentally. Too much power to the 'outer mental consciousness and mental lasciviousness' destroys 'the very blood in our bodies' (F, 176), and one of Lawrence's solutions, at least, is a culture-wide reveille:

> Every man and woman should be forced out of bed soon after the sun has
> risen: particularly the nervous ones. And forced into physical activity. Soon
> after dawn the vast majority of people should be hard at work. If not, they
> will soon be nervously diseased. (F, 177)

If *so*, the world will be turned the right-(Lawrentian)-side-up again, the
lights will be turned out on sexuality, and 'outer mental consciousness'
will be suppressed by physical labour, the proper activity of daylight. It
all sounds so eminently normal, so what is at stake here to make Lawrence
feel so strongly about us getting a good *night*'s sleep followed by a hard
day's work?

A knottier anxiety lies at the bottom of this, the issue of the primacy
and encroaching power of visual sexuality. Underpinning Lawrence's
discourse on visuality is his more basic philosophy of sexual difference.
Against the grain of our culture and (as feminism has identifed) its
masculinisation of the gaze and powers of illumination, Lawrence
identifies femininity with the values of the rising sun – with cerebral
powers of illumination, and the desire to see and penetrate visually – and
thus cannot bear to see them encroach upon his celebrated darkness. If
women are aligned with vision and light, the (feminine) invasion of
Lawrence's dark continent of (masculine) sexuality reclaims the night. For
Lawrence, it is important to go to bed when it gets dark (to be unconscious
in darkness) and wake up at dawn (to be conscious in the light), actually
and metaphorically, primarily because to do otherwise threatens the
whole balance of power between 'visual, ideal consciousness' (the
feminine) and Phallic, and blind, 'blood life'. To make 'the mistake of
turning life inside-out, of dragging the day-self into night, and spreading
the night-self over into the day' is also to make the mistake of prioritising
conscious ways of seeing: in this way, Lawrence argues, we also make
'love and sex a matter of seeing and hearing and of day-conscious
manipulation' (both quotations, F, 175). In short, we then make love and
sex feminine rather than Phallic, visual rather than blind. This is the range
of reversals and binarities upon which Lawrence pins his whole sexual and
visual discourse.

Whilst *Fantasia of the Unconscious* often reads like a highly systemised
but certifiable schizo-rant, setting out an elaborate vision of social and
individual organisation based on the intricate relationship between the
solar plexus, the lumbar ganglion, and the sun and the moon ('I may as
well say straight off that I stick to the solar plexus'[2]) its discussion of dark
and seeing selves is crucial, and clearly sets out this model. *Fantasia* begins
with an analysis of how the individual develops from infancy, and ends
in a eulogy to the delights of 'having a wife', the moment of heterosexual
fulfilment achieved when the woefully '"intelligent" wom[a]n' leaves her
mind (and her eyes) behind, '*believes* in you and submits to your purpose

that is beyond her' (F, 193). There are *some* dark women in Lawrence, like Winifred at the start of *England, My England* who, 'having once known the glow of male power . . . would not easily turn to the cold white light of feminine independence' (EME, 20). Such women are not, however, as interesting as the visionary ones. To be eyeless in paradise is the goal for us all, but women have further to go to get there.

Ignoring for the moment the banal sexism of this, *Fantasia* demonstrates most clearly Lawrence's ideas about the development of men and women from childhood through modern (but unfulfilled) adulthood, towards the possibility of real (Lawrentian) arrival. It is a key text, and despite its premise of an argument with Freud, one might say that it is Lawrence's metapsychological statement, offering a strong sense of his psychobiological topography, with a narrative which traces individual development and leaves fulfilment as yet to be achieved by most of us. It is also the case history of our culture, following the growth of Lawrence's (male) Everyman whose progress to a conclusive moment of dark healing is traced through the terms of looking and vision. Individual identity is born at the moment when the infant can see that the other – the rest of the world – is visually separate from itself. This is taken to extremes in modern individuality, and Lawrence fixes on and repeatedly represents the figure of the twentieth-century self which organises the world and understands most things primarily through the sense of sight. To go one (Lawrentian) stage further, people must transcend vision into a new, renewing, experience of darkness. This development has a parallel gender dynamic, which is that Lawrence's Everyman is feminised – 'it' changes sex – as it becomes more and more reliant on vision. A curious evolution takes place, then, through which a child is born into darkness, emerges into the light which is progressively identified with femininity, and then has to undergo a culminative experience of darkness in order to find its way 'home' again. The seers and perverse knowers of Lawrence's narratives are generally female, and so the final stage of immersion in darkness, of willed blindness, involves a submission of knowing femininity to the positively weighted 'unknowing' Phallus. Light and looking in their perverse forms are feminine,[3] and so darkness comes only when the feminine submits. Essentially, all selves are 'dark', but we have forgotten this. Full human arrival depends upon losing, forgetting or destroying our visual apparatus, and living 'below the waist':

> below the waist, we have our being in darkness. Below the waist we are sightless. When, in the daytime, our life is polarised upwards, towards the open sun-wakened eyes and the mind which sees in vision, then the powerful dynamic centres of the lower body act in subservience. . . . And then we flow upwards, we go forth seeking the universe, in vision, speech, and thought – we go forth to see all things, to hear all things, to know all things by acquaintance and by knowledge. (F, 179)

This is the 'daytime self', the thinking, seeing and writing self, the self which, moreover, writes (Lawrence's) books. This 'wide-eyed spirit [which seeks] to bring all the universe into the range of our conscious activity' appears here to be set in equal, respectful, opposition to the 'other' self in which Lawrence is more interested. This is not, however, the case: in modern times the 'wide-eyed spirit' has become female, its corporate form takes on a sadistic, possessive and disproportionate shape as the cocksure woman.

'Bringing *all* the universe into the range of our conscious activity' is, then, the woman's obsession. Women have become so relentlessly 'wide-eyed' that their desire to look and to know is pathologically epistemophilic (to deploy a slice of jargon from Melanie Klein). Epistemophilia is 'the impulse to search for knowledge', a possessive desire which Klein aligns with primal sadism and other active infant drives.[4] Lawrence's modern woman is the epistemophile *par excellence*; she has cathected all of her sexual desire onto the drive to know. Her will to know has possessed and perverted her 'natural' desires, and so she takes more into her conscious system than is good for her. When sex comes into the head, it is matched with an attitude to knowledge and thought which is passionate and (for Lawrence, perversely) sexualised. Sex in the head is twinned with the *desire* to know.

This is not unlike a comment made by Jacques Lacan, as quoted by Catherine Clément: 'Desire, domesticated by the educators, put to sleep by moralists, betrayed by the Academies, has taken refuge in the passion to know.'[5] Read one way this seems like an acutely Lawrentian statement, except that Lawrence would never term knowledge a refuge, nor would he allow that the will to know could be truly passionate. But certainly, desire is betrayed, enervated, caged and – crucially – emasculated,[6] when it is expressed as the desire for knowledge. And because the 'wide-eyed spirit' is more predictably vilified across the range of Lawrence's corpus and frequently *only* appears as the perverse 'passion to know', it cannot be seen to exist in simple and equal opposition to the darker, sightless self, rather coyly situated 'below the waist' (the writer of *Lady Chatterley's Lover* obviously hasn't yet summoned up the courage to call a John Thomas a John Thomas). Indeed, Lawrence goes on to establish the 'night-time self' as primary, the lost but fundamental core of sexual subjectivity. To experience *positively* this Lawrentian version of the dark night of the soul would be to rebalance our different internal selves so that the unconscious is given its fundamental priority again.

What we should do, then (and Lawrence here reaches a crescendo of prescription), is to reclaim the night of the self:

We wanted first to have nothing but nice daytime selves, awfully nice and kind and refined. But it didn't work. Because, whether we want it or not, we've got night-time selves. And the most spiritual woman ever born or made has to perform her natural functions just like anybody else.

We must *always* keep in line with this fact.

Well, then, we have night-time selves. And the night-self is the very basis of the dynamic self. The blood-consciousness and the blood-passion is the very source and origin of us. . . .

We have to sink back into the darkness and the elemental consciousness of the blood. And from this rise again. But there is no rising until the bath of darkness and extinction is accomplished (F, 182–3)

Returning to 'the very source and origin of us', we must submit to 'the bath of darkness' and only build conscious life on top of this natural foundation. To see things first, rather than know them darkly, is to fatally mistake the natural order of things. At this point in *Fantasia of the Unconscious* (the final chapter, 'The Lower Self'), Lawrence slips increasingly into what one hopes is self-parody, but which undoubtedly isn't. 'And so we resolve back towards our elementals. We dissolve back, out of the upper consciousness, out of mind and sight and speech, back, down into the deep and massive, swaying consciousness of the dark, living blood' (F, 184).

Blindness and insight[7]

For Lawrence, then, the metaphysical split between, on the one hand, 'mind and sight and speech' and on the other, 'dark, living blood', does not exist in a gender vacuum; the virtues of Darkness and the vices of visual consciousness are inevitably bound up with his thinking on gender and authentic sexuality. Jonathan Dollimore discusses the way in which 'Lawrence audaciously sexualises Western metaphysics' in a brilliant argument about Lawrence's voice as both *'blindingly heterosexist and desperately homoerotic'*.[8] I am interested in the way that Lawrence visualises this gendered metaphysic, but also in the way in which he turns the visual and sexual power politics of metaphysics on its head, still prioritising masculinity but in the form of a dark, Utopian unconsciousness, set against a femininity which is degenerately knowing and visually obsessed.

As Lawrence's work develops, he consolidates the link between different experiences of darkness and light as sexual/spiritual states and possibilities of sexuality and gendered identity. Unconscious blindness is offered as a doorway to sexual insight, but Lawrence wants always to characterise this as a masculine mode of being. Looking, the desire to be looked at, and the need to verify experience visually, are consequently characterised as feminine (or inauthentically 'knowing') states of mind.

Thus the act of looking is feminised, and then criticised – or rather it is feminised in order to be more systematically criticised. The power of blindness and the experience of Darkness is made masculine, and then valorised.

Lawrence's short story of 1918, 'The Blind Man', offers a clear example of how this metaphysical split begins to be sexualised. The eponymous hero is blessed by virtue of being blind. In a sense, this story is a trial run for *Lady Chatterley's Lover* which turns it inside out, inverting the key events and the significance of the protagonists. 'The Blind Man' is the longer novel's earlier shadow – it makes war injury and handicap positive, and the healthy stranger (the Mellors figure) fails to seduce the woman because he is visually intact. The whole story revolves around the negative role of sight, and so it explores the underside of *Lady Chatterley* – the possibility that war can positively destroy human capabilities which, for Lawrence, are themselves negative. The negative of war acts upon the negative sense of sight to enable a positive, sexualised and essentially dark relationship with the natural world. In *Lady Chatterley*, Connie's husband loses his sexual potency and becomes ever more a visually defined asexual figure of vilification; in 'The Blind Man' Isabel's husband – the title character – finds his darkness and connection when he physically loses his eyes. Isabel actually *gains* her husband, in the true Lawrentian sense, when his sight is destroyed in the trenches, and he returns home to a sensual paradise regained:

> Life was still very full and strangely serene for the blind man, peaceful with the almost incomprehensible peace of immediate contact in darkness. With his wife he had a whole world, rich and real and invisible.
>
> They were newly and remotely happy. He did not even regret the loss of his sight in these times of dark, palpable joy. A certain exultance swelled his soul. (EME, 55)

The story develops this strong implication that the blind man's world is 'rich and real' *because* it is invisible. The 'almost incomprehensible peace of immediate contact in darkness' is often offered in Lawrence's corpus (very similar terms of description being repeated) as the highest form of experience. One should not strive for a contact *with* darkness – this would maintain the self as a separate experiencing being; rather one should immerse oneself *in* it, like the writer in the forest. True 'contact' comes with*in* darkness.

Sight, for Lawrence, maintains the self's edges. Indeed, in *Fantasia of the Unconscious* he suggests that when a baby develops the ability to look at its mother critically, it has reached a significant moment of self-consciousness. In a passage which is a kind of hybrid of Lacan's Mirror Stage and Freud's fort/da game, he suggests that seeing thrusts the other away from the self, and thus the self's edges are created. Having 'relinquished' the mother in order to realise the *difference*, 'the wonder of other things', the child sees her consciously for the first time as a separate entity:

> if she tries to force its love to play upon her again, like light revealing her to herself, then the child turns away. Or it will lie and look at her with the strange, odd, curious look of knowledge, like a little imp who is spying her out. This is the curious look that many mothers cannot bear. Involuntarily it arouses a sort of hate in them – the look of scrutinizing curiosity, apart, and as it were studying, balancing them up. . . . The mother is suddenly set apart, as an object of curiosity, coldly, sometimes dreamily, sometimes puzzled, sometimes mockingly observed. (F, 40)

Here, then, the child relates to its mother as a visual object, and it has found the ability to be aggressive along with the new sense of its own self as a growing individual. The process clearly relies upon a key moment of (visual) recognition, and in this sense its relationship with Hegel's Master–Slave dialectic is important. In this sequence (perhaps the most famous phase of the *Phenomemology of Spirit*), the ideal pair of consciousnesses, One and Other, are differentiated by, and gain self-consciousness through, their ability to recognise each and the other as separate. The moment of recognition is the point at which their equal difference is marked. Crucially, each needs the other as a mirror to give itself its sense of self, of separateness: 'They recognise themselves as mutually recognizing one another'.[9] This recognition is the key to self-consciousness for Hegel. From this moment, however, the imbalances and inequalities begin to build up; one and other enter into a relationship of domination (the master and slave of the title), the spark from which early Marxist theories of consciousness and power were to grow.

In *The Bonds of Love*, Jessica Benjamin discusses the echoes of Hegel's work on recognition in psychological theories of infant development, particularly various theories of separation–individuation to be found in ego psychology from the 1960s onwards, as well as D.W. Winnicott's object relations theory.[10] Returning to Lawrence via Winnicott, the act of recognition and of being recognised becomes part of a fantasy dynamic of destruction and survival, in which attacking the other must be seen as part of a process of separation and self-knowledge. The need for an individuating moment of recognition inherent in the act of 'seeing' the mother (separating from her) which is discussed in *Fantasia*, therefore needs to be seen as an aggressive act through which the self begins to recognise itself. Lawrence's infant is destructively dispassionate and, as Benjamin says of Winnicott's work, 'Destruction . . . is an effort to differentiate. . . . When I act upon the other it is vital that he be affected,

so that I know that I exist – but not completely destroyed, so that I know
he also exists.'[11] For Lawrence, then, seeing is an effort to differentiate:
when the child sees the other it is vital that it knows it is seen, in order
that it may know itself as seer.

Thus, when the mother is set apart the baby is set up – sight is integral
to the creation of the conscious self. In *Fantasia*, despite the larger weight
of Lawrence's polemic, this is not necessarily a negative process – it is the
first moment in a chain of individual evolution which *should* end in a
return to sexualised (mature) darkness. The baby's look is the first instance
of what Lawrence calls 'the extravagance of spiritual *will*', whose
qualities are:

> nervous, critical objectivity, the deliberate forcing of sympathy, the play
> upon pity and tenderness, the plaintive bullying of love, . . . eager curiosity,
> . . . the delightful desire to pick things to pieces, and the desire to put them
> together again, the desire to 'find out', and the desire to invent. . . . (F, 41)

This positive gloss on 'the desire to "find out"', the cerebral – and soon-
to-be-feminine – preserve, is, however, quite rare.

Early in *The Rainbow* Ursula's child-identity is crystallised in an
Oedipal moment of awakening through the father. At this moment she
comes into her own as a visual and conscious little girl, the eldest and first
to mark herself off from sensory reality through the separating desire of
the father:

> Her father was the dawn wherein her consciousness woke up. . . . The clasp
> of his hands and the power of his breast woke her up almost in pain from
> the transient unconsciousness of childhood. Wide-eyed, unseeing, she was
> awake before she knew how to see. She was wakened too soon.[12]

Were this a boy-child under discussion, these would be quite conventional
Oedipal terms for the painful break away from the mother as the child
aligns itself with the father and the order of the Symbolic. That it is a girl,
and a girl who learns to wake up to the 'dawn' through her *desire* for the
father, twists this individual development–narrative crucially. This is also
remarkable for its assertion of a love which is precisely *not* blind, and of
desire as a material magnetism which excludes Ursula's mother ('[Ursula]
set towards him like a quivering needle. All of her life was directed by her
awareness of him, her wakefulness to his being. And she was against her
mother' (R, 221)). But the girl is not becoming a boy in aligning herself
with her father, and neither is she following a straightforwardly female–
Oedipal route, for in loving him she also learns to look. This, then, is a
desire for the father which actually *opens* the girl's eyes: boy-like, she takes
her place in the Symbolic ('her consciousness woke up') when the presence
of the father 'dawns', but what she is learning is how to be a *woman* who
sees, and all of this happens with the *growth* of father–child desire, not

its violent termination. Were Ursula destined for a more negative role, this would certainly signal the dawning of a 'cocksure' nature. The seeing woman is Lawrence's hermaphrodite, and never more so than when Ursula – vehicle for all of the sympathies of *The Rainbow* – finds out who she is. She follows what is usually a masculine path of looking and knowing, but this is enacted through a taboo experience of incest. The visual femininity of the grown woman allows this: women learn to see and to know better than men, but it is still love for the first man which kick-starts the process. This is remarkable for the way in which it combines a statement of the importance of vision in the growth of the self, with an exploration of the twist which femininity adds to the tale. But for her father, Ursula realises, 'she might have gone on like the other children . . . one with the flowers and insects and playthings, having no existence apart from the concrete object of her attention' (R, 221).

For Lawrence, when the baby fully *sees* its mother, it says, 'Here I only know the delightful revelation that you are you. The wonder is no longer within me, my own dark, centrifugal, exultant self. . . . And I can no longer exult and know myself the dark, central sun of the universe' (F, 38). 'You' is a delight here – moving from the essential darkness of self to the light of other is undoubtedly positive at this point. But it is not finally enough for Lawrence. His last moment of fulfilment is both beyond and before this choice of dark self (which does not even know that it is blind) or illuminated other (which acts as a Hegelian mirror which mediates the self's image of itself). The third, synthetic moment of connection with the (sexual) other, and with the material world, in a state of blessed blindness, is where Lawrence's heart lies and where his full philosophy is consolidated. This is the third phase of his history of individual development, the final moment of fulfilment which passes beyond 'visual consciousness', and beyond any possibility of visual sex. 'The Blind Man' consolidates Lawrence's much more characteristic advocation of a dark state of connection, a moment when the falling into vision is forgiven by a literally immediate (i.e. unmediated) undistanced contact with the natural world as darkness falls across the reconnected self.

Lawrence's progression of healthy human development is quite crudely dialectical, and plainly teleological. Normal development leads to the third moment of dark consummation, even though most of us are trapped, fatally, in the moment of visual consciousness, cut off from each other by the fact that we want to *see* each other, preferring to 'make eyes of love.' Lawrence is clear that, if we do everything right, and are prepared to lie back and close our eyes, the connection must take place: 'In one direction, all life works up to the one supreme moment of coition' (F, 18). At this moment, visual beauty is irrelevant, and left far behind: Lawrence's couples do it with the lights off, mentally if not actually. In practice he breaks his own rules enough (he puts on sufficient lights) to allow masculinity to be seen and celebrated as the prime spectacle of that 'one supreme moment of coition'. All of his fictional sex scenes are characterised by a dynamic of voyeurism and exhibitionism which breaks the rules, rules which in his non-fiction dictate that true sexual connection should take place blindly, in a realm way beyond the excitements of the gaze:

> this has nothing to do with pretty faces or white skin or rosy breasts or any of the rest of the trappings of sexual love. These trappings belong to the day. Neither eyes nor hands nor mouth have anything to do with the final massive and dark collision of the blood in the sex crisis. . . . (F, 174)

It is easy to see how statements such as this have to some extent endeared Lawrence to some female, and even feminist, readers. Lawrence rejects the common sexual emphasis of our culture which for some feminists, dominates and objectifies women by visually referring them to an ideal image (the familiar subjection of sexual worth to a narrow range of centrefold stereotypes). Lawrence's rejection of the hallmarks of ideals of beauty would be refreshing, if it didn't simply replace one sexual prescription and range of expectations with another. He still loves women for their bodies, but what they look like is less important than their readiness to close their eyes at the crucial moment. What matters is that they can achieve 'the final massive and dark collision of the blood'. Forget how you look, do not be the slave of your mirror any longer (and *never*, like Hermione Roddice, actually *enjoy* your mirror) – as long as you are ready to submit to a darkness which is essentially phallic, you can leave off submitting to the demands of looking good. If feminism laments the limitations of our culture's ideals of feminine beauty, Lawrence answers by charging us not to look at all, but, like a nun deprived of a mirror, his dark solutions are hardly liberating. We may be limited by an overemphasis on the contemporary equivalent of 'pretty faces or white skin or rosy breasts', but in throwing out this bathwater we also lose the baby – the possibility of using powerfully and pleasurably a wider range of visual and other 'trappings'.

Let me recap on Lawrence's various stages of man – the framework of ideal development which he outlines in *Fantasia* will form a clear backdrop to my discussions of Lawrence below. The individual moves through vision back into darkness again, a move which involves a significant sleight of hand: Lawrence seems to build darkness out of light, the final heterosexual consummation out of the individual and dividual incompletion of the single, conscious self. Only in passing through the first two moments – the first being the 'root' moment of 'dynamic, pre-mental knowledge, such as cannot be transferred into thought' (F, 34), the second being the birth of thought itself, and which is constituted by the purest form of transference, the exchange of images between mother and child – can the third moment of 'living Darkness' between two (heterosexual) people be achieved. Unfortunately for Lawrence's women, most of them remain stuck at the stage of looking and mental primacy, knowing their identity through visually assured difference, since they refuse to forgo the intellect and embrace instead the nebulous, not to say dubious, rewards of the 'living darkness'. In a sense, 'inauthentically feminine' women (cocksure or 'mental-conscious' women, who drag modern men down with them) are trapped at a retarded stage of development, bound to their babies and by their mental love for their babies, never progressing into adult darkness. The 'finally obscene love-will of the mother' ensures that 'the modern child' is, 'born out of the mental-conscious love-will, born to be another unit of self-conscious love-will: an ideal-born beastly little entity with a devil's own will of its own, benevolent, of course, and a Satan's own seraphic self-consciousness, like a beastly Botticelli brat' (F, 144). Whilst this rant against ideal humanity ends in a eulogy to poison-gas, elsewhere a simpler solution is advocated: turning off the lights of consciousness, blotting out mother-love with heterosexual sex, enforcing an all-consuming, blind genital submission which turns cocksure mothers into *authentically* feminine Lawrentian heroines. Beyond sight is where Lawrence would have us, at the end of the journey to dark maturity:

> They say it is better to travel than to arrive. It's not been my experience, at least. The journey of love has been rather a lacerating, if well-worth-it, journey. But to come at last to a nice place under the trees with your 'amiable spouse' who has at last learned to hold her tongue and not to bother about rights and wrongs: her own particularly. And then to pitch a camp, and cook your rabbit, and eat him: and to possess your own soul in silence, and to feel all the clamour lapse. That is the best I know . . . we all make a very, very bad start today, with our idea of love in our head, and our sex in our head as well. (F, 138)

Until we each achieve our place in this tableau of arrival, we are not fully developed. Beneath the humility of 'That is the best I know' lies a developmental prescription: *arrive* here, do not get stuck on the journey. The sun has gone down, the woman lowers her eyes and shuts her mouth, darkness is anticipated, and the soul is ready for it, allowing the clamour of consciousness to 'lapse'.

This is where – to cut across again to the short story in question – the blind man finds himself, a stage further along in Lawrence's theory of development by virtue of his 'disability'. So closely identified with each other are visual sense and 'sex in the head' that when one is lost the other goes too. Not being able to see is more than made up for by having your sex knocked out of your head and back into your 'blood'. When visual power is lost, so is the 'ideal of love'; blindness 'cauterizes' the disease of sex in the head. Beyond sight is also before it, and when the blind man finds the spatial world closing in on him again, he experiences a healing of the gap which sight had gouged between self and thing in the painful creation of his conscious self. When Darkness falls, miraculously, he not only reconnects with what would in another discourse be called a pre-Oedipal sense of immediate contact, he also gets the girl.

'The Blind Man' is an exemplary statement of Lawrence's philosophy: it offers a fantasy narrative of a nexus of ideas about gender, authenticity and knowledge which all connect on the issue of Lawrence's philosophy of vision. In short, what he advocates is any experience which strips one of sight, as a way back to pre-visual bliss – the immersion of the self (at the risk of losing it) in an experience of unmediated darkness. Blindness is an aid to truth, a guarantee of insight. As Lawrence writes of the production of *Hamlet* he saw in Italy,

> It is a strange thing, if a man covers his face, and speaks with his eyes blinded, how significant and poignant he becomes. The ghost of this Hamlet was very simple. He was wrapped down to the knees in a great white cloth, and over his face was an open-work woollen shawl. But the naive blind helplessness and verity of his voice was strangely convincing. He seemed the most real thing in the play.[13]

The ghost, then, is real by virtue of his inability to see, the one being an index of the other. Because he is 'a voice out of the dark' he becomes more 'strangely real' (Italy, 82) than what we might call any 'sighted voice'.

This is one of the concerns of 'The Blind Man', but here Lawrence also develops his discussion of the relationship between sight and self. The ability to see is integral to the construction of the conscious self as a thing separate from the natural world – the self which characterises itself as other than the object it perceives. Blindness, on the other hand, allows 'unspeakable nearness'; denigrated by a visually orientated (and, for Lawrence, a degenerate) culture as a state of deprivation, here blindness is a state of grace which heals the fatal gap between self and other, a gap opened up by the conscious self's ability to see, to see the world *as* other. The 'unspeakable', 'incomprehensible' self which is born of the shadowy reunion between blind self and dark otherness is Lawrence's final, authentic goal. The fact that 'he did not think much' (EME, 64) is offered as a positive state on a par with the fact that he cannot see. What is being celebrated here is an unknowing, prelinguistic self – a self cut off from visual images, which wants to 'unthink' thought, a self which wants to slip into a blank space before language. How, then, can this self be literary? How is Lawrence to write about that self which undermines the act of writing? How is he to make it speak? How can one write with approval of (and visually scrutinise) a self which is ostensibly in the process of undoing itself as a speaking – and looking – subject?

Vision and splitting

The 'immediate' quality of the blind man's contact is thus a crucial part of the positive destruction of his self. Sight, which marks distances between objects and allows a conscious knowledge of those objects, is replaced by what Lawrence calls, in a moment of near self-parody, 'blood-prescience'. Vision is, then, the basis of distinction; it marks differences and not only verifies but actually brings about the fatal gap between the self and the natural world. It is this which casts one from Edenic Dark immediacy to post-lapsarian visual separation. Yet Maurice the blind man has the chance to go back. The claims Lawrence makes for this state of 'pure' and unmediated contact are extraordinary:

> So long as he kept this sheer immediacy of blood-contact with the substantial world he was happy, he wanted no intervention of visual consciousness. In this state there was a certain rich positivity, bordering sometimes on rapture. Life seemed to move in him like a tide lapping, lapping, and advancing, enveloping all things darkly. It was a pleasure to stretch forth the hand and meet the unseen object, clasp it, and possess it in pure contact. He did not try to remember, to visualise. He did not want to. The new way of consciousness substituted itself in him. (EME, 64)

The wild, unseeing self is awakened when darkness falls, but the cost of this is ultimately loss of consciousness, or a 'new way of consciousness.' 'Visual consciousness', on the other hand, only acts to differentiate. Vision is an 'intervention' in the rapturous union of authentic self with the natural world. It brings about a fundamental split in the self, between its past and present, self and others. For Lawrence, the dawning of visual consciousness, in cultural or individual history, constitutes the fall from grace.

The fact that it is a male character who rejects visual consciousness here is no accident, and this is not because of the contingencies which have sent him to the trenches in the first place. The whole story sets up darkness as intrinsically masculine, and positions Isabel as helpless seer of masculine darkness throughout. This becomes clear at a few key moments:

> She pressed his arm close to her, as she went. But she longed to see him, to look at him. She was nervous. He walked erect, with face rather lifted, but with a curious tentative movement of his powerful, muscular legs.
>
> She could feel the clever, careful, strong contact of his feet with the earth, as she balanced against him. For a moment he was a tower of darkness to her, as if he rose out of the earth. (EME, 63)

The more Isabel struggles to see Maurice the less she is able to connect with him – she is weak because she looks. When she is plunged fully into darkness, however, she has to submit to something of his sense of things, and a split takes place between the Isabel which still strives to see and a wilder self which finds other things in the darkness. This is both thrilling and threatening: 'She did not stir, because she was aware of the presence of the dark hindquarters of the horses, though she could not see them, and she was afraid. Something wild stirred in her heart' (EME, 61). Here Isabel's brush with darkness threatens her controlling self enough to allow an other, more immediate, self to emerge. She is both the wild thing stirring and the fearful, conscious onlooker, straining to control the 'presences' which are neither near nor far. Distance is subverted, and thus the spatial relationships between things are unclear or undone. Non-visual awareness of a natural 'presence' invites the wild ones out from within, but whilst one continues to experience through a conscious, seeing self, the other will continue to be afraid. This spilt self is, of course, a familiar one, but Lawrence explores it consistently, linking the visual with speech and offering both as key components of the conscious self. Isabel is torn between the second moment of Lawrence's dialectic, and the third which would allow her full contact with Maurice. When she cannot control through sight, she tries through speech. Speaking when she finds the immediacy of darkness too disturbing, her language becomes a way of marking a difference between herself and the undermining dark morass which Maurice occupies and Lawrence sanctifies:

> How near he was, and how invisible! The darkness seemed to be in a strange swirl of violent life, just upon her. She turned giddy.
>   Her presence of mind made her call, quietly and musically:
>   'Maurice! Maurice – dea-ar!'
>   'Yes,' he answered. 'Isabel?'
> She saw nothing, and the sound of his voice seemed to touch her.
>   'Hello!' she answered cheerfully, straining her eyes to see him.
> He was still busy, attending to the horses near her, but she saw only darkness. It made her almost desperate.... She wished he would come away.
>   While he was so utterly invisible she was afraid of him. (EME, 62)

Maurice, of course, is perfectly capable and unafraid in actual darkness – for him there is no difference. The whole story is carefully phrased to valorise Maurice's handicap: not even knowing, as night falls, that the lamps are unlit, he moves confidently in his world of unmediated touch:

> She saw him mount into the darkness, unseeing and unchanging. He did not know that the lamps on the upper corridor were unlighted. He went on into the darkness with unchanging step....
>   ... He seemed to know the presence of objects before he touched them. (EME, 64)

Isabel, on the other hand, is limited by her reliance on sight – for her, Maurice disappears into the darkness, and is lost visually – it is his *in*visibility which she most fears. For Maurice, darkness is all-encompassing, and it does not make visual phenomena disappear – all things are constantly present in another realm which is not dictated by the absence or presence of light. Thus Maurice's blindness is not perceived by him in this context as a deficiency at all – he is empowered by his indifference to light. It is the sighted here who are passive, unmoving, incapable of penetrating the element of the blind: Maurice dextrously *acts* ('he went away, . . . he went on . . .', and the fact that 'he did not know' that there was no light is given as a blessing, a capacity – 'he *did*', he was capable), whilst Isabel passively watches.

I am reminded of the joke in which a Rabbi and a Priest play golf together, behind a party of blind men, who are also playing golf, but understandably rather slowly. Whilst the Priest sympathises and understands, the Rabbi testily asks, 'But why can't they play at *night*?'. Like the blind golfers, Maurice doesn't notice the dark – he is, we might say, visually amphibious. The Priest and the Rabbi, however, can only play golf in the day, and Isabel is similarly limited. Her helpless voyeurism of Maurice's capable blindness dominates her experience of the world, and whilst Maurice moves around and *does*, she can only waver between inactive visual struggle and passive gazing – 'She saw nothing . . . [she] strain[ed] her eyes to see him . . . she saw only darkness . . . While he was so utterly invisible she was afraid of him . . . She disliked to answer into the dark . . . She longed to see him, to look at him. She was nervous . . .' (EME, 63). Vision is a curse, and the looker is its worse victim. Maurice is indifferent to whether Isabel can see or not, whilst she is constantly pinned down by her need to see what he is doing – the blind man visually obsesses her. In his poem 'Know Deeply, Know Thyself More Deeply' Lawrence advocates female blindness in response to this: 'Go down into your deep old heart, woman, and lose sight of yourself./And lose sight of me' (Poems, 477).

Phallus in wonderland

But Lawrence isn't simply interested in valorising the darkness within which Maurice moves 'almost unconsciously in his familiar surroundings, dark though eveything was'. With the next move, silence is celebrated along with darkness, and throughout Lawrence's work, the transcendence of speech is one of the key rewards of darkness. In his element Maurice is in touch and apparently multi-sensed. Blindness gives access to a form of synaesthesia, but voices still have purchase as a way of gaining control.

For Isabel, speech must act as a marker between herself and things, since vision cannot, and always the experience is threatening. Impossibly, she sees darkness, and she fears Maurice's invisibility.

Darkness and wordlessness are married in authenticity, as illumination and language are cast out. In the culminative 'Excurse' chapter of *Women in Love*, Birkin goes shopping, but as he enters the illuminated stage of the store[14] 'he remained dark and magic, the living silence seemed the body of reality in him'. To be 'dark' is now evidently not enough; phallic heroes must also be 'magic' and, most significantly, 'silent', and strong enough in this to carry the darkness and silence through with them into the illuminated public world. This, in turn affects or infects Ursula ('She too was dark and fulfilled in silence') (WL, all quotations 401), but what is most strange is that Lawrence is managing to labour the virtues of silence and the non-verbal using so many words. As Ursula contines to watch him she thinks, 'The dark, subtle reality of him, never to be translated, liberated her into perfection', and it is here that Lawrence most particularly betrays his objection to language. Both vision and speech divide the self off from dark immersion, but whereas vision marks a spatial distance, speech is a 'translation'. Words are silent inner truths uneasily reworked at one remove. In submitting to Birkin, Ursula rejects this process of 'translation', which would turn Lawrence's essential self into an image, a linguistic simulacrum or visual representation, of itself.

Darkness as an object for writing is one thing, however, but silence? The Romanticism of this, persisting in arguments for silence made by such a prolifically verbal cultural figure, the perverse advocation of the pre-linguistic through language, is striking. Despite Lawrence's historical and cultural moment, and – as Tony Pinkney has argued[15] – his obsession with the forms and possibilities of modernism, a bubbling Romanticism can be traced throughout his work. But in tandem with this familiar Romantic eruption comes another paradox: the desperate argument for dark unseeing which takes place even while the narrative is itself fixated on images, on the look of things (all this is happening, remember, as Ursula *watches* Birkin in 'the lighted, public place'). Ursula's thought continues:

> To speak, to see, was nothing. It was a travesty to look and to comprehend the man there. Darkness and silence must fall perfectly on her, then she could know mystically, in unrevealed touch. She must lightly, mindlessly connect with him, have the knowledge which is the death of knowledge, the reality of surety in not knowing. (WL, 402)

This is a clear statement of alternative knowledges, and it is an idea which keeps recurring, particularly in what is perhaps Lawrence's darkest novel, *The Plumed Serpent*. Cautiously circling a concept which, by its own definition, should not be defined, this elliptical sense of saying something which should properly be left 'unrevealed', 'untranslated' into discourse, is a hallmark of his writing. What we are confronting in phrases like 'the knowledge which is the death of knowledge', or in the visual presentation of a figure who nevertheless should properly be left 'in unrevealed touch', is a characteristic conceptual knot which is tied when Lawrence is both urged to represent ('translate') and holds back because of what he deems the inauthenticity or violence of representation. In his desperation to say the impossible, Lawrence decides to do both at once – to speak and not to speak, to see and go blind.

I do not want to say much here about the extensive eulogies to darkness which occur in later Lawrence – a few muddy moments of mystification from *The Plumed Serpent* will give the unfamiliar reader the general idea. At one point in Chapter 13, Ramón retreats alone into the darkness, strips off his clothes, and then (one can only assume) masturbates his way into a deeper darkness. Here he is 'invisible', because, like the child who covers its eyes, he can see no one seeing him, and so he must be invisible – actually not there if no-one's eyes find him out. This is an exemplary piece of Lawrentian mystification, and I quote it simply as a prime example of the phallic ideal around which *The Plumed Serpent* circles:

> Till the black waves began to wash over his consciousness, over his mind, waves of darkness broke over his memory over his being, like an incoming tide, till at last it was full tide and he trembled, and fell to rest. Invisible in the darkness, he stood soft and relaxed, staring with wide eyes at the dark, and feeling the dark fecundity of the inner tide washing over his heart, over his belly, his mind dissolved away in the greater, dark mind, which is undisturbed by thoughts.
>
> He covered his face with his hands, and stood still, in pure unconsciousness, neither hearing nor feeling nor knowing, like a dark sea-weed deep in the sea. With no Time and no World, in the deeps that are timeless and worldless. (PS, 205–6)

Literally thoughtless, this is as pure a transcendence of feminine epistemophilia and scopophilia as one is likely to find in Lawrence, and as such it represents some sort of ideal. Ramón's prayer-state eschews any reference to the external,[16] and as such it connects with several other moments when Lawrence advocates the circular return of the masculine self to itself for release from the bounds of knowledge, vision and inauthenticity.

Indeed, Lawrence's male is repeatedly caught in the act of withdrawing into the privacy of his sovereign self and speaking the silence which apparently cannot be spoken. Returning to the self in a state of misogynistic prayer is a homecoming and a kind of orgasmic death, more generally, a defiance of the straight-line logic of modern times: 'If I have a way to go', he writes in *Mornings in Mexico*, 'it will be round the swoop of a bend impinging centripetal towards the centre. The straight course is hacked out in wounds, against the will of the world.'[17] Like Ramón's deeps that are 'Timeless and Wordless', the Indian Round Dance, described in 'Indians and Entertainment',

> is the homeward pulling of the blood, as the feet fall in the soft, heavy rhythm, endlessly. It is the dark blood falling back from the mind, from the sight and speech and knowing, back to the great central source where is rest and unspeakable renewal. (Mexico, 58)

The Indians dance a centripetal dance, a possibility of return being found in darkness, where the blood falls back. The Round Dance defies the term 'entertainment', meeting several of the criteria for authentic experience we have already encountered: 'It has no name. It has no words. It means nothing at all. There is no spectacle, no spectator' (Mexico, 58). Lawrence's better-known philosophy of spiritual exogamy, of leaving and reaching out into an unknown 'beyond', has then been abandoned in favour of a kind of cultural narcissism. Both Ramón's rejection of the outside, and the Indian emphasis *back* to the centre, are connected forms of return. Narcissism is then understood as the return to the self, or to an original point of origin, the 'homeward pulling of the blood'. The centrifugal movement of modernist exodus is rejected in favour of a spiralling dance back to the start, with the dark inner self as point of entry.

This constant reference to the structures and desires of 'home' is, of course, exactly what Lawrence pinpoints in *Fantasia of the Unconscious* as a fundamental problem with the Freudian world of family romance and incestuous relations. Here his cherishd Indians dance out a pattern which replicates the return to the self and the start.[18] Even the Christian Cathedrals of 'Market Day' in *Mornings in Mexico* are subverted backwards, their towers 'slowly leaning, seeking the curve of return' (Mexico, 51), and Lawrence's 'home' has to be understood as always male. Cipriano dances the same round dance in *The Plumed Serpent*, and comes to Kate with the same spirit searching for this 'renewal', but the acting out of this, and what it means in terms of the general epistemological and sexual message of the book, is that in touching her he touches himself, once she is suitably submissive. For all the novel's insistence on reciprocity, 'renewal' is simply for the male – women act as mediators of male desire, the junctions through which it passes on its way back to the self or, as we shall see in Chapter 3, on its way to encountering another male body. For the female the act which renews Cipriano's 'huge erection' is 'a mystery of prone submission', closing eyes and lying back:

> the supreme passivity, like the earth below the twilight, consummate in living lifelessness, the sheer solid mystery of passivity. Ah, what an abandon, what an abandon, what an abandon! – of so many things she wanted to abandon. (PS, 325)

The man renews himself; the woman abandons herself.

Desire of the masculine and of the self as masculine consequently exists in tandem with an equal desire to negate femininity – the return to the dark self is part of a movement of negation *outwards* (of the visionary woman) as well as an *inward* affirmation. If Ramón's slipping away is narcissistic, it is a form of narcissism tainted by the nagging desire to have one's experience in reference to another who is *not* there, who is *not* having it too. Darkness is always set up with reference to an absent, seeing woman.

At the heart of Lawrence's metaphysic is a argument for the sanctity of silence used to evade the problems of language, a plea for darkness made in tandem with a nefarious pleasure in the gaze. Ramón's narcissism, then, never exists in and for itself as something which is primarily interested in itself. For all the solitude of this experience, the hostile message between the lines is: this is a darkness which is found in spite of the light which threatens the edges, a blind insight indulged despite the prying eyes of women which have first to be excluded. In the next chapter I will look directly at those eyes.

Chapter Two

◆

'... my eyes are like hooks ...'
Sadism and the female gaze

There is a notorious moment in *The Plumed Serpent* when the consequences for men of the woman's look are clearly spelled out. A man might stand there, innocently minding his own business, and what does a woman want to do, to what do her thoughts turn? Not to sex but violence – all she can think of is sticking a knife in his back:

> He stood thus, naked to the waist, his black hair ruffled and splendid, his back to the women, looking out at the lake. . . .
> Kate saw the sigh lift the soft, quiescent, cream-brown shoulders. The soft, cream-brown skin of his back, of a smooth *pure* sensuality, made her shudder. The broad, square, rather high shoulders, with neck and head rising steep, proudly. The full-fleshed, deep-chested, rich body of the man made her feel dizzy. In spite of herself, she could not help imagining a knife stuck between those pure, male shoulders. . . . Kate's heart suddenly shrank in her breast. This was how Salome had looked at John. (PS, 194-5)

Kate looks at Ramón as Salome looks at John the Baptist; for both women, in Paul Virilio's words, 'the eyes' function being the function of a weapon'.[1] Two pages later she admits again that she 'knew how Salome felt. She knew how John the Baptist had been, with his terrible, aloof beauty, inaccessible, yet so potent' (PS, 196). Ramón, who here becomes blind by virtue of his turned back (his eyes are blind to Kate's desire) has done nothing but 'look good', aloof, perfect, the prime masculine specimen and spectacle – an image *asking* to be pinned down.

Kate's act is doubly criminal, not only murderous but cowardly, stealing the moment of violation when the victim's back is turned (she later castigates herself as the inhabitant of 'our paltry, prying, sneak-thieving day'). Just like a woman to fight dirty – just like a woman to look at all. Despite the fact that no sooner has the knife appeared in the other's back than it is turned around onto Kate herself, as she indulges in a frenzy of self-recrimination, her gaze has marked her out as murderer. Feminist film theorists have continued to question what happens when the woman looks,[2] but for Lawrence the answer is clear: looking and killing, sight and a violent will, are inextricably bound up with each other, and if 'Darkness' fails then we must submit to the illuminated, voyeuristic desires of that degenerate female sexuality which even manages to well up in our heroine Kate. Lawrence's anti-ocular polemic cannot finally be separated from his sexism, as female looking and murder collapse into each other.

The section on vision in Diane Ackerman's *A Natural History of the Senses* begins,

> Look in the mirror. The face that pins you with its double gaze reveals a chastening secret: You are looking into a predator's eyes. . . . Our instincts stay sharp, and, when necessary, we just decree one another prey and have done with it.[3]

This sense that predation is the reason for looking, violence the conclusion of vision, runs through Lawrence's work as an angry seam which hardly changes. Whilst whole swathes of his philosophy and style mutate as he moves through the stages of his writing life, on this issue there is little development, and whilst this book notes the dates and historical position of Lawrence's individual works as often as possible, an early work is likely to be making exactly the same point on this issue as a late one: our eyes have murder built into them, but it is the woman's look which is most dangerous of all.

This connection between a dependence on looking and a violent streak is also played out in the disastrous relationship between Hermione and Birkin in *Women in Love*. 'Hermione loved to watch', we are told (WL, 148). She looks at Birkin 'with leering eyes' (WL, 162), and she looks 'down at Ursula with that long, detached, scrutinizing gaze that excited the younger woman' (WL, 88). These are, however, the symptoms of a degenerate sexuality, and on this Birkin offers the final word when he rages at her early in the novel in Ursula's classroom:

> 'You've got that mirror, your own fixed will, your immortal understanding, your own tight conscious world, and there is nothing beyond it. There, in the mirror, you must have everything. . . . what you want is pornography – looking at yourself in mirrors, watching your naked animal actions in mirrors, so that you can have it all in your consciousness, make it all mental.'
> (WL, 91–2)

The 'sense of violation in the air' here comes from too much truth spoken, as well as Birkin's desire to crack Hermione's skull 'like a nut' (setting her sex in the head free of its mental bounds) as surgery for her pornographic looking-disease. In 'The Border Line' Katherine is touched by the darkness of her first husband, and afterwards 'as she undressed, she avoided the sight of her own face in the mirror. She must not rupture the spell of his presence' (WRA, 98). Hermione is less touched by Birkin, her love of the mirror and of her own gaze disrupting the 'normal' heterosexual exchange Lawrence would support. It is Hermione perhaps who speaks in the poem 'Intimates': 'Don't you care for my love? she said bitterly./I handed her the mirror and said: Please address these questions to the proper person!' (Poems, 604). Whilst Lawrence's dark men are positively encouraged to return to the self in the Round Dance, to an act (like Ramón's) of non-visual self-connection, for women the situation is not the same. It is not simply, as Jenijoy La Belle argues, that Hermione is unfaithful to Birkin in taking the mirror as substitute male,[4] but that her whole mode of sexual organisation and desire is visual. Birkin may say too much, but Hermione's crime is greatest. Her love of looking is part of a bigger, modern, chain of violations with which she connects.

The defamation takes place in Ursula's schoolroom, in a bitter argument between the couple watched over by Ursula herself. It is curious that such a vitriolic debate about the power and evils of looking should itself take place under the gaze of another, and in its early stages under the gaze of a whole roomful of people ('And then only she turned to Ursula, who, with all the class, had been watching the little scene' (WL, 86)). The spectacle of intimacy, even intimate hatred, has a large audience, whose presence the players disavow: Lawrence is nothing if not fond of making ironic spectacles of his actors, as they debate the power of sight and sex.

But in Birkin's diagnosis lies a prediction of Hermione's later violence. Having it all in your consciousness, making it all mental – these are acts of force, through which everything is squeezed into the frame of the mirror, into the tight bounds or bonds of consciousness and image. Already, then, Hermione has violated the *outside* through her 'porno-graphic' (for which read narcissistic, self-referential, mentally and visually enclosed) relationship with herself, with the *inside*. It can only be a matter of time, then, before she does something worse:

> Terrible shocks ran over her body, like shocks of electricity, as if many volts of electricity suddenly struck her down. She was aware of him sitting silently there, an unthinkable evil obstruction. Only this blotted out her mind . . . his silent, stooping back, the back of his head.
>
> A terrible voluptuous thrill ran down her arms . . . Her hand closed on a blue, beautiful ball of lapis lazuli that stood on her desk for a paper-weight. . . . She moved towards him and stood behind him for a moment in ecstasy. . . .
>
> Then swiftly, in a flame that drenched down her body like fluid lightning and gave her a perfect, unutterable consummation, unutterable satisfaction, she brought down the ball of jewel stone with all her force, crash on his head. But her fingers were in the way and deadened the blow. Nevertheless,

down went his head on the table on which his book lay, the stone slid aside and over his ear, it was one convulsion of pure bliss for her, lit up by the crushed pain of her fingers. (WL, 162–3)

In this passage, which reads like an actualisation of Kate's fantasy violation of Ramón, the woman once again turns on a man whose back is turned. The consequences of perverse looking are not only murderous, but cowardly: look she might, but look him in the eye she won't. Again, the negative force of will and vision is 'electric': the terms in which her compulsion is described are those of a specifically modern 'current', alien to darker Lawrentian energies – the current, indeed, which by now has allowed the light (actual and metaphorical) to go on in a million modern homes. Beyond this, the terms of her 'voluptuousness' are those of illumination: flames, lightning, and that extra spasm of sado-masochistic ecstasy in the final sentence as pain 'lights up' her 'convulsion of bliss', taking it one notch higher. Hermione is a desperate figure of visionary violence and vice, for whom looking can only end in tears.

These are women who cannot help but see sadistically. Another example of the connection which Lawrence makes between vision and violation in its relationship to femininity comes in Lawrence's unfinished story 'The Wilful Woman', whose eponymous heroine has eyes with the futurist potency of an illuminating drill – she can pin you down with a look from hell:

Her thick, dark brows like curved horns over the naïve-looking face; and her bright, hazel-grey eyes, clear at the first glance as candour and unquenchable youth, at the second glance made up of all devilish grey and yellow bits, as opals are, and the bright candour of youth resolving into something dangerous as the headlights of a great machine coming full at you in the night.[5]

The vampish sadism of the female look here marks women out once more as the sex in visual and physically violent control, but there is another layer to this. Modern technology, in the form of mass lighting (flicking a switch and banishing the night, or turning on your car headlights and combining light with speed), offers an apt range of analogies for Lawrence's analysis of the female gaze. Women and 'the great [modern] machine' combine to form a vortex of negative elements.

Is the gaze female?

In her recent book *The Woman at the Keyhole: Feminism and Women's Cinema*, Judith Mayne sums up the critical impact of the work of Laura Mulvey:

if there is any single notion which underlies virtually all feminist analyses of the dominant cinema, it is that of the film as spectacle, and more specifically, of the woman as object of spectacle. . . . [T]he equation between film and spectacle has been used to describe the ideal spectator of film as male and the typical object of spectacle as female. . . . It has become commonplace to note that however diverse the manifestations of spectacle in the cinema, they are all – sooner or later – about men looking at women. In Mulvey's words, the classic cinema puts forth man as bearer of the look, woman as its object.[6]

My concern in this chapter, however, is with woman as 'bearer of the look'. The title above echoes that of E. Ann Kaplan's famous essay, 'Is the Gaze Male?',[7] which discusses a variety of feminist positions emerging from film theory which align visual power and pleasure with masculinity. Lawrence's wilful or cocksure woman can be interpreted as a negative answer to Kaplan's question – the gaze is feminine, and it is the woman's gaze which holds the power. One of the concerns of this chapter is to ask, if feminism argues that women have difficulty in looking, how do we account for all of the women in Lawrence who look, and who look in a way which feminism characteristically deems 'male'? The eyes of the Wilful Woman are organs of her lust for domination. The gaze of Hermione Roddice is that of the female fetishist, fixating on her image-in-the-mirror, having all her sex in her head. Kate is the heroine of *The Plumed Serpent*, but she is also the bearer of eyes which are 'like hooks' capable of pinning a man down.

So when Lawrence makes his women 'bearer of the look' he establishes an intriguing configuration of agreement and clash between his work and feminist theory. For both Lawrence and much film theory of the 1970s and 80s, the gaze is aligned with activity, epistemological power, sadism. This much is agreed – the contention lies in how this is gendered. Mulvey's influential essay on the problem of women and the audience of classic Hollywood films, situates the cinematic gaze – of the audience, of the camera, and of the screen characters – in terms of voyeurism and sadism, as a male phenomenon. The image of the woman on the screen 'masculinises' the spectator regardless of the actual sex of the individual viewer of the film. In the light of Mulvey's work, as Constance Penley puts it,

> feminists have no choice but to reject the forms of classical cinema inasmuch as they are constructed on the basis of a male fantasy entirely detrimental to women, one which inevitably makes the woman a passive recipient of the aggressive male look.[8]

Later feminism has followed this by mapping the male gaze onto a range of other masculine qualities which are pitted in binarity against feminine passivity. Thus the oppositions and pairs which Hélène Cixous cites in her essay 'Sorties' –

> Thought has always worked through opposition.
> Speaking/Writing
> Parole/Ecriture
> High/Low[9]

can logically be supplemented with the cinematic opposition Voyeur/ Exhibit, Seer/Seen, Male Gaze/Female Spectacle. For the most part, Lawrence is systematically consistent: time is white, Western, conscious, it is a cultural imposition on the darkness of the 'moment'. Darkness itself is alternatively aligned with a 'quick' natural being outside of time or before history. Visual perception, reason, time and the intellect lie on the side of consciousness. In his preferences Lawrence is an exemplary irrationalist. Where his philosophical world turns upside down is on the issue of how this opposition is gendered. The gaze is culturally *female*: it is women's sight which is 'sharp', women who thirst after the look and its cerebral pleasures, and men who conversely are urged to retreat into an eroticised blindness. This emphasis cuts against the strongest thread in feminist film criticism to date; Lawrence could not be further from Linda Williams' account of what happens 'When the Woman Looks' in silent cinema:

> Like the female spectator, the female protagonist often fails to look, to return the gaze of the male who desires her. In the classic narrative cinema, to see is to desire. It comes as no surprise, then, that many of the 'good girl' heroines of the silent screen were often figuratively, or even literally, blind.[10]

Lawrence, on the other hand, emphasises the power of women's eyes, their unnatural ability to fixate and pin down whatever their gaze rests upon, their role as the organs and agents of conscious control. Lawrence's women seldom fail to see, often initiate desire with a look, and, as we saw in the last chapter, it is the 'good boys' of his silent screen who slip into a virtuous blindness.

Lawrence's emphasis on women's vision, then, turns feminism's gendered world upside down. The result, however, is no less sexist. At the start of 'Sorties', Cixous asks,

> Where is she?
> Activity/passivity
> Sun/Moon
> Culture/Nature
> Day/Night,

but Lawrence answers this in quite other terms: 'she' reigns in the former camp rather than the latter – the agent of light, logic, looking. The gaze

is aligned with conscious experience, intellectualisation, feminine matriarchal control. Women's eyes are used vicariously to enjoy the spectacle
of *men*, yet feminism has identified the primacy of *woman* as spectacle,
the difficulty of female spectatorship. When women look, it is argued, they
adopt a twisted position in relation to their own reflected images. So what
are the consequences of Lawrence's challenge to the great metaphysical
coupling which has fixed women in Cixous' patriarchal 'double braid'?
How does he manage to subscribe to the traditional psychoanalytic view
(which deems looking active, powerful, primally sadistic) whilst still
ensuring that *whatever* her position – seer or seen – a woman cannot win?

Looking and being looked at are situated both in psychoanalysis and in
recent film theory as active and passive modes of being respectively. The
activity of looking is aligned with a range of other masculine 'activities',
whilst the passivity of being the object of the gaze is situated alongside
other forms of 'feminine' passivity. For Freud, activity and passivity are
more fundamental than the two other pairings crucial to the development
of the subject – masculine/feminine and phallic/castrated.[11] Activity and
passivity are thus early shadow-forms of what it is to be masculine and
feminine, but in and of themselves this pair forms the fundamental
and first set of choices which the developing subject makes, as the purest
and most basic power division the subject is involved in. The subject's
relationship to the look, and its gender-identification, is then mapped
directly onto this primary opposition. Freud makes the connection between
looking and activity, and being-looked-at and passivity, in several places,
but most clearly in his *Three Essays on the Theory of Sexuality*: 'in the
perversions which are directed towards looking and being looked at, we
come across a very remarkable characteristic . . . : the sexual aim ocurs in
two forms, an *active* and a *passive* one'.[12] Despite the pejorative use of
the word 'perversion' which blights much of Freud's work, it is here that
he identifies voyeurism as simply an extreme form of everyone's 'normal'
instinct to gain enjoyment from erotic looking. He terms this an 'active'
sexual aim, and conversely argues that the 'passive' sexual aim of
exhibitionism is simply the extreme – if perverse – conclusion of everyone's
natural desire to recreate themselves as objects of beauty. Thus the gendered
positioning of the look is clearly suggested, although Freud does not go
so far here as to deem men natural voyeurs and women the converse.

In the next section of the *Three Essays*, however, sexual activity and
passivity are further mapped onto sadism and masochism, and by
implication looking is reinforced as an act of aggression, with exhibitionism underlined as a form of visual submission. The binary opposition of
each pairing can be mapped onto the others: activity/passivity, voyeurism/
exhibitionism, sadism/masochism. As Freud writes, 'We find, then, that
certain among the impulses to perversion occur regularly as *pairs of*

opposites,[13] but it is also clear that we are not simply dealing with perversion or extreme states here, since finally each of these pairs can also be mapped onto the pair masculine/feminine. Beyond and before this, however, to some extent Freudianism founds human subjectivity on a bedrock of primal scopophilic instincts which, working hand-in-hand with the Kleinian notion of epistemophilia, characterises the infant and young child's rampant and dominant desire to know through seeing. For Freud and Klein, the instinct which engenders the infant thirst for visual knowledge is one of the primary foundations of adult scopophilia and aesthetic appreciation. It is important to note, however, that for Freud, this 'original' state of primal sadism is not essentially characterised by a desire to destroy or inflict pain: this more familiar form of reactive sadism is a secondary response, dependent upon the reactions of another, masochistic partner.[14] Sadism is another term for an essentially innocent primal activity, the primary drive to impress or inscribe oneself upon the world. In voyeurism, fetishism and exhibitionism this primary, outward-thrusting activity becomes twisted and distorted into a reactive aggression, the female voyeurism of Lawrence which sates its visual thirst on the sexualised male object.

From this psychoanalytic model of scopophilia has sprung a wealth of theories concerned with the power of the gaze, particularly Christian Metz's discussion of the voyeurism of cinema and Laura Mulvey's important reading of cinematic pleasure rooted in masculine access to the powerful gaze, established in a relationship with female exhibitionism and objectification. Although Mulvey's essay appeared some time ago now, its key points are still debated; in the late 1980s studies of the problems and pleasures of female spectatorship have formed a veritable publishing growth industry.[15] When the female spectator *can* find a space (e.g. with the audiences of so-called 'women's films'), it is, as Constance Penley writes, 'an awkward and difficult one: she is a sort of transvestite, forced to assume another role in order to "read" the image'.[16] In gazing, woman becomes vicariously male. This is Constance Penley, discussing the work of Mary Ann Doane:

> Citing Julia Kristeva's description of the double or triple twists of female homosexuality, Doane compares it to the position of the female spectator of [women's] films: 'I am looking, as a man would, for a woman'; or else 'I submit myself, as if I were a man who thought he was a woman, to a woman who thinks she is a man.' Why is female looking so problematic in these films? ... This desire to look is quickly transformed into a desire to be looked at. Significantly, though, the desire to be looked at is itself transformed into a paranoid fear of being looked at. ... It is almost as if the films are compelled to act out the difficulty or impossibility of contructing a position for a woman spectator.[17]

Moreover, it is also almost as if the position of the woman spectator acts out the twists of primary sadism and secondary masochism, her visual actions dancing between penetration and submission. Even a book called *The Female Gaze* begins:

> Why write a book about women *looking*? At men or at each other? In most popular representations it seems that men look and women are looked at. In film, on television, in the press and in most popular narratives men are shown to be in control of the gaze, women are controlled by it. Men act; women are acted upon. This is patriarchy.[18]

But as the book itself shows, things are not so simple. There are many gazes; women's eyes are constantly seduced from all fronts, by magazines, advertising, television, films and literature, and if this adds up to a more complex idea about what it is for women to have power imposed upon them, then that is still not the same as being passive in relation to the necessarily male gaze. Lawrence, however, does not attempt to theorise the basis of the female gaze, instead assuming an unproblematic connection between cocksure mentality and sadistic looking which slides across the questions feminism raises about sexual difference. Lawrence's women do not gain from their visual power or pleasure, moving only from the reactive pleasures of 'sharp sight' to self-castigation and back again. Consequently, Lawrence's bigger critique of the metaphysical prioritisation of the conscious and the visual is not a radical stroke for the unconscious or genuinely transgressive possibilities. It is, rather, a blow for sexism. The predominant narrative voice thus militates against a voyeuristic and sadistic femininity which wants visually to 'pin down' the male image, and I now want to turn to some examples of this.

Distance and modernism

Women in Love opens with a chain of scenes which offer a miniature visual drama of the shock of modernism, and some of its visual possibilities. The first chapter is nothing if not a skilled example of stage management, scene-setting and shifting. It is also part of a peculiarly modern investigation of visual positions and the clash of cultural perspectives. Gudrun and Ursula are first seen sitting at a window, drawing and sewing whilst also looking out. They discuss marriage, they discuss fulfilment and independence, and then they go to view a local society wedding – 'view' being exactly what they do: they do not take part, they watch from afar, they visually assess and observe. Lawrence's concern with the female gaze, with visual art, and with the eyes and image of Gudrun the artist, is present from the first few sentences. Gudrun's powerful gaze is one of the cornerstones of the novel. '[W]ide and large and wondering' (WL, 429) or 'round and dark and staring, her full soft face impassive . . . so that she seemed to be backing away in antagonism even whilst she was advancing' (WL, 223), Gudrun's look is never innocent, always suggesting her relative position in a power network – as here, when she can aggressively retreat *and* advance with the same glance. Elsewhere the look of a woman becomes more clearly murderous – women's eyes are called knives, fish-hooks, their gaze is castrating. I now want to look at the convergence of these two strands: Lawrence's analysis of (sadistic) visual priority and his account of femininity.

Women in Love starts as it means to go on, as series of 'scenes' are paraded before the eyes of Gudrun and Ursula. Five pages into the book, the women leave the house, setting off to walk through an extraordinary sequence of social tableaux. Their journey is a series of views – they see and are seen – the effect being a long procession of people gazing at each other. This technique sets the visual tone of the whole novel: the women are positioned so as to facilitate their looking, which kicks off a developing exploration of ways of seeing, focusing particularly on the eyes of Gudrun. The narrative sticks to the viewpoint of the women, and so even though they move through it, it is the scenery which seems to move past them (and us): first, the high street, in which Gudrun, in 'her grass-green stockings, her large grass-green velour hat, her full soft coat, of a strong blue colour', is 'exposed to every stare' (WL, 58), then past staring mining women, and then into the sight of the other wedding-watchers: '"What price the stockings!" said a voice at the back of Gudrun. . . . How she hated walking up the churchyard path, along the red carpet, continuing in motion, in their sight' (WL, 59–60).

To the 'Women, their arms folded over their coarse aprons . . . [who] stared after the Brangwen sisters with that long, unwearying stare of aborigines' (WL, 58), the 'girls' (*sic*) are the exotics, and the 'aboriginal' stare of the colliery women is that of those who are at home, witnessing the passage of two travelling strangers, whose cosmopolitanism and aesthetic pretentions ensure that they no longer belong. Lawrence is clearly uneasy on this point: his earlier warmth towards this community has to struggle to emerge from beneath the burden of the perspective of those who have moved on, as he was himself in the process of doing when *Women in Love* was written.[19] Lawrence's gaze is itself a travelling one. Moving from the perspective of his class origins, he begins to see with the eyes of the middle-class intelligensia, 'trying on' their gaze as his own. *Women in Love* is a crisis-text in this development of social cross-gazing. From the perspective of *Sons and Lovers*, the term 'aboriginal' could only have been pejorative, but by now, it is Gudrun and Ursula who are the outsiders, the Midlands becoming a dark continent of threatening foreigners. Yet their strangeness is temporal rather than spatial: the mining women stare out from another time (that of pre-modernism), rather than from another continent, although the implication that the girls are occidental travellers in an oriental space is still there. From this point of view, the staring mining people seem little more than components in a late nineteenth-century tableau vivant, past-images which still hang onto the flesh. The passage is haunted by an uncanny sense that the girls have wandered back in time by walking forward in space, giving this moment of cultural cross-gazing a curious atmosphere somewhere between science fiction and travelogue. From the position of modernist subjectivity which Lawrence ascribes to Gudrun, the real world has turned into a representation of itself, and these spectres of a (for her, past) community can only be seen in the chilling terms of artifice:

> Gudrun watched them closely with objective curiosity. She saw each one as a complete figure, like a character in a book, or a subject in a picture, or a marionette in a theatre, a finished creation. She loved to recognise their various characteristics, to place them in their true light, give them their own surroundings, settle them forever as they passed before her along the path to the church. She knew them, they were finished, sealed and stamped and finished with, for her. (WL, 60–1)

This is ripe for narrative condemnation; 'knowing' a living thing – be it book or beast – so that it is 'sealed and stamped and finished with' is the kiss of death to it. Gudrun's modernist gaze, her 'objective curiosity', may be obsessed over as one of the central concerns of *Women in Love*, but it cannot finally be celebrated. As the text's developing fascination with cold artistic vision and its relationship to sadistic feminine sexuality is pushed to an extreme, so Gudrun's ability to connect authentically with the 'living' world degenerates. As the book progresses, so the gap between herself and the object of her scrutiny widens, eventually opening so wide that she is lost somewhere in between – her soul is sacrificed to the chasm of distance. Gerald might actually die for his failure to 'connect' (Forster's 'only connect' being, as Tony Pinkney notes, one of the touchstone statements of the moment), but Gudrun's fate is no happier. For the final Gudrun, bitter and hard and wilfully nasty, seeing is an index of not-being, conscious-knowing excluding any hope of 'dark'-knowledge for ever – 'this awful, inhuman distance . . . would always be interposed between her and the other being' (WL, 432):

> Gudrun saw all [the mountains'] loveliness, she *knew* how immortally beautiful they were, great pistils of rose-coloured, snow-fed fire in the blue twilight of the heaven. She could *see* it, she knew it, but she was not of it. She was divorced, debarred, a soul shut out. (WL, 494)

Spiritual death is, then, the price the artist-seer has to pay for being far enough away from her object to represent it. The bleak tone of Gudrun's encounter with the mountains is not echoed in other accounts of her distance: elsewhere she gains malicious pleasure from the cold irresponsibility which distance bestows upon her ('it gave her pleasure to sit there, cheeks flushed, eyes black and sullen, seeing them all objectively, as put away from her, like creatures in some menagerie of apish degraded souls' (WL, 471)). More dangerous for the would be blind man which the last chapter introduced us to, however, is that on one level Gudrun has to be read as something of a portrait of the artist: her objective curiosity causes her to see people as Lawrence does, 'a character in a book', significantly aligned with subjects in pictures or marionettes in theatres. Lawrence's analysis of the female gaze might also then be a self-analysis. Gudrun shares the author's perspective, who must then himself recognise the fate of being 'divorced, debarred, a soul shut out', in a world which is 'put away from him'.

A less triumphant version of this distance had already been marked out by Miriam in *Sons and Lovers*. In Miriam we find the germ of the form of feminine scopophilia which becomes a raging disease in some of Lawrence's later texts, with the scopophilic woman established as culturally dominant and occupying the position of power in relation to the gaze. Here, however, Miriam's act of looking is implicated in her victimage and suffering, her lack of 'quickness' (the spontaneity of spirit which is to become the hallmark of Dark Passion), being an index of her need for mental possession. The fact that she sees, at a distance, that she 'thinks' rather than 'is', is crucial to her impotence in the text. Paul's 'God doesn't *know* things, He *is* things';[20] but Miriam chooses knowledge, and a gap between her need to know and her ability to 'be' is painfully marked out as a gap of personal failure. Just as a baby's coming into vision – seeing the other at a distance – is articulated as a kind of fall from darkness in *Fantasia*, so Miriam's inability to connect darkly is an effect of her conscious self-distance, or self-conscious distance. She can only 'take' Paul visually: 'She felt as if she watched the very quivering stuff of life in him' (S&L, 305). The conflict of Paul and Miriam is, then, expressed in visual and epistemological terms; their battle and her defeat are articulated as differing attitudes to looking and knowing ('But I wish to know – ' she replied. He laughed resentfully' (S&L, 270)). In *Sons and Lovers* we see the beginning of the interchangeability of certain gender positions with certain epistemological ones: the feminine (specifically Miriam and Mrs Morel) as synonymous with a cerebral–visual fixation and the prioritising of conscious knowledge, the masculine as increasingly identifiable with a quest for dark sexuality and mystical knowledge. As Lawrence's career develops, both sexual/epistemological poles are so nearly always placed in the same gender camps as to be almost anatomically grounded truths of gender. Women want to 'have' things visually, and their judgements take place at a conscious distance from the object. This in turn enacts a kind of violence against the object: mental possession, 'watching the quivering stuff of life' rather than *being* it yourself, founds Lawrence's critique of modernism and modern femininity.

That all this shows Lawrence experimenting with ways of seeing, as well as indulging his nefarious enjoyment in the gaze, is clear. More specifically, in *Women in Love* Lawrence fixes upon Gudrun as a visually sadistic subject, a character saturated in the force and consequences of looking. Not only does she herself see, witness, observe, she is viewed and assessed as a visually powerful object on a number of occasions, eyed-up and jeered at: 'exposed to every stare, she passed on through a stretch of torment. It was strange that she should have chosen to come back and test the full effect of this shapeless, barren ugliness upon herself' (WL, 57). Here, then, we have a seer who is seen, playing out the ambiguity suggested by the title of a recent collection of essays on gay film, *How Do I Look?* As Teresa de Lauretis notes in that volume,[21] the relationship between looking (seeing) and one's own 'looks' (one's image and visage, the spectacle one makes) is close, and for Gudrun one constantly slips into the other: 'Yet she must sit and watch, watch. . . . From every side of the Café, eyes turned half furtively, half jeeringly at her, men looking over their shoulders, women under their hats' (WL, 471). The vampish woman has often been offered up as a classic female fetish-image, visually intriguing *because* she is brave enough to look: 'The vamp is one of the few female stereotypes who is allowed to gaze uninhibitedly at men, Mae West is an example, who directly links the denigrating "sizing up a hunk of meat" look with her sexual ambitions.'[22] Gudrun is Lawrence's strongest vamp, precisely because she constitutes a particular, magnetic object by virtue of her aggressive gaze. It is as if Gudrun's look is itself magnetic, looking in a way which attracts the look. She is both object and seer-judge, a canvas of early twentieth-century Bohemian fashion upon which the public eye is tested out, a representation of someone with eyes, someone whose artistic business it is to represent. For a writer who has conventionally been misread as a pre-modernist modern, this is strikingly self-referential: Lawrence shows Gudrun erecting herself as a visual testing ground, before scrutinising the stares of others as they bounce off her body by virtue of her own, overarchingly powerful visual understanding. For Carol J. Clover the relationship is clear: 'Inside every Peeping Tom is a peeped-at child, trying incessantly to master his own pain by re-viewing it in the person of another.'[23] Freud's voyeur is also something of an exhibitionist, and Gudrun is both subject and object of the look. Being seen in all her thoroughly modern chic is a kind of martyrdom, as she is subjected to the (for her, 'new from her life in Chelsea and Sussex') debased viewpoint of common people. She is visually magnetic precisely because she has visual power, both in the sense of an understanding of the gaze which she then turns on others, and as a stunning, violently dressed, *attractive* object herself.

The 'whip hand' of vision

Much is made of the relationship between the gaze of the detached women and the spectacle of what they see, their first sightings of the men they focus on from afar who are to become their lovers: 'Gudrun lighted on [Gerald] at once . . . His gleaming beauty, maleness, like a young, good-humoured, smiling wolf, did not blind her to the significant, almost sinister stillness in his bearing, the lurking danger of his unsubdued temper' (WL, 61). Ursula, too, sees Birkin before he sees her: 'He piqued her, attracted her, annoyed her' (WL, 68). Whilst the men are a little threatening, this does not override the primary fact that whoever sees first holds the power, as in that parting reply to the unwanted soul who leaves saying 'See you soon' – 'Not if I see you first'. In her recent book on spectatorship, which contains a brilliant analysis of the visual dynamic of Valentino's films, Miriam Hansen argues that 'Whenever Rudolph Valentino lays his eyes on a woman first, we can be sure that she will turn out to be the woman of his dreams, the legitimate partner in the romantic relationship.'[24] This is a specific example of Linda Williams' bigger point, that 'In the classic narrative cinema, to see is to desire'.[25] The wedding scene in *Women in Love* follows this strongly in spirit, if not in gender: Hansen goes on to argue that 'Whenever a woman initiates the look, she is invariably marked as a vamp, to be condemned and defeated in the course of the narrative.' This is both true and not true of Lawrence: the women see their men first, sealing destiny with a look, but only Gudrun emerges as a vamp, although both are differently defeated. Lawrence is experimenting with two possible consequences of the women's different 'first looks'. Ursula watches and wants Birkin before he knows she exists, but as neither a vamp nor a victim; she is ambivalent both in her oppositional questioning and in her bouts of submission to Birkin's dark truths. Hansen's point, that Valentino's gaze is hardly that of the macho superhero (when his 'eyes get riveted on the woman of his choice, he seems to become paralyzed rather than aggressive or menacing, behaving like the rabbit rather than the snake'[26]), is certainly more applicable to Ursula's gaze, which oscillates between active and passive, than it is to Gudrun's.

If looks could kill, then it is Gudrun who would be the mass-murderer. Her gaze might come with an actual physical blow, or it might implicate its object in a sticky web of power which finds her finally in control. The dynamic between Gudrun and Gerald in particular plays out both of these possibilities. Of the moment at which their love crystallises, Lawrence writes,

> She was watching him all the time with her dark, dilated, inchoate eyes. She leaned forward and swung round her arm, catching him a light blow on the face with the back of her hand. . . .
>
> And she felt in her soul an unconquerable desire for deep violence against him. (WL, 236)

This sets the tone for much of their relationship, in which mutual visual scrutiny is accompanied by bubbling threat and power-play. Despite Gerald's obvious gender advantage, there is never any doubt about who is in control; this Gerald knows, from the moment earlier in the book when he 'watched Gudrun closely, whilst she repulsed Hermione. There was a body of cold power in her. . . . He saw her a dangerous, hostile spirit, that could stand undiminished and unabated' (WL, 181). But Gudrun's cold power is not developed alone – it cannot exist except in a relationship of dominance, and as Gerald is observing this of Gudrun, she is fixing him as her partner in what Lawrence calls 'a sort of diabolic free-masonry' (WL, 181). As Birkin says early in the book, 'It takes two people to make a murder: a murderer and a murderee' (WL, 82), and so Gerald slips into his role as submissive to Gudrun's dominant. Any negotiation in between about these roles must always be read as sexual experiment or playing with loaded dice, for Gudrun *has* to win.

Lawrence's rabbits are not, however, as meek as Rudolph Valentino, and the scene of power which takes place around the violence of Bismark the rabbit is particularly revealing. Indeed, the whole is punctuated or punctured by moments in which the gaze itself reveals its subjects, dilated pupils standing for ripped veils in a shock of revelation ('he saw her eyes black as night in her pallid face, she looked almost unearthly. The scream of the rabbit . . . seemed to have torn the veil of her consciousness' (WL, 316); 'The long, shallow red rip [in Gudrun's arm] seemed torn across his own brain, tearing the surface of his ultimate consciousness, letting through the for ever unconscious, unthinkable red ether of the beyond, the obscene beyond' (WL, 317)). The membrane of vision is ripped, letting the outside in and the inside out, the repetition of the tearing action signalling that these red seepages across the divide are involuntary, they cannot be controlled. In the violent scene – the struggle with the animal, Gudrun's wound, their visual exchange – some fundamental divisions have blurred, the seams between people, between inside and outside, have come undone, and the sign of this violence is not blood from a single body but an 'unthinkable red ether of the beyond'. This is not simply Lawrence being wilfully mystifying; the 'red' is an unclaimed substance, which seems to bleed from all the bodies in this encounter, in cries, discharge and action. The chaos of experience here may be rendered primarily in visual terms, but what is really going on is a violent synaesthesia involving several bodies uneasily parted. Gudrun's wound is felt as a rip in the screen between 'his own brain' and 'the obscene beyond', the rabbit's scream tears the veil of Gudrun's consciousness, the rabbit itself is undivided and undirected (its 'black open eye . . . perhaps was looking at them, perhaps was not'), infecting all who touch it with its own violence. It is only in these moments of eruption that Gudrun's look does not divide her from the thing she sees. Whilst participation in these extreme scenes tears certain elements apart (Gerald's mind, the veil of consciousness, Gudrun's flesh), it also allows the gap between vision and thing to close.

These nasty mergings might indicate that the division between Gudrun and Gerald is sado-masochistically unclear, for who is the master and who is the slave when Gudrun's wound can itself become the weapon to slice Gerald's brain? Lawrence often plays with scenes in which tenable moral positions or clear sides (like who is the victim and who the violator) can only be resolved or achieved after a struggle. Several scenes with animals, such as this one, or Gerald's overpowering of his horse in Chapter 9, or the bullfight scene which opens *The Plumed Serpent*, manifest a disturbing excitement without (at first) a single fixed object or division of sides. But for the most part roles are resolved, and Gudrun's role is aggressive. Against her knowledge that 'she was revealed', that she is exposed ('She lifted her arm and showed a deep red score down the silken white flesh'), each scene – this one included – is consolidated with Gudrun as Gerald's dominatrix.

Another significant struggle for power, with Gudrun finally coming out on top but only after a battle, takes place much later in the book, and is acted out almost entirely through the looking-glass, and near to Gerald's death. If Hermione's sexual reality takes place in the mirror ('There, in the mirror, you must have everything'), Gudrun's power games are played out there too. Lawrence's women know the rules of the looking-glass world. Gerald stands behind her watching her in the flesh, whilst she watches his unknowing reflection in the mirror in which she is looking at herself. Kate, remember, turns on a man whose back is turned, twisting the mental knife, and Hermione can only hit the back of Birkin's head. These are violences acted out when one's gaze isn't met; these are women taking advantage of visual mis-meetings. In the mirror, looking at Gerald who does not meet her gaze, Gudrun experiences a crisis of confidence and dominance ('For her life, she could not turn round and face him' (WL, 508)) which gathers and breaks without Gerald apparently knowing anything about it. She weakens, and is brought to the point at which she is *almost* 'grovelling at his feet, letting him destroy her', before finally turning back and taking control, with Gerald aware of nothing. Everything is projected onto his unseeing image in the mirror, in the face of his 'obtuse blindness', and Gudrun collects herself 'Thank[ing] God he could see nothing': 'She had the whip hand over him now.' The pleasures of the process through which this resolution is reached are, however, as important as the goal (the satisfactions of achieved sadism and submission). The woman might eventually wield the whip, her victory may be a sure thing from the word go, but Lawrence takes no short-cuts on the way. Neither does he assume that in the interval of play, positions of power are dictated by gender. Whilst all the contradictory machinations of sexual negotiation may be present, they are never resolutely gendered, allowing male and female to exchange power and impotence before the woman inevitably wins. On the way to these moments of resolution, the two negotiate the possibility that each can be both active and passive in the same moment of desire:

> Gudrun looked at Gerald with strange, darkened eyes, strained with underworld knowledge, almost supplicating, like those of a creature which is at his mercy, yet which is his ultimate victor. He did not know what to say to her. He felt the mutual hellish recognition. And he felt he ought to say something to cover it. He had the power of lightning in his nerves, she seemed like a soft recipient of his magical, hideous white fire. (WL, 316–17)

She 'almost' supplicates, is *like* a creature which is at his mercy, but these are only some of the tactics of mimicry which comprise Gudrun's bigger sadistic strategy: this is masochism used to trap. It disarms him, he is lost for words, embarrassed, overpowered: she is 'his ultimate victor'. Yet at the same time she is, submissively, the 'soft recipient of his magical, hideous white fire'. Lawrence cannot resolve this yet, not until she strikes him again with a look a little later. To understand how Gudrun's looking back can be so 'finally' destructive, we might turn again to the cinematic *femme fatale* who dares to return the gaze of camera or man, or to Miriam Hansen's doomed women who look first. Gertrude Koch celebrates a particularly transgressive moment in Ingmar Bergman's *Summer with Monica* (1952), when Harriet Andersson looks directly at the camera, out of the screen and at the spectator, 'break[ing] the taboo on the gaze':

> if woman dares to gaze then there is nobody who can freely reply to her . . . The autonomous, freely gazing woman will never find anyone who can stand up to her gaze, who will not try to deflect and subjugate her gaze.[27]

Koch's feminist idealism is lost on Lawrence, who prefers to show Gudrun's visual daring as sexually dangerous. Nevertheless, it is finally only her ability to look back which signals her menace: 'Her eyes looked up at him with shocking nonchalance. . . . he felt again as if she had hit him across the face – or rather as if she had torn him across the breast, dully, finally' (WL, 318).

These savage scenes are important for several reasons. First, the by now traditional feminist criticism of Lawrence's violent misogyny, which ostensibly casts women as victim and author as violator, has to be reworked in order to take on board the obvious pleasure the novel takes in the fantasy figure of Gudrun. For Emile Delavenay Lawrence's forceful women are symptoms of a personal 'psychodrama', 'the embodiment of the desires and fears of a masochistic author'.[28] 'What of Alvina Houghton in *The Lost Girl*', he asks, who 'felt as if, with her hands, she could tear any man, any male creature limb from limb', or, 'Ursula in *The Rainbow* ("Her hands and wrists felt immeasurably hard and strong, like blades," . . .), or Annie, the Midlands Bacchante in "Tickets Please"'? If characters like Gudrun are 'ready to tear the male to pieces with their hands of steel', it is, for Delavenay, because they represent 'the desires and fears of a masochistic author'. Delavenay's conclusion is that these women symbolise 'those "behaviour patterns of bondage and humiliation" which are known to have been those of the young Lawrence towards his mother, and in his later life towards Frieda'.[29] Yet Alvina finds her fulfilment in submission to her primitive husband, and Ursula submits so absolutely to Birkin that even those female readers who passionately identify with her in *The Rainbow* largely cast her off as a role model when she steps into *Women in Love*. An authorial paranoia might site the position of the critically appropriating female reader as its greatest threat, but it then also goes on to ensure that the sadistic female character has the red blood drained from her. Gudrun ends up gazing bleakly at despair.

Castration and civilisation

If the woman looks, the spectacle provokes, castration is in the air, the Medusa's head is not far off.[30]

Having mentally knifed Ramón in the back, Kate in *The Plumed Serpent* turns on herself in an act of masochistic penitence. Her definitions of the female gaze are more telling than the banal, misogynistic fact of her visual repentance, in a passage which is perhaps the single most significant statement on female vision in Lawrence:

Let me close my prying, *seeing* eyes and sit in the dark stillness along with these two men. . . . They have got rid of that itching of the eye, and the desire that works through the eye. The itching, prurient, *knowing*, imagining eye, I am cursed with it, I am hampered up in it. It is my curse of curses, the curse

of Eve. The curse of Eve is upon me, my eyes are like hooks, my knowledge
is like a fish-hook through my gills, pulling me in spasmodic desire. Oh who
will free me from the grappling of my eyes, from the impurity of sharp sight!
Daughter of Eve, of greedy vision, why don't these men save me from the
sharpness of my own eyes! (PS, 196–7, Lawrence's italics)

Here, then, women's eyes are sharp weapons with large appetites: vision
is greedy, it itches, it grapples. Kate is initially defined by her visual need,
her first words in the novel being 'Oh yes, I think we must see it' (PS, 11).
Vision hampers the seer, as well as catching and pinning down the seen.
And eyes are not so much the windows of the soul as the instruments of
knowledge. Kate's eyes are hooks on which to trap others, but they are
also the portals through which *she* is pulled 'in spasmodic desire', the
desire to know. Eyes have power in both directions, they are barbed to
catch both subject and object, fixing the seer and the seen alike. The male
object may be possessed by the woman who sees him, but she is equally
possessed – hampered, used – by her own will to knowledge. It is eyes,
not bleeding, mortal wombs, which are women's true 'curse'; and whereas
the more traditional 'curse' of menstruation concerns only the woman
herself, this curse has a double effect. It lashes out as well as in, hooking
and cutting its objects as well as bending Kate to its will. Women's curse
is man's too: their sharp sight, which serves a voracious desire to know,
cuts the flesh they see.

It is only a short step from this outrageous nexus of images, to the seeing,
knowing woman as castrator. In his essay 'Enslaved by Civilization',
Lawrence charges educating women with exactly that, taking the part of
5-year old Johnny against an army of sadistic old-maid schoolmistresses,
inciting him to rebel against woman's project to teach him to write. If
visual intellectuality is a curse, if it takes you to an early grave, it is also
at the root of a number of other more sadistic violences:

> Nothing is more insidiously clever than an old maid's fingers at picking off
> the little shoots of manhood as they sprout out from a growing boy, and
> turning him into that neutral object, a good little boy. It is a subtle, loving
> form of mutilation, and mothers absolutely believe in it. (Px, 483)

This is an extraordinary image: female teaching as systematic mutilation,
a diligent pruning of machismo, which appears as easy to tame as a
tomato plant. And, in another revision of Oedipus, it isn't the father's No
which suggests to the little boy the threat of castration; it is the mother's
neurotic fingers which socialise through a bizarre sexual horticulture. I am
reminded of another pedagogic witch condemned by Philip Rieff in his
chapter on Lawrence in *The Triumph of the Therapeutic*, who – to Rieff's
horror – even manages to emasculate Shakespeare: 'The pleasure of
Shakespeare has been destroyed for generations of schoolboy readers, who

have encountered him thus with the blood let out under the sterile guardianship of old maid teachers.'[31] Rieff's primary anxiety here is of a castrating (feminist?) literary criticism which threatens to read *anything* 'with the blood let out'.

The virulently mental old maid is only one guise which the cocksure woman-as-educator takes on in Lawrence's corpus. In a number of places he identifies the mother not with irrationality and instinct but with pedagogy, in another reversal of a classic metaphysical identification.[32] Intellectuality is the matriarchal realm, instinct and intuition the father's mode. This parental distinction is present in Lawrence's discussion of the family in *Fantasia of the Unconscious*, in the battle between Carlota and Ramón over their sons in *The Plumed Serpent*, and of course in *Sons and Lovers* (in which, it has to be said, Lawrence's sympathies obviously still lie with both mother and – to some extent – mind). But in the later *Studies in Classic American Literature*, he writes (with a nasty autobiographical emphasis):

> My father hated books, hated the sight of anyone reading or writing.
> My mother hated the thought that any of her sons should be condemned
> to manual labour. Her sons must have something higher than that.
> She won. But she died first.
> He laughs longest who laughs last. (Studies, 92)

It is clear from this that Lawrence *is not* laughing – he is writing books, divided between identification with masculine unknowing and a writing life which intrinsically cuts him off from it. The paradox is that when Lawrence-the-grown-up-Johnny makes his exhortation against writing and the women who teach him it, he is deriding the very skill by which he earns his living.

Another cocksure woman whose tastes do not run to red-blooded men is Winifred Inger, Ursula's lesbian teacher in *The Rainbow*. She is 'a fearless-seeming clean type of modern girl' with 'an unyielding mind' (R, 336) (this old maid is a girl despite the fact that she's 28), driven to sexual 'perversion' by her already perverse spirit, that of the blue-stocking. Whilst the old maid would intellectually pick the quick shoots of machismo from the small boy, and whilst Kate can string a man up on her hook-eyes, Winifred sexually threatens to smother Ursula's own 'flame' with her grotesquely feminine body ('her female hips' come to seem 'big and earthy, her ankles and her arms were too thick', her passion is a 'heavy cleaving of moist clay' (R, 344)). And whilst rejection at the hands of Ursula is Winifred's punishment, other female characters are not so lucky. With an unfortunate regularity which feminist critics have noticed, Lawrence's cocksure women are put to the stake. This is Scott Sanders:

The emasculating women suffer appropriately horrible fates: the woman in *The Fox* has a tree fall on her; the one in *The Captain's Doll* falls out of a window; the heroine of 'None of That' is raped and murdered by a gang of thugs; the heroine of 'The Woman Who Rode Away' is stripped of her identity and ritually stabbed to death; and in *The Plumed Serpent* Carlota suffers a stroke and while dying must listen to the egoistic rantings of Cipriano.[33]

Lawrence makes no bones about the political and poetic importance of cocksure consciousness: in addition, Winifred is, of course, 'interested in the Women's Movement' (R, 343). Kate's 'prurient, *knowing*, imagining eye' has a political role, and this is connected with her inability to connect with the 'richness' of men. Women gain access to an effective armoury in the sex war through a combination of writing and suffragism, but in the process they succumb to the curse of Eve, a barren fruitlessness:

> So we have the tragedy of cocksure women. They find, so often, that instead of having laid an egg, they have laid a vote, or an empty ink-bottle, or some other absolutely unhatchable object, which means nothing to them (Essays, 33)

Ursula's reasons for rejecting Winifred, then, can be translated into the terms of Lawrence's castigation of the emasculating schoolmistress, the woman who can 'hatch' nothing. Ursula, it has often been said, is 'the Lawrence character' in this novel, the vessel of a developing phallic consciousness, a heroine as surrogate hero. For her part, Ursula graduates to discovering the 'Riches' of Birkin's masculine loins in *Women in Love*, to fail her degree, and to categorically reject the profession of schoolteaching.

Lawrence, unfortunately, is not so lucky, for what has he done in the writing of all this except lay an empty ink-bottle? The lingering possibility is that access to the unknowing phallic Eden is probably lost from the minute a boy learns to read and write; let us remember that this is the man who, in *Fantasia*, would rather like to prevent ordinary people from learning to read ('I would like him to give me back books and newspapers and theories. And I would like to give him back, in return, his old insouciance, and rich, original spontaneity and fullness of life' (F, 116)). So what is he doing championing *in writing* a pre-linguistic realm which by its very nature is cut off from the writer himself? And how does this knot implicate intellectual women? Lawrence works under the continual nagging fear that in writing he has erased his name from the Book of (Lawrentian) Life and cut himself off from real phallic consciousness.

We may seem a long way from vision here, but on the issue of Lawrence's image of mental life, visual obsession and the violent organisation of the world by the female gaze is central to that situation 'when a woman gets her sex into her head'. Castrating cocksure women are also those who look, who 'have' through looking. And the Lawrentian paradox can also be written in visual terms: Lawrence is a writer who so often looks at the world through women's eyes, only to denigrate them for looking. These threads can be woven together if we look briefly at a specific form of the female gaze – that of the female reader, who figures as a character particularly strongly in *Mr Noon*.

Nailing the text

> Remember, you girning, snarl-voiced hell-bird of a detestable reader that you are, . . you bitch, that the fight is over nothing at all, if it isn't everything. . . . Therefore you sniffing mongrel bitch of a reader, you can't sniff out any specific why or any specific wherefore, with your carrion-smelling psycho-analysing nose, because there *is* no why and wherefore.[34]

In *Mr Noon* Lawrence overtly declares war on his female reader. His 'dear readerly' asides betray a number of authorial anxieties: across his text, the narrator fears, the critical woman will cast her gaze and hook a specific meaning, a particular 'psycho-analysing . . . why and wherefore' from its living body. The sex of the text enters the head of the reader, and so, Lawrence writes elsewhere, 'the book bleeds', its red-blooded life is shed at the whim of a female critical knife. Lawrence writes novels, the novel being 'the one bright book of life'; these are, apparently, *living* presences which should be treated with the respect of an organism: 'In the great novel, the felt but unknown flame stands behind all the characters, and in their words and gestures there is a flicker of the presence' (Px, 165). Van Gogh's sunflowers, less visually accurate than a camera's image, are better for their intangibility and inexplicability: 'You cannot weigh nor measure nor even describe the vision on the canvas' (Px, 175). Similarly, criticism should not weigh nor measure nor describe the text, a vulnerable, sexualised body prone to the sharp sight of the critical gaze. In *Mr Noon* that sadistic gaze is specifically feminised and particularly focused on the vulnerabilities of a masculine body of writing: this 'hell-bird of a detestable reader' is not the general reader, the reading public at large, but specifically a female reader whose gender is 'essential' to the reading she constructs. From '*Gentille lecteuse, gentilissima lettrice*' (Noon, 141) she becomes the psychoanalysing, 'sniffing mongrel bitch of a reader', the 'rampageous reader, ferocious reader, surly, rabid reader, hell-cat of a reader, a tartar, a termagant, a tanger' (Noon, 205). This last charge merits an explanatory note in the Cambridge edition: she is 'a sharp, stinging person' (Noon, 324). The critical will to know a text apparently becomes more dangerously pointed when the critic is female, bearer of a sadistic gaze and a thorny sexuality which perversely and pruriently walks all over the body of a man, his text and his authorial intentions.

For the Lawrence of *Mr Noon*, then, a reader's pleasure in the text is characterised by her cocksure will to know and see it – its red-blooded masculinity is finally only meaningful if it is useful to this devouring female[35]. The female reader is a 'sniffing mongrel bitch', whilst the mother (here in *Aaron's Rod*) is 'a bitch in the manger' who uses man 'as if he was nothing but an instrument to get and rear children'.[36] As he writes in an unpublished letter in 1917:

> All I can say is, that in the tearing asunder of the sexes lies the universal death, in the assuming of the male activities by the female, there takes place the horrid swallowing of her own young, by the woman . . . I am sure woman will destroy man, intrinsically, in this country. But there is something in me, which stops still and becomes dark, when I think of it . . . I am sure there is some ghastly Clytemnestra victory ahead, for the women.[37]

It may seem contrived to attribute any of this certainty to a growing awareness of both women's ways of seeing and knowing, and the relationship of this with the image of the self being developed at this time by psychoanalysis. But Lawrence's writing career can be seen as a slow developing polemic against Freud, and the critical persuasion of *Mr Noon*'s projected reader signals Lawrence's developing understanding of psychoanalysis as a kind of 'Clytemnestra victory' over the misogynies of his text itself. As Emile Delavenay notes, by 1928 Lawrence was sufficiently 'alive to the possible clinical interpretation of his adolescent symptoms' which were manifested in his early poetry that he went back to it and censored it, cutting out the bits which might be food for growing psychoanalytic thought.[38] For a further gloss on Lawrence's image of psychoanalysis as a particularly feminine reading tool we could refer across to *Psychoanalysis and the Unconscious*, written just before *Mr Noon* was started in 1920, and to *Fantasia of the Unconscious*, written several months after *Mr Noon* was abandoned in 1921. Lawrence's polemics against his analytic women readers are thus sandwiched between his two central psychoanalytic statements, the latter being also the other text in which Lawrence has most malicious fun at his 'dear reader's' expense ('I *will* drive you home to yourself, do you hear? You've been poaching in my private atmospheric grounds long enough' (F, 26, Lawrence's emphasis)).

For the Lawrence of *Fantasia*, psychoanalysis crystallises and celebrates what he considers to be the sovereign conscious subject, the modern soul who threatens culturally to eclipse his preferred darker self: psycho-analysis is thus bracketed together by Lawrence with a pathological femininity which would know him. By this token, Freudianism is cast as a kind of prurient ego-psychology, an agent of epistemological closure, a means of explaining everything in terms of an unproblematic sexuality, rather than a means by which the sexual ambiguity in phenomena might be suggested. The feminine consciousness which the narrator 'sniffs out', and the psychoanalytic movement itself, come into being at the same historical moment, as symptoms of the same modern spiritual malaise: that of delimiting the bounds of a wild, dark life which should rightly be left to its own ambiguities with the lights resolutely *off*. Both psychoanalysis and women thus, in effect, threaten to define and determine the limits of knowledge of his text. They appropriate or 'use'[39] only to substantiate their own interpretations.

Here is another account of female misuse of the male object, this time from *Lady Chatterley's Lover*:

> ... 'Gradually I got sick of it: and she got worse. She sort of got harder and harder to bring off, and she'd sort of tear at me down there, as if it was a beak tearing at me. By God, you think a woman's soft down there, like a fig. But I tell you the old rampers have beaks between their legs, and they tear at you with it till you're sick. Self! Self! Self! all self! tearing and shouting! They talk about men's selfishness, but I doubt if it can ever touch a woman's blind beakishness, once she's gone that way. Like an old trull!'[40]

This 'blind beakishness' leaves the man torn apart, absent, consumed. Bertha, it is clear, uses him as he is supposed to use her. What is most striking, however, is the way that word 'blind' appears here as an index of her unconscious frenzy, a blindness which would be advocated if it were masculine. This is a 'beakishness' which causes sickness, as the woman starves and depletes the man: she is able both to use and to waste him (that she 'didn't get me a proper dinner when I came home from work' (Lady, 210) adds insult to injury; in *John Thomas and Lady Jane* the fact that Bertha 'wouldn't cook my dinner – an' wouldn't sleep with me' – the one implicated in the other – causes Parkin to become 'sick, body-sick an' soul-sick'[41]). In *The Plumed Serpent* Kate remembers an old self whose primary desire was clitorally to 'know' her husbands with a 'beak-like friction of Aphrodite of the foam'. Like Bertha's, Kate's clitoral sexuality is frictional, like her own eyes it is 'sharp', phallic, a weapon needing to know. But although it is frenzied it is not blind, it is a 'seething electric female ecstasy' which thrives in the white light of consciousness, in 'one final spasm of white ecstasy which was like sheer knowing'.

Cipriano denies Kate such pleasures, preferring a vaginal 'mindless communion of the blood' which is 'curiously beyond her knowing', and Mellors meets Bertha's voracity with an equally insatiable misogyny which only betrays its puritanical desire in the coyness of the phrase 'down

there' ('you think a woman's soft down there'). However, Bertha's nether
regions are eminently Knowable and Seeable, and Lawrence doesn't hold
back from describing them. The 'beak' indeed takes on a far more phallic
significance that Mellors' own 'column of blood', which Lawrence
emphasises is a round, soft, bud-like entity. The aggression of the Phallic
Man lies, then, not in his member, but in his verbal representation of the
female genitalia. Mellors imbues it with a prickly violence, with the
penetrating power to violate him:

> 'She had to work the thing herself, grind her own coffee. And it came back
> on her like a raving necessity, she had to let herself go, and tear, tear, tear,
> as if she had no sensation in her except in the top of her beak, the very
> outside top tip, that rubbed and tore. That's how old whores used to be, so
> men used to say. It was a low kind of self-will in her, a raving sort of self-
> will: like in a woman who drinks.' (Lady, 210–11)

We return to the perversity of feminine self-will. The woman who 'grinds
her own coffee', whose anatomy – visual or genital – can tear away at a
man like a knife, needs in Lawrence's mythology a man similarly armed
to defend himself. A woman might have a keen sight or an eager sex, and
so the sharp adjectives keep occurring: beaks, hooks, blades, stings, all
can stand in for eyes, clitorises, critical faculties. Remember that the
female critic of *Mr Noon* is a 'hell-bird', a 'hell-cat', a psychoanalysing
'bitch', sharp words signalling teeth, beaks and a bad attitude – a critical
anatomy bent on tearing away at enshrined masculinity.

This disturbing account of Bertha is effectively analogous to the
paradox in Lawrence's writing with which we are concerned here, which
plays itself out in the sexual relations of the novels and stories. Bertha
wields the pointed object, the stiletto, the pen-shaped instrument. She
hacks away at her 'material'. It is a perversion of the 'proper' authorial
position, in which, as Hilary Simpson puts it, 'femininity [is] "raw
material" and masculinity [is] "shaping force"'.[42] It might be said, then,
that this very feminine 'style' enables any description of it: her sexuality
has enough of the qualities of inscription to suggest that she perversely
represents the power of literary definition. And yet, since we reach her
through Mellors, we are forced to attribute our shock at this excessiveness
to the voice from which it comes. We do not have access to any 'Bertha'
other than Mellors'; we only encounter the violent excesses of his
description. Any horror which comes from the image of deadly and
insatiable penetration must moreover be horror at Mellors' linguistic
vulgarity. It is the text's need to make an excessive femininity exhaustively
'known' to us which provokes shock. A certain feminine sexuality lies
visibly prone on the page, and we are excessively encouraged to despise
its excesses.

In the same way Lawrence imbues his projected reader, his fantasy of a critic, with a rampageous will to know, an epistemophilia which he knows about only because of 'his own' desire to know her. He reads his reader, sniffing out that which he finds unsympathetic, and wills her destruction with the sting of his words. Bertha's desire to inscribe herself, to rearrange a masculine desire to 'grind her coffee' for her, is thus shown to be a perverted writerly activity. The woman takes up the pen in a parody of masculine inscription; she is a critic who uses the masculine text. Mellors projects this role sexually onto Bertha. In reading his reader in this way Lawrence submits to a monumental authorial paranoia.

The woman who would know, then, is bearer of the phallus in any social and epistemological sense. She takes up the instrument of penetration in order to know her object, and to exhaust it. Bertha's insatiability, her power to deplete her object, is exactly that of the critic Lawrence anticipates at the beginning of *Apocalypse*, where criticism is synonymous with the power to exhaust: 'Now a book lives as long as it is unfathomed. Once it is fathomed, it dies at once. . . . Once a book is fathomed, once it is *known*, and its meaning is fixed or established, it is dead.'[43] That this fear is repeatedly invoked underlines its ability to threaten acutely. There is something obsessive about this worry: 'Once it is fathomed', 'Once a book is fathomed' – 'it is dead'. For the self-styled prophet of 'the one bright book of *life*', this is his 'darkest' nightmare: to be critically 'fathomed'. In 'Morality and the Novel' he writes 'If you try to nail anything down, in the novel, either it kills the novel, or the novel gets up and walks away with the nail' (Px, 177). It is this, finally, which lies at the root of many of the anxieties discussed in this chapter. What Lawrence designates as the two linked key female 'perversions' – scopophilia and epistemophilia – are each attempts to 'nail' reality down, through visual images and possession, and through knowledge, capturing reality in what Virginia Woolf calls 'nuggets of pure truth'. With an awareness of readerly powers – or rather, of the reader's *writerly* powers – Lawrence begins to fantasise about how a book (perhaps even his own) can be fathomed through the gaze and cashed out into nuggets of contained, literary critical knowledge. Add to this sense of a criticism which can utterly fathom a text a further panic about the excessive femininity which can come and come again, and you have in one modern female body the advantageous qualities of both masculine and feminine sexualities (according to the popular myth of potency). A critic can enter the text and take (cut, sting, hook, peck, scrutinise), exhausting the text yet exceeding it (nailing it down and then moving on). The anxiety provoked by this devastating conglomeration of possibilities feeds into Lawrence's hungry authorial paranoia.

The spectator-in-the-text

Women in Lawrence are not just anticipated readers or 'spectators *of* the text', however. They are, more than anything else, spectators-*in*-the-text. Nick Browne uses this term in his important reading of *Stagecoach*, in which he argues that having a spectator-in-the-text is one answer to 'the rhetorical problem of telling a story, of showing an action to a spectator'.[44] If the reader is 'the spectator', then Lawrence's looking women, like the women through whose point of view the discussed section of *Stagecoach* is seen and narrated, are our eyes-in-the-text. One of the effects of Lawrence's repetitive style is the constant referral back to the experience of the central character, through whose eyes we see the action. In a key scene in *Women in Love* which I shall discuss in detail in the next chapter, within which Gudrun watches Gerald forcing his horse into submission, constant reference back to Gudrun's gaze reminds us that we are *with her watching him* – Gudrun in reverse-shot gives us a direct perspective on the scene, her look 'allows us in'. To paraphrase Browne, the image of Gerald,

> is paradigmatically referred to the authority of the glance of the 'absent one,'
> [Gudrun] the offscreen character within the story who in the countershot is
> depicted within the frame; the spectator [us] 'identifies' with the visual field
> of the 'owner' of the glance.

The version of this scene in Ken Russell's film succeeds, I feel, because it powerfully follows the frenetic shot/counter-shot editing of the text itself: we see the scene, we see Gudrun watching the scene, and then we see the scene again, etc. Russell, predictably, exceeds the demands of invisible or continuity editing here, focusing heavily on Gudrun's gaze, on her sexually spellbound eyes, on her pleasure in looking – as, indeed, does the text. What is remarkable is that Lawrence's original writes this editing technique into its dynamic despite his more polemical position on cinema.

Perhaps this is simply the extrapolation of an obvious point – Lawrence often chooses women as his protagonists, and it is through their eyes and experience that we understand the world of the text. Their experience is the dominant framing device, their visual images of the world narrate the journeys of the novels, their images of men are the texts' pleasure, although it is painfully true that the way a woman looks is frequently criticised by a greater masculinist narrative voice. Nevertheless, Ursula in *The Rainbow*, Kate in *The Plumed Serpent*, the Connie character in all three versions of *Lady Chatterley's Lover*, all are overtly our spectators-in-the-text. In countless other places, women's central function is this: to see what Lawrence wants us to see on our behalf, to guide the action through their visual experience. There is nothing unusual in this; using a character's point of view to move the action on is a common mode of picaresque narrative. But despite Lawrence's theoretical position on cinema, this picaresque technique is overtly visualised; indeed, Lawrence's narrative strategy becomes progressively less 'literary' and more cinematic, the prioritised point of view becoming less verbally impressionistic and more visually direct. Despite his voiced opinion of cinema, he cannot help but take the term 'point of view' at face value. When he uses a character's perspective to move the action on, he does so quite literally: their *view* is what we 'see.' That he pushes point-of-view ever nearer to the territory of cinema is interesting given his antipathy to it.

We see through the eyes of women, but women are denigrated for seeing. We see Gerald pleasurably through Gudrun's eyes, and yet Gudrun is finally criticised for being too sadistically, visually orientated. We see women looking, indeed, we often see only *because* women look, and yet the consequence of this looking, of the 'sharp sight of the highly bred white woman', is punishment and a sexist backlash. Nick Browne confronts a similar paradox in *Stagecoach*: 'how can I desribe my "position" as spectator in identifying with the humiliated position of one of the depicted characters, Dallas, when my views of her belong to those of another, fictional character, Lucy, who is in the act of rejecting her?' A simple Lawrentian analogy might come from *Sons and Lovers*, and Browne's question would translate thus: How can I describe my position of identification with Miriam in her humiliation, when my view of her belongs to another character, Paul, who is in the act of rejecting her?

For Browne, the problem is simply that the text as a whole is arguing for sympathy with Dallas whilst paradoxically looking at Dallas through the eyes of one who feels no sympathy for her. For many readers of Lawrence, the problem is that we can see a validity in the position of the woman who sees, against the grain of the novel's polemic. *Sons and Lovers* makes us share Paul Morel's perspective (his 'literal geographical position of viewing'), and it *tries* to commit us to sharing his 'figurative point of view', Morel's moral position. But a visual point of view is not the same as a moral or emotional one, and at times, despite the polemical weight of much of Lawrence's writing, we can take a different view through the same lens. This, for Browne, is crucial to the decentring experience of cinema:

> Identification asks us as spectators to be two places at once, where the camera is and 'with' the depicted person – thus its double structure of viewer/viewed. As a powerful emotional process it thus throws into question any account of the position of the spectator as centred at a single point or at the centre of any simple optical system. Identification . . . necessarily has a double structure in the way it implicates the spectator in the position of both the one seeing and the one seen.

This splitting and doubling is also present in the multiple narratives of
Lawrence. We see through Paul's eyes, but we also identify with Miriam,
and although these are contradictory possibilities (given the strength of
Paul's vehemence, and backed up by the pressure of a Leavisian party line
which until recently encouraged us to applaud his defeat of her), they do
not cancel each other out. Not only is Lawrence playing with visual
perspectives, the text can never finally force a unified view. The
relationship of reader and text mirrors that of Lawrence's women and
their men: 'Her he *drove* into thought, drove inexorably into knowledge
– and then execrated her for it.' Despite the weight of a critical history
which has sought to enforce a single Leavisian perspective on the text, the
experience of reading is finally a double one. Alison Light's reponse to
Kate Millett's reading of *Sons and Lovers* effectively underlines this:

> In my own reading at seventeen I identified desperately with Miriam, and
> contrived to reject Paul even though I was well aware that I was often
> reading against the grain. My objections, however, point to my recognition
> that if Lawrence *is* Paul, he is also Paul's mother and girl-friends, and if, as
> Millett does, we take their part, we haven't somehow escaped Lawrence,
> but exposed the way in which novels, as constructs of the imagination, might
> be atttempts at 'ungendering', and however unsuccessful, at dispersing or
> even at transgressing the gendered experience of an author and its usual
> restraints.[45]

If seeing women are the prime target, then how does this correspond to
Lawrence's textual image of himself, the writer, the intellectual, visually
powerful novelist? Or to Miriam as an image of Lawrence himself? The
female victim of the polemic – who thinks, reads, and looks at men and
at herself – may be a fantasy or phantom of an authorial identity which
Lawrence disavows, but must also uneasily acknowledge. Lashing out
from this perspective would then be a self-violence, enacted in a displaced
way via the body of a woman.

In setting up female characters of intelligence, articulacy and vision,
Lawrence is thus experimenting with images of, and his own perception
of, the authorial position. Through these representations of knowing
women the novels encounter a range of images of authorship. It could be
argued that in *The Lifted Veil* George Eliot is playing out and working
through the worse scenario of omniscience: the realist writer as total
clairvoyant, uncontrollably witnessing the leakages of other subjects,
feeling on the *outside* of other selves that which should 'properly' be kept
within, dark, private.[46] In the same way Lawrence must come to terms
with the speaking and seeing subject which he would prefer not to be. He
does this in a displaced way, through women, but in doing it *at all* through
women, he is also identifying himself *as female*. Rather than producing,
as Simone de Beauvoir puts it, blueprints for women's behaviour,[47] his

novels work through, and his female characters play out, a possible blueprint for authors. Lawrence's version of Eliot's worst-case authorial scenario is then explored through the role of seeing and knowing women. In his discussion of women, one of the things that he is doing is working through his responses to how authorship is constituted in our culture, contributing to the revision of the terms of authorship which is one of the hallmarks of modernism. To extend Light's point, it might be said that 'Lawrence' is not Rupert Birkin, but Hermione Roddice, 'he' is not Paul Morel or Don Ramón but Miriam Leivers or Kate Leslie.

In 'killing off' his thinking, articulate woman Lawrence is then doing something much more twisted, indulging an authorial masochism keen to fantasise and feel its own destruction. In lashing out at the only object in the text which is anything like an authorial self, he is enacting a kind of authorial suicide played out via the representation of a knowing woman. Or, to put it another way, the fate of woman in Lawrence is not that of feminism's innocent victim; the drama which focuses on women in Lawrence allows a kind of relished confession of the shortcomings of an author in love not with language and light but with dark, silence and masculine primitivism.

This would be one answer to the question of why, if Lawrence hates cocksure women so much, if he reviles the act of seeing with one's own eyes so strongly, if sex in the head is abhorrent, does he continue to return to each of these with such passion and fascination? Another answer would be that these were the evils which Lawrence's historical moment had thrown rudely into his path, and negotiate them he must, even if that negotiation takes the form of reviling a discourse as it enters its cultural ascendancy. Whilst his talent may not have been that of backing the right cultural horse, he did, however, display many of the symptoms of a modernist writer who was himself undergoing 'the shock of the new', kicking against burgeoning new forms of femininity and cultural visualisation. Paul Virilio reads this moment in a rather different, but connected way. In *War and Cinema* the First World War is roughly the point at which two technologies converge: that of cinema and the military, with each facilitating the advancement of the other throughout the century. Without making the explicit connection, Lawrence's unease about femininity and possession is symptomatic of the anxiety concerning this energetic convergence of vision and violence. For Lawrence, however, everything – even this connection – is essentially gendered: it may be men who primarily engage in actual violence, but it is women for whom the statement, 'once you can see the target, you can expect to destroy it' is true.[48]

One of the first paintings which Lawrence produced is a bizarre study of voyeurism and exhibitionism called 'Boccaccio Story', depicting a darkly

Chapter Three

♦

Putting on his glory

Lawrence's male spectacles

For D.H. Lawrence, peacocks, like men, are beautiful simply for the sake of it. Their finery has little to do with attracting the female of the species, and much more to do with the splendour of display for display's sake. Sexual difference, in the world of birds and men, is staged through a dynamic of the visible and the unseen, although usually this exchange is consolidated as the seeing woman asserting her prurience over the would-be-dark male. But when masculinity takes centre stage – be it peacocks or men – something interesting happens:

> If I had ever seen a peahen gazing with rapt attention on her lord's flamboyancy, I might believe that he had put on all those fine feathers just to 'attract' her. But she never looks at him. Only she seems to get a little perky when he shudders all his quills at her, like a storm in the trees. Then she does seem to notice, just casually, his presence.
> These theories of sex are amazing. A peacock puts on his glory for the sake of a wall-eyed peahen who never looks at him. Imagine a scientist being so naive as to credit the peahen with a profound, dynamic appreciation of a peacock's colour and pattern. Oh, highly aesthetic peahen! (Essays, 13–14)

And so, the peacock does it just for fun – for the sheer pleasure of spectacle, without even a spectator, since his wall-eyed hen is too stupid to notice. Lawrence's aesthetics are vigorously non-functional: 'beauty is a mystery. You can neither eat it nor make a flannel out of it.' Nor, it seems here, can you mate with it or even make cross-gender contact because of it. Whilst elsewhere in Lawrence's work women are castigated for their rampant desire to look, here the female's main quality is her indifference, her aesthetic frigidity, and whilst Lawrence's irony speaks some respect for her blithe indifference to scientific causality, the overall picture is of a profound misunderstanding – misrecognition – between the sexes on the issue of the gaze and its object. One looks away whilst the other offers himself up, or perhaps the exhibitionism is an act outside of an economy of (what I will call, for want of a more elegant term) 'voyeuro-exhibitionism' – the interrelationship of need which exists between the seeing and the seen. Here it seems that visual beauty is fine as long as no one is looking at you. Perhaps the peacock needs no eyes – except his own, seeing and unseeing – to indulge in his splendour. For Lawrence, this is some kind of ideal, and it is fitting that the animal is male. The peacock has something which exceeds his mate's interpretative ability: what he has she cannot even see, and yet he continues to display it. This is a show without an audience, a spectacle with no spectator, a display without a function. In his attempt to challenge our rationalising question – 'What's the point?' – Lawrence also sets up a paradigm for the understanding of sexual difference as a dynamic of display and *mis*recognition, exhibition-ism, voyeurism, and *mis-seeing*, which is present in all sexual situations throughout his work. Sometimes men and women meet, but they do not necessarily meet each other's gaze.

For Lawrence – known so well as the writer of heterosexuality *par excellence* – masculinity finally stands alone, the spectacle to end all spectacles, *blindingly* beautiful. Peacocks are not men, but his men too are spectacular, and it is with reference to both birds and men that Lawrence's standard of beauty is established in his 1928 essay 'Sex Versus Loveliness', from which this bird-talk comes. What is particularly interesting about this essay, however, is that the next image Lawrence offers as the exemplar of beauty isn't a dark male, and neither is it a creature freed of the need to be beautiful for his women: it is a movie star.

Charlie Chaplin is truly an odd choice as the image of 'essential beauty', and for more reasons than are immediately obvious. First there is Lawrence's utter hatred of cinema, and the very fact of visual display for entertainment's sake, not to mention the more obvious qualities of the little tramp himself. So when Lawrence turns positively to the image of Chaplin, something intriguing is evidently going on: 'there is a greater essential beauty in Charlie Chaplin's odd face than ever there was in Valentino's. There is a bit of true beauty in Chaplin's brows and eyes, a gleam of something pure' (Essays, 15). Here, then, the first great movie star, flickering on a million screens as prime symbol of the cinematic culture so despised by Lawrence, is admitted as the relative standard of 'essential beauty'. Valentino, as I argued in the Introduction, had a key part in galvanising the female gaze as a mass force in the silent era, guaranteeing his role as a prime target for the 'highbrow' literary establishment. It is partly sour grapes which causes Lawrence to plump for the peculiar Chaplin over the heart-throb Rudolph, who during his life had been the focus of a cult, as Miriam Hansen puts it, 'staged by women, to the exclusion of men . . . [T]he Valentino cult gave public expression to a force specific to relations *among* women'.[1] In keeping with this, Lawrence lamented the modern sensibility which *thinks* that 'a lovely woman must look like Lillian Gish, a handsome man must look like Rudoph Valentino. So we *think*'. Nevertheless, Lawrence does not counter this by choosing, as his image of beauty, a woman, or a figure outside of the world of cinema. He chooses the most powerful cinematic property around. In the midst of a philosophy of dark and unseeing but *essentially felt* experience, the moving image of a man's face can nevertheless embody 'a bit of true beauty' – Lawrence's characteristic repetitions emphasise the value, the quality. What is going on here?

This chapter will identify a number of contradictions at the heart of Lawrence's work, contradictions which allow this against-the-grain celebration of Chaplin's cinematic face to slip through. Specifically, the gap I want to identify is that between the overt positive valuation of heterosexual darkness and the actual practice of setting up pleasurable voyeuristic scenes with men as object, between Lawrence's attempt to blinker the female gaze and his focusing of that very gaze onto some of the most powerful images of male beauty which literature offers us. Lawrence's pleasure in the face of Chaplin – whose next film (three years after Lawrence's essay) was to be *City Lights*, a film about blindness and vision, within which Chaplin's role is to be the eyes to a blind woman – is only the starting-point in this series of visual contradictions, and it is to Lawrence's central spectacles of masculinity that I want to turn in a simultaneous further investigation of his critique of 'visual vices'.

Given that Lawrence spends so much energy on his suspicion of looking, it is curious that one of the characteristics of his work is the way that it stages a particular fantasy of masculinity as the object of the gaze of women in the narrative. This is done partly (and in quite a banal way), in order to punish those women for looking – it sets them up (makes a spectacle of them) as agents of the 'prurient gaze' so that the punishment for looking at men possessively can be displayed. This scene of displayed punishment, in which the wrongdoer is made a spectacle of and visibly sacrificed, has been analysed by both Nietzsche and Foucault in interesting ways. For Nietzsche in particular, the spectacle of punishing the wrongdoer is fundamental to our whole moral framework,[2] and the impact of this on disciplines such as film studies in which the relationship between looking, power and morality is central, is clearly important.

But it is with men's bodies, rather than women's ways of seeing them, that I want to begin this chapter – although, as with all good voyeur/poseur relationships, the flesh and the gaze cannot easily be distinguished. It is often said that Lawrence writes about men's bodies as a way of indulging his desire for them, an activity which George H. Ford in 1964 coyly called 'one of Lawrence's idiosyncracies': 'Rarely does he bring his women characters before us as physical presences, whereas his male characters are distinguished by descriptions of their bodies. Often these descriptions focus attention on male loins or thighs.'[3] This is about as far as Ford goes with the analysis, and Lawrence's 'view' of men (his visual pleasure in their images) is only really developed through the sporadic discussions of his homosexuality which have appeared at intervals over the years, the most important work of which has been done by Jeffrey Meyers.[4] One may have expected that the publication of the explicitly homoerotic Prologue to *Women in Love* would have concluded the 'is he or isn't he' debate (with an affirmative verdict). Yet its ghost still haunts even such recent work as Tony Pinkney's 1990 reading, which substitutes Fredric Jameson's modernist 'Male Pseudo-Couple' for what Pinkney terms a 'reduction' of Lawrence's sexual dynamics to 'unconscious homosexuality'. For Pinkney, homosexuality is only 'a communication code that Lawrence will sometimes employ'.[5] I want to go much further than this here, not by 'outing' Lawrence through an act of reading against the grain, which succeeds where others have failed in unearthing whatever lies latent between the lines of the text, but by looking hard at what we most obviously see: rapturous male bodies, gazed at by women. What I am interested in is the negotiation of a double taboo which occurs in Lawrence when men are viewed: the mutual satisfaction of same-sex desire and voyeurism, both of which – as we have graphically seen – are quite overtly castigated by the 'conscious' polemic (except at rare moments such as the *Women in Love* Prologue), yet nefariously indulged in a variety of ways.

If Lawrence's compulsive offerings of beautiful and highly sexualised images of men, represented through the eyes of women, are evidence of disavowed homosexuality, then it is a form of homosexuality which is primarily manifested as voyeurism, and generally it is a woman who acts as voyeur, and who is therefore clearly able to mediate masculine desire *for men*. This relationship might work according to the logic of Luce Irigaray's reading of women's role as mediator in all economic relationships between men; 'all economic organization is homosexual. That of desire as well, even the desire for women. Woman exists only as an occasion for mediation, transaction, transference, between man and his fellow man, between man and himself.'[6] If we take a second look at what happens in Lawrence when women look at men with desire, something of this is certainly taking place. Women's eyes are used to faciliate 'our' – the narrative's – masculinised desire for the male object. Women mediate a desire to look at men which comes from somewhere other than themselves. It is the male spectacle which figures as the sexiest thing in Lawrence, the object which finally interests him most, but it is women who do the looking. I will pick up on this again, having looked a\ some men through women's eyes, as directed by Lawrence.

Already this is becoming wierder than Leavisite criticism of Lawrence would countenance: one of our century's primary writers of machismo dressing in drag – or perhaps we should say 'cross-gazing' rather than 'cross-dressing' – in order to gaze upon the spectacle of his own sex. However, the more uninspired, psychobiographical discussion of homosexuality which Lawrence criticism has attempted has got nowhere, assuming a clear division between the heterosexuality of the texts which then act as a closet behind which a rather more homosexual life was lived. Far more interesting are the texts themselves, as scenes of a range of desires which include the visual desire to enjoy men, which is primarily acted out through the eyes of women. 'Lawrence', then, must be understood not simply as occupying the position of narrative controller who denigrates women for looking, but also as trying out and playing with the position of the woman who looks at the men who are frequently set up as spectacle. As we saw in Chapter 2, the important discussion of the male gaze and woman as its object which has taken place in feminist film theory has only recently been developed and reassessed to account for the gender-dynamic of a situation within which woman occupies the ostensibly powerful position of the gaze. For these reasons and more, Lawrence is an important site upon which recent work on masculinity as spectacle (which has, again, had most purchase in film studies) can be discussed and developed in more literary terms. Whilst celebrating pre-linguistic, blind states of dark unknowing, Lawrence produces an 'illuminated' cultural corpus which shows, enjoys and celebrates men as sexual objects, vicariously indulging in – according to him – the 'feminine' positions of looking, knowing and naming. Despite himself, through women's eyes he becomes a prime if nefarious partaker of visual vice.

There are many instances of women looking at men in this way in Lawrence's work; the spectale of the dark, naked Indian figures as a key formation of ideal masculinity in *The Plumed Serpent*, 'The Woman who Rode Away' and (from a different point of view, since this is a travel book and thus more clearly narrated by 'Lawrence's voice') *Mornings in Mexico. The Lost Girl* is an early development of this strain, dramatising Alvina's gradual narrowing of vision, as her world becomes increasingly focused on her dark Italian husband. In the first part of this chapter my primary focus will be *Women in Love*, specifically the image of Gerald which the novel keeps returning to through the sadistic eyes of Gudrun. Lawrence's work progressively focuses on the world of physical masculinity as seen by the woman – in a sense, he becomes increasingly a writer of the woman's 'point-of-view shot' – but as a channel for male desire, rather than a writer who continues to explore the multitude of visual angles or perspectives which his early (more dialogistic) work had revealed. I will also look closely at some men in the bath – or more specifically at what happens to women when they come upon men in a vulnerable state of undress. The spectacle of the man washing – 'privates' made public – overseen by unseen women who enjoy their nakedness from the classic position of the (usually male) voyeur, is a scene which Lawrence compulsively repeats. It appears in all of the versions of *Lady Chatterley* (such a scene being the moment when Connie first falls in lust, in a text which focuses almost entirely on her view and image of Mellors), in 'Jimmy and the Desperate Woman' and in *Women in Love*, and I will look at all of these towards the end of this chapter.

Brief encounters: on voyeurism and concealment

Whilst feminist criticism has established its arguments against images of women in Lawrence as one of its primary battlegrounds, it is not women as image in any simple sense which concerns me here, but rather the image of women as imagers, seers, visual subjects rather than objects, whose power and fatal flaw is their scopophilic thirst. In imaging and visually objectifying the men around them they in turn become the key representatives of the evil of the gaze. In short, they become negative images by virtue of their visual desire and prowess.

Here is a short passage from *The Plumed Serpent*:

> Ramón sat forward in his rocking-chair, holding his cup in his hand, his breasts rising in relief. And on his thighs the thin linen seemed to reveal almost more than his own dark nakedness revealed him. She understood why the cotton pantaloons were forbidden on the *plaza*. The living flesh seemed to emanate through them. (PS, 196)

This scene-within-a-scene takes on a special significance because it is set apart from the rest of the text as a self-contained paragraph all by itself. In this one look Lawrence condenses a heady mixture of nefarious voyeuristic pleasures. First, here is a scene within which a woman, despite herself, indulges in an act of undressing-with-a-look, a brief encounter with a man in his briefs. Having made the tea, and in passing him his cup, we are told that the first and only thing Carlota's gaze falls upon is her husband's groin. Moreover, she doesn't need to do much to 'undress him' with her look, because the provocatively thin (and banned) trousers he is wearing are even more erotically revealing than nakedness. The male object is charged but aloof; and it is Carlota's gazing desire which, in its ability to make the sitting man 'seem' erotically charged, turns this brief encounter into something quite transgressive. In reading the significance and insubstantiality of the linen and what lies underneath it, Carlota does the work of the voyeur, and we all join in. It is to the woman looking that all 'seems' to be imbued with sexuality. When 'the thin linen *seemed* to reveal almost more', and when 'the living flesh *seemed* to emanate through', it is Carlota's eroticising gaze which does the *seeming*. This is of course another instance of (to use Angela Carter's term) 'Lorenzo as Closet Queen'[7] noting that the linen was thin, that here is an article of clothing which functions like classic fetish underwear in its ability to reveal and conceal simultaneously. The fabric covers but unclothes; it is worse than nothing, for it frames and accentuates in its (literally) thin attempt at modesty. Ramón's 'living flesh' is eroticised just like the female pudenda in classic erotic imagery. Just as Roland Barthes' striptease artiste is 'desexualised at the very moment when she is stripped naked',[8] so Ramón is here 'reveal[ed] almost more' when so inadequately clothed than he would be if entirely stripped.

The despised Carlota is here our spectator-in-the-text, since with her we are *all* forced to rest our gaze on Ramón's groin, like it or not. She certainly stands in for any *female* viewer (since, the text implies, isn't this what we all do, all the time?), and the difference or slippage between her view of Ramón and what is obviously Kate's view of Ramón which comes in the next paragraph is hardly mentioned. Without a change of position or point of view being overtly signalled, we now see this through the eyes of another – through Kate's (the other woman present) rather than Carlota's eyes:

> With the blue sash round his waist, pressing a fold into the flesh, the thin linen seeming to gleam with the life of his hips and thighs, he emanated a fascination almost like a narcotic, asserting his pure, fine sensuality against her. (PS, 196)

As the chapter continues with a longer view of the 'handsome, almost horribly handsome' man, it becomes clear that we are now looking through the second woman's eyes rather than the first (we are reminded of Carlota's vision a page later only when she returns with the frustrated 'Ramón! . . . Won't you put something on?'). In the next paragraph it is Kate who takes over the look, and the transition from one woman's gaze to the other is only evident if you look carefully. In a sense, it doesn't matter: for all women apparently see the same. They see the beauty of men – they see, but their gaze is not reciprocated, and they see what they're not supposed to see. Most importantly, women's eyes function as the legitimate (read heterosexual) lens through which men can be viewed and enjoyed. As is evident even from this small scene in *The Plumed Serpent*, characters such as Carlota and Kate almost seem to be doing us the service of allowing us to look alongside them at the primary erotic object. In these places, punishment of the women for doing the looking comes only as a guilty backlash after the enjoyed event.

The account of scopophilia which I gave in Chapter 2 now needs to be developed in terms of this classic encounter. The section in Freud's *Three Essays on the Theory of Sexuality* in which the vicissitudes of vision are discussed is important for many reasons: Freud is not simply offering a local analysis of what might seem to be a marginal 'perversion'. More than this, he offers a much larger image of how we respond to visual stimulation, and its absence. Alongside his discussion of the way in which we all at root participate in the voyeur–exhibitionist pact (since we all gain some pleasure from looking and being looked at), Freud most clearly analyses the role of physical beauty in sexual life, and it is here that he first uses the important term 'sublimation'. Indeed, Freud's discussion of voyeurism and exhibitionism founds his whole theory of art, for in arguing that we all respond to the erotic potential of the gaze he apparently stumbles upon the idea that works of art are created to fill the gaps which our culture inserts through censorship. The more we cover up, the more our imagination can make use of excess sexual energy in symbolically filling the gaps in what it can see and constucting art works to fit. In terms of this model, this would make Carlota a form of artist, in her ability to focus in on the *not*-seen and fill it with erotic potential. Freud puts it rather more elegantly:

> The progressive concealment of the body which goes along with civilization keeps sexual curiosity awake. This curiosity seeks to complete the sexual object by revealing its hidden parts. It can, however, be diverted ('sublimated') in the direction of art, if its interest can be shifted away from the genitals on to the shape of the body as a whole. It is usual for most normal people to linger to some extent over the intermediate sexual aim of looking that has a sexual tinge to it; indeed, this offers them a possibility of directing some proportion of their libido on to higher artistic aims.[9]

Thus the *concealment* of the body engenders imaginative images of revelation, artistic or erotic, and Freud is offering here what could form the basis of a powerful theory of the relationship between pornography and 'higher' art forms. For pornography itself does not succeed on the nakedness and total revelation of the bodies of its objects; rather, the way that it charges a whole 'scene' with this potential concealment/revelation dynamic is crucial to its success. These ideas might account theoretically for the prevalence of the classic porn props – the persistence of bits of clothing (underwear, clothes peeping open or spread apart, translucent fabrics and fetish clothes which frame parts of the body) which conceal in order to reveal – and all that is so manifestly present in Ramón's thin 'gleaming' linen pantaloons. Freud is arguing that the more we 'censor' – be it through the 'clothing' processes of civilisation, or through the moral functioning of wider-scale censorship processes – the more *artistically* active our voyeuristic instincts will become, and Carlota's gaze bears this out. Ramón is a pornographic object here in the sense that he uses clothing – albeit passively and 'unknowingly' – as a way of playing with a viewer's 'curiosity'. Just before this scene, he wishes for 'the *veils* of isolation' (p. 193, my italics), *visual* barriers against other people which can hardly act as substantial walls, and which, as we have seen with the tantalisingly veiling pantaloons, may even provoke curiosity. This idea has been argued through in many forms: people do not stop wanting to look when you remove their visual objects; voyeurism, indeed, is fed by its playful prevention.

Yet situations within which men, not women, are objects of beauty are rarely analysed, even if they are often represented. Stephen Neale's important and very influential 1983 article 'Masculinity as Spectacle'[10] extends Laura Mulvey's earlier work by analysing the 'images and functions of heterosexual masculinity': how images of men are staged and established as visual objects of pleasure. Spectacle is instrinsic to cinema, and Neale's point is that it is the *masculine* spectacle which has been neglected by film theory hitherto, except in gay theory which has often focused specifically on images of gay men. Neale's work is useful, since despite Lawrence's ostensible loathing for the look, he goes to great lengths to ensure that characterisation is visually established, that the written text goes as far as it can in framing, showing exchanges of looks or furtive voyeurism, displaying the male object centre-stage. The sleight of hand which Lawrence almost got away with in our brief passage is astonishing: he gave us the image of Ramón's body, and he even filled in the gaps, whilst still being able to blame Carlota for looking. We, and he, are off the hook: it was *Carlota's* 'curiosity [which sought] to complete the sexual object by revealing its hidden parts'. Certainly, Ramón cannot immediately be seen to be culpable.

Before turning to the spectacle of Gerald, let us again think through what must be going on here, in order to understand what happens when the woman – Gudrun – looks. Despite the polemical thrust of this, we are concerned here with something other than a one-way flow of aggressive looking, which has hitherto characterised the female gaze in Lawrence's topography. When a masculine object is featured centre-stage, it becomes to some extent exhibitionistic, even if the man – like the peacock – doesn't *show* that he knows he is being viewed. Exhibitionism, like masochism, is never innocent: it exploits, uses and enjoys the gaze of the other. Despite their difference and distance, voyeurism and exhibitionism are interdependent, and can be understood as such with reference to psychoanalytic notions of reversal and need. Scopophilia incorporates two drives which seem mutually exclusive but which are not; exhibitionism is, then, part of the same basic drive as voyeurism, but the drive is reversed. Consequently, Freud argues, all voyeurs are to some extent exhibitionists, just as all sadists share the pleasures of masochism. In 'Instincts and their Vicissitudes',[11] the passive form of a drive (exhibitionism) is understood as the reversal of the active form (voyeurism), so that even when people identify themselves wholly with one side – active or passive – they still share and embody the desire of the opposite. In more Hegelian, but rather different, terms, the master (voyeur) needs the slave (poseur) as much as the slave needs the master – the relationship of power is still a relationship of interdependence, so that each relate to the other in terms of a mutual need. Ramón the human peacock cannot therefore be set up so blatantly as desired spectacle without this inviting our suspicion about his culpability, involvement, pleasure. When the woman looks, she cannot be *simply* guilty; when the man is viewed he cannot simply rest as the passive victim of her sharp sight.

Spectacle of will: Gerald

This was the glistening forbidden apple, this face of a man (WL, 416)

A clear view of the spectacle of masculinity can be found in *Women in Love*, in the image and body of Gerald Crich. Gerald is viewed throughout the book, particularly by Gudrun, as a stunning figure of action; in one of his earliest entrances he dashes across Gudrun and Ursula's field of vision as he dives into a lake:

> And she stood motionless gazing over the water at the face which washed up and down on the flood, as he swam steadily. From his separate element he saw them and he exulted to himself because of his own advantage, his possession of a world to himself. He was immune and perfect. . . . He could see the girls watching him a way off, outside, and that pleased him. (p. 51)

This sets up many of the terms I will focus on in this chapter: Gerald's physical perfection, his separateness, his disavowed knowledge of the women's look and Gudrun's intense gaze. I want to focus particularly on the first few pages of Chapter 9 ('Coal-Dust'), famous for its dramatic opening which features Gerald forcing his terrified horse to suffer at close quarters the passing of a noisy train, as Gudrun and Ursula look on.[12] Whilst we get much on how Gerald 'sees himself' subjectively which eventually justifies his death (we are told repeatedly that he felt 'exposed', and he conveniently enough ends up dying of exposure, a fitting end for one so visible), what I want to concentrate on is how he is seen. The chapter directly stages Gerald's most striking quality: his *masculine* 'to-be-looked-at-ness' (a phrase Laura Mulvey uses in relation to the female object of the look[13]), but as a whole the chapter is divided between and explores many ways of seeing. Like the opening of the book, it is essentially a sequence of scenes within which spectacles are set up to be viewed: Ursula and Gudrun watch Gerald, and then, walking on, become themselves objects of the gaze of two labourers who look and comment from afar, and this is followed by a final scene in which the women chance upon the spectacle of a half-naked miner washing himself in his back yard.

Few scenes in literary history are quite so saturated in perversity as this opening one, however, infused with a surreal sense that proportion has been forfeited to the demands of spectacle. It is also a scene which could be inserted anywhere in the book, existing as a disembodied image which stands alone and needs no context to generate the distress and arousal which are displayed in four brief pages. Beyond or before the sense of the scene as allegory – the wilful man forcing the creature to submit to his industrial will to power – it is shocking spectacle. There is, however, little actual physical violence to be seen here, although one might emerge from a reading of the scene feeling that it had involved actual painful violations – whipping at the very least. Yet Gerald does not whip the horse (as he does in the version of this scene in Ken Russell's film), and the battle is one of wills rather than a physical exchange of subjection: 'Gerald pulled her back and held her head to the gate'; he 'was heavy with the mare, and forced her back'; 'He bit himself down on the mare like a keen edge biting home, and *forced* her round.' *Force* is a word Lawrence is reluctant to go beyond here, and whilst the agent of Gerald's force is the bit in her mouth, it seems that his whole body has become a devouring set of teeth, a 'keen edge' with the ability to manipulate her so fundamentally that she will do exactly what she least wants to do, she will act against (her own perception of) her own interests, and she will bleed in the process. But it is only at the end of the scene that Gerald's spurs come into use; until that point he plays on her own fear, using it against her and entering into a pact with the train to intensify the experience. It is the locomotive, not Gerald, which 'broke with more and more force on her', which repeatedly strikes her with 'sharp blows of unknown, terrifying noise', but it is undoubtedly Gerald who turns this into his tool.

Yet whilst a violence is undoubtedly being *done to* the mare (she 'rebounded like a drop of water from hot iron'), its origin is not simple; Gerald is no simple sadist, and there is no single responsible agent. He manipulates her against herself, making her face her own fear, and this engagement is what is visually witnessed. It is more than a simple master–slave, one-way domination: 'It seemed [to Gudrun and Ursula, presumably] as if he sank into her magnetically and could thrust her back against herself', and 'Both man and horse were sweating with violence'. Who is doing what to whom is only finally clear, as the scene establishes master and slave out of a conflict in which Gerald and the horse are physically locked and briefly undifferentiated. In the process of subjection both bodies are bound together in a mutual experience of violence which is indulged intersubjectively. There is a victim here, and a variety of physical and mental violences are being done, but the agent of these is not, at first, obvious. Something has been released to make the whole scene one of pursuit and desired domination, and it is the whole consequent spectacle which is viewed and interpreted:

> But he sat glistening and obstinate, forcing the wheeling mare, which spun and swerved like a wind, and yet could not get out of the grasp of his will, nor escape from the mad clamour of terror that resounded through her, as the trucks thumped slowly, heavily, horrifyingly, one after the other, one pursuing the other, over the rails of the crossing.

Thus even the train needs to join in this relationship of domination, and the next sentence is even more telling: 'the locomotive, as if wanting to see what could be done, put on the brakes, and back came the trucks rebounding on the iron buffers, striking like horrible cymbals. . .' Since this only makes the situation worse, 'what could be done' here has to be read as a need to push things even further – the will of the train is patently *not* to make peace, but to intensify the scene of subjection. A bigger point needs to be made in relation to the scene itself, as a whole. Gerald engulfs the horse, and together the two become one spectacle, a single being with two halves, violater and violated: 'the man closed round her, and brought her down, almost as if she were part of his own physique.' The difference is marked by pleasure, as every trace of emotion which flickers across the rider is scrutinised in detail: whilst the horse can only respond reactively, in pain, 'recoiling' and 'rebounding' and bleeding, 'a glistening, half-smiling look came into Gerald's face'.

The passage is also strikingly close to a scene in E.M. Hull's 1919 desert potboiler *The Sheik* on which, ironically, Rudolph Valentino's hugely successful 1921 film was based, a connection made by Billie Melman in *Women and the Popular Imagination in the Twenties: Flappers and Nymphs*. Although a direct line of influence cannot be traced between Hull's account and the similar scene in *Women in Love*, and notwithstanding the division of high and low culture which ostensibly separates the two texts, readerly pleasures in these set pieces are arguably the same. Hull focuses on the captive heroine's transfixed stare as she witnesses the sheik subduing a wild colt, and the parallels with Gudrun's look are clear: 'Diana was almost sick with horror from the beginning; she longed to turn away, but her eyes clung fascinated to the battle that was going on.'[14] But if Hull did not know *Women in Love*, Lawrence certainly knew *The Sheik* by the time he wrote 'Surgery for the Novel – or a Bomb' in 1923, in which he manages to criticise it for its flagrant sado-masochism. As Melman notes, the 1920s desert romance puts primitive masculinity centre-stage, even in its eponymous titles (*Sons of the Sheik, The Desert Healer, The Hawk of Egypt*). If Lawrence doesn't do this in his titles he makes up for it in the narrative itself; men are visually central, and Melman's comment on Lawrence's lowbrow contemporaries serves as an apt comment on the scenes we are concerned with here: 'Typically, scenes of ravishment are prepared for by conventional passages in which the distressed victim scrutinises appreciatively the magnificent physique of the aggressor.'[15]

What we see, then, is subjection as spectacle, a violent image of mutuality, of the interdependence of sadism and masochism in the act of power. Just as the seer and the seen need each other, so – despite the raging passion of this – Gerald and horse on one level quite dispassionately unite in a pact which finds each meeting the other's need as dominant and submissive. Yet Gerald at this point is undoubtedly in the aggressive role, so how this connects with his *other* role as object of Gudrun's gaze is complicated. Gerald, it seems, can be both active force against the horse and passive flesh for Gudrun's look. One thing which is going on in this crisis of power is that the two fundamental drives of sado-masochism and scopophilia are beginning to collapse into each other, or rather, are being powerfully edited together. Spliced with an image of Gerald-the-sadist is Gerald-the-'thing-to-be-looked-at', one coming hard on the other as the scene reverberates with a shot/reverse-shot dynamic. Gerald, then, can be *both* potent whip-wielder *and* passive (or as Gudrun calls him) 'picturesque', object.

The picturesque

So what visual relationships are at work here? The scene opens in this relatively peaceful way:

> Whilst the two girls waited, Gerald Crich trotted up on a red Arab mare. He rode well and softly, pleased with the delicate quivering of the creature between his knees. And he was very picturesque, at least in Gudrun's eyes, sitting soft and close on the slender red mare, whose long tail flowed on the air. He saluted the two girls, . . . In spite of her ironic smile at his picturesqueness, Gudrun liked to look at him. He was well set and easy, his face with its warm tan showed up his whitish, coarse moustache, and his blue eyes were full of sharp light as he watched the distance.

'Gudrun liked to look', and the scene's 'picturesqueness' is mediated through Gudrun's eyes. After a brief recognition, Gerald does not acknowledge the presence of the women: they watch him and he watches the distance. Whilst this may be because he has eyes for greater things but they only have eyes for him, it is more consistent with Gerald and Gudrun's embryonic relationship that she should gaze at him without her gaze being returned. The women, but Gudrun in particular, can view the spectacle unchecked; Gerald – we know from his greeting – knows that he is being watched, but it is important that his actions disavow this. His frenzied absorption in the act of subjecting the horse is one hallmark of this, as is the use of the word 'picturesque' in Gudrun's thought. Picturesque is an odd word to use in relation to a human being, referring as it usually does to inanimate landscapes which appear to mimic art rather than the other way around, the natural world as *almost* beautiful or pleasing enough to be a picture – life aping or aspiring to its representation. The Shorter OED gives us, 'In the style of a picture' or 'in the style of a painter'; 'Like a picture; fit to be the subject of an effective picture; possessing pleasing and interesting qualities of form and colour' as definitions of picturesque, and the slide between 'picture' and 'painter' is interesting. Indeed, it is Gudrun who 'thinks' the word 'picturesque', and it is thus Gudrun who imbues the scene with the qualities and likenesses of a work of visual art, turning the 'life' of the spectacle of Gerald into visual art and naming it 'picturesque.' The word, then, frames the experience, and offers a context for our reading of it: to Gudrun, through whose eyes we see and interpret the scene, it is primarily spectacle, and in this Gerald is complicit.

Let me unpack this a little more. Gudrun has to represent Gerald as 'picturesque' to herself whilst she is in the act of looking at him. But there is movement here, passion and sadistic action. He is not a fixed image, he *acts* again and again, and it is her visual realisation of his actions and reactions as a range of images moving in time which cause her to 'faint with poignant dizziness'. In his 'picturesqueness' Gerald is not a still image, and moreover his sexual sigificance relies on Gerald's representation of him to herself as an object at a distance. What Gudrun is doing is turning Gerald from a live performer into a representation of a live performer, thus reinforcing the distance between her gaze and the object of it in a way which is necessary to the satisfaction of voyeuristic desire. If Gerald were actually, physically and tangibly Gerald – if she were 'really feeling' his sadism or even knowing that he is looking back – then the distance between them which her pleasure in gazing depends upon would be fundamentally challenged.

Christian Metz makes this point in *Psychoanalysis and Cinema* when he distinguishes between the experiences of cinema-going and theatre-going, two activities which may seem to appeal to the same voyeurism of the audience. Metz's bigger point about the distance which the voyeur requires between his gaze and its object is a crucial context for this discussion. For Metz, voyeuristic desire depends on distance, as the voyeur anxiously establishes, patrols and indulges in the space between his eyes and the object:

> The voyeur is very careful to maintain a gulf, an empty space, between the object and the eye, the object and his own body: his look fastens the object at the right distance, as with those cinema spectators who take care to avoid being too close to or too far from the screen.[16]

'Too far away' would be to not see the scene at all, whilst 'too close' would also place it impossibly out of focus. But translate this into Gudrun's view, and the result of closeness would be to see Gerald *as Gerald*, a man she *can* sexually contact through touch, and *not* a visual object. For Gudrun, distance is necessary to the pleasure of looking, and to be looked at Gerald must be represented as the image of himself. Metz continues:

> To fill in this distance would threaten to overwhelm the subject, to lead him to consume the object (the object which is now too close so that he cannot see it anymore), to bring him to orgasm and the pleasure of his own body, hence to the exercise of other drives, mobilising the senses of contact and putting an end to the scopic arrangement.[17]

This the voyeur does not want to do. Voyeuristic desire depends upon the distance between the organ (the eyes of the seer) and source of the drive (the object) – always at a distance, always the unattainable, obscure and therefore perfect object of desire. And desire, as Metz the good Lacanian reminds us, is ever dependent on 'the infinite pursuit of its absent object'. *Absent*, yes, but visually *present* also: look, don't touch, and visually you shall 'have' what you want.

I want to turn briefly to Rock Hudson for help with this. More specifically, I want to use Richard Meyer's brilliant analysis of the iconography of Hudson's body, and of what makes a good male pin-up. Meyer quotes Richard Dyer's point that the pin-up plays out 'the contradiction between the fact of being looked at and the model's attempt to deny it'. Meyer continues: 'This denial usually takes the form of the male model either ignoring the camera as though unaware of its presence . . . or acknowledging its gaze with a sort of phallic defiance, a looking past or through its vision.'[18] Now whilst Gerald is not a 'real man' in the sense of a body being viewed by a camera (except when he 'becomes' Oliver Reed), he *is* a prime piece of literary beefcake. His subjectivity is constantly redefined in terms of Gudrun's gaze and his response to it, which usually takes the form of a disavowal of all response. And not only is he beefcake for Gudrun, but for Birkin too, whose love for Gerald (as expressed both in the supressed 'Prologue' and the final novel) is bound up with the image which Gerald, the 'hard-limbed traveller and sportsman',[19] makes; Birkin, after all, 'was more of a presence than a visible object;. . . Whereas Gerald himself was concrete and noticeable, a piece of pure final substance' (WL, 347–8). But he is a 'piece of substance' which refuses to look back, and it perhaps is this which makes him a pin-up more than his concrete noticeability. Gerald's literary body is specularised in a way which mimics this real relationship between viewer and pin-up, and thus Gudrun can experience the pleasures of *not* having her gaze returned: 'Unique among these beefcake kings, Hudson could accommodate the intrinsic passivity of the pin-up stance, could visibly acquiesce to his position of "to-be-looked-at-ness".'[20]

Desire, then, is in the eye of the beholder, and this Gudrun knows. In order to keep her desire alive, in order to keep giving herself that exquisite experience in which 'the world reeled and passed into nothingness', her eyes spellbound and dilated (an experience, let us remember, which she does not get in *actual* sex with Gerald), she must stand back and render him 'picturesque'. Perhaps what is most inappropriate now about the word is not its application to a human object, but its curious asexuality. Yet in terms of the whole voyeuristic economy at work here it does at least serve to make Gerald into the visual object she needs him to be. Dispassionate it may be, but Gudrun's visual sexuality must above all make her man into a spectacle of masculinity before she can lose herself to the sight of him. It is this which marks theatre off from cinema for Christian Metz. He writes:

> the theatre really does 'give' this given, or at least slightly more really: it is physically present, in the same space as the spectator. The cinema only gives it in effigy, inaccessible from the outset, in a primordial *elsewhere*, infinitely desirable (= never possible), on another scene which is that of absence and which nonetheless represents the absent in detail, thus making it very present, but by a different itinerary. Not only am I at a distance from the object, as in the theatre, but what remains in that distance is now no longer the object itself, it is a delegate it has sent me while itself withdrawing.[21]

I am not arguing that Gudrun turns Gerald into a film of himself in order to enjoy the sight of him, although the cinematic qualities of the scene of Gerald presented to us in the book might account for its success as a key scene in Ken Russell's film. However, it is clear that *she is represented as needing to make Gerald into a representation*, and at a proper cinematic distance. Her anger at Ursula's intervention is a protest at the betrayal of distance; Ursula's words betray the fact that they are both *there* with Gerald, and thus that he is not an 'effigy', inaccessible, existing in the 'primordial elsewhere' of Gudrun's scopic fantasy. If Ursula can shout in anger then Gerald can respond, which is exactly what Gudrun doesn't want him to do. In this anger, as well as in her vision of his 'picturesqueness', Gudrun marks and defends the distance between herself and the visual representation of her desire. And thus Gerald is turned into a particular form of spectacle – a framed image *over there*, not a present actor and no longer even 'the object itself [but] a delegate it has sent me while itself withdrawing'. This is Gerald as spectacle, the creation of both Gudrun's desire and his own will to disavowal.

Disavowal and distance

All of this is going on whilst Gerald gazes fixedly into the beyond, displaying only the expressions of disinterested sadistic pleasure. He does not seem to know that he is being watched, and yet we know that he does. This contract of disavowal is important, and aligns the scene more closely with a publicly displayed enactment of a contract between voyeurism and exhibitionism than with a truly cinematic scenario. As Metz goes on to argue, one of the reasons that cinema satisfies voyeuristic desire is that cinematic events are not only at a spatial distance (the space between one's eyes and the screen), but they are at a temporal distance too: the events filmed are not only a fiction, but a fiction which has long since happened:

> in the cinema, the actor was present when the spectator was not (= shooting), and the spectator is present when the actor is no longer (= projection): a failure to meet of the voyeur and the exhibitionist whose approaches no longer coincide (they have 'missed' one another).[22]

This is patently not the case with the scene in question: Gudrun and Gerald 'meet', although their meeting can only succeed on these sexually charged terms on the condition that they pretend that they have not. Certainly, they are placed as characters in a scene at one and the same time. Beside the question of Gerald's 'picturesqueness', then, the distance between them rests on the more conventional contract of 'voyeuro-exhibitionism' which does not require the temporal gulf which marks out cinematic voyeurism. Like its violent sister sado-masochism, this relationship requires an act of consent which is then playfully denied. Gerald is one half of what Metz calls the 'true perverse couples' of 'domestic voyeurism'. Aided 'by a certain dose of bad faith and happy illusion' he is 'the passive actor (the one seen), simply because he is bodily present, because he does not go away, is presumed to consent, to cooperate deliberately'.[23] Thus whilst he cannot be a 'cinematic spectacle' to Gudrun (since he is present to her – she has not 'missed him' and experienced him only in retrospect), he does still satisfy one of the essential principles of voyeurism; he here obeys, as Metz again puts it, the 'recipe' that 'the actor should never look directly at the audience': he is 'something that *lets* itself be seen without *presenting* itself to be seen'.[24] The human spectacle's disavowal of himself as spectacle is crucial to the pleasurable maintenance of distance.

And so Gerald's expressions tell Gudrun everything she needs to know – whilst, of course, not admitting that they are actively communicating anything. This passivity, or rather this studied non-contact which Gerald displays, is all going on at the same time as his quite furious contact with the horse. Not engaging with his audience, he does nothing *other than* engage with (make his presence felt to) the horse. He both imposes his body on another, and distances himself from all contact with others, whilst allowing the expressions of excitement to still flit across his face. It is these 'looks' crossing his face which stir Gudrun most, and the relationship between observation of his action and her response resembles in structure the cinematic editing practice, intrinsic to so-called invisible or continuity editing, of shot/reverse-shot. In this respect, Ken Russell's version of this scene, rapidly and frenetically edited, outdoes the dynamic of the text, but even on the page this is a superbly 'edited' scene: from 'Gudrun liked to look at him' to Gerald watching the distance, from Gerald's 'half-smiling look' to Gudrun's sexually astonished response ('Gudrun was looking at him with black-dilated, spellbound eyes'), a structure of looking is established which allows Gudrun to watch Gerald, but does not involve him looking back, although he knows and enjoys himself as spectacle. As a classic voyeuristic scenario, it involves the aroused viewer witnessing a virtuoso performance from the key player who sticks to his exhibitionistic role by disavowing the existence of the audience. And all this occurs under the watchful eye of 'The one-legged man in the little signal-hut . . . [who] stared out from his security, like a crab from a snail-shell', a gratuitously bizarre detail thrown in to remind us that this is not just a scene set up by two sides (the watcher and the watched) but that the whole is framed by a third gaze, thus establishing a layering of voyeurism. Still more telling than the presence of the eyes of the one-legged man is the moving presence of the man on the train, for it is he – anonymous, isolated by his act of passing through, of moving on – who sees the whole framed as a scene with edges:

> The guard's-van came up, and passed slowly, the guard staring out in his transition on the spectacle in the road. And, through the man in the closed wagon Gudrun could see the whole scene spectacularly, isolated and momentary, like a vision isolated in eternity.

The first use of 'spectacle' here is I think quite colloquial – it is undoubtedly a 'scene' in the ordinary sense of a scandalous or extraordinary public event, or rather a private event (the dirty washing of sadism and desire) made public 'in the road': these people are making a scene, displaying themselves in a vulgar and violent manner, they are making spectacles of themselves. It is the second use of the term ('through the man in the closed wagon Gudrun could see the whole scene spectacularly') which requires, as it were, a second look. Lawrence is of course a notoriously repetitive writer, but the layering of vision here is significant, pushing towards a complex possibility of looking.

The guard is 'in his transition', he is isolated by his movement, the fact that he's subject to time: he will pass by. But through his eyes Gudrun also sees the spectacle 'like a vision isolated in eternity'. This is the perspective of a relative viewer, whose view is defined primarily by the fact that it is constantly changing as he tracks by. But it is also a view of the whole scene, which only the guard can see from a variety of angles. There is something cubist about this multi-perspective, but the image I am left with is, again, more cinematic than painted. On one level the guard watches like a camera mounted on a dolly, and, indeed, tracking shots are often made possible by the dolly being mounted on a track, like a train. I am not suggesting that Lawrence is consciously visualising a way of seeing which was only just becoming possible in cinema itself; although dollies were first used in 1899, they weren't used in American cinema until 1915, nor in British cinema until 1926. Perhaps it is now impossible to read this movement outside of the visions which cinema has given us as readers. Perhaps a century of cinema has distorted or redefined the limits of our interpretation of literary images such as this: we can no longer do anything, even read, outside of the interpretative framework which cinema has forged. We can, perhaps, only *know* such a scene, visually 'isolated in eternity' yet seen in passing, from several angles, with reference to cinematic knowledge. More historically speaking, perhaps Lawrence is symptomatic of a cultural moment which needed to be able to articulate reality through the tracking shot, and whilst cinema comes to realise this most fully, Lawrence is here visualising in literary terms a way of seeing which his wider cultural moment was determining and rendering necessary.

The man tracks by the scene, then, a scene with which he is sublimely unconnected. And so the relative becomes the essential: *because* he stares 'out in his transition' his fragmented vision can frame, close, render an endless story 'isolated and momentary'. A twisted scene becomes a subliminal frame outside of time, or rather a frozen sequence of frames, 'isolated in eternity'. The connection between movement (the eyes of the seer tracking past) and fixity (the closed, essential moving image which this whole scene becomes for the man on the train) is complex. Moving within and being subject to time are the prerequisites for a clear image of what is 'really' going on, and so, to borrow a definition of cinema from Gilles Deleuze, this image has at the heart of it an understanding of what is intrinsically cinematic: 'cinema does not give us an image to which movement is added, it immediately gives us a movement-image. It does not give us a section, but a section which is mobile, not an immobile section + abstract movement.'[25] I want to argue that Lawrence's phrase 'staring out in his transition on the spectacle' is playing with possibilities of looking which are not just voyeuristic, but which are intrinsically cinematic: do not motion picture cameras do exactly this? The man's view is that of the 'movement-image', whilst Gudrun's identification with his view turns her into the audience identifying with the camera's viewpoint. This is cinema as image-in-movement, not a simple sequence of still photographs or the effect of a magic lantern show. Finally, precisely because the man is moving and thus cannot see how this scene has unfolded, his perspective paradoxically takes on an 'eternal' quality. His movement – his becoming – constitutes the 'being' of the scene. To paraphrase Mulvey again, the flow of action is 'frozen' in a moment of 'erotic contemplation', although it is not the spectacle of woman which does this. The guard's picture stands in for (represents) all of the complex relationships between these people, but for a moment it is Gudrun's 'truth', becoming as Being.

Seeing and being

Since, as I have argued, the seer and the seen are bound fast to each other's need, I want to take the liberty of shifting the emphasis of this slightly, from Gerald's flesh back to Gudrun's gaze. Sometime later in *Women in Love*, Gerald again becomes Gudrun's object:

> She looked at him, as he leaned back against the faint crystal of the lantern-light. She could see his face, although it was a pure shadow.
> But it was a piece of twilight. And her breast was keen with passion for him, he was so beautiful in his male stillness and mystery. It was a certain pure effluence of maleness, like an aroma from his softly, firmly moulded contours, a certain rich perfection of his presence, that touched her with an ecstasy, a thrill of pure intoxication. She loved to look at him. For the present she did not want to touch him, to know the further, satisfying substance of his living body. He was purely intangible, yet so near. Her hands lay on the paddle like slumber, she only wanted to see him, like a crystal shadow, to feel his essential presence. (WL, 244–5)

Here Gudrun wants to look, and only to look. Gerald once again is the spectacular male presence who is to be 'had' more fully here through vision than in any other way. This is implicit too in the passage (from 'Coal Dust') which we have just looked at. Within the context of the gaze of the guard on the train and the one-legged man the exchange between Gudrun and the disavowing Gerald continues: 'he leaned forward, his face shining with fixed amusement. . . . It made Gudrun faint with poignant dizziness, which seemed to penetrate her heart . . . A sharpened look came on Gerald's face', and finally:

Gudrun looked and saw the trickles of blood on the sides of the mare, and she turned white. And then on the very wound the bright spurs came down, pressing relentlessly. The world reeled and passed into nothingness for Gudrun, she could not know anymore.

Whereas the spectacle for Ursula has consolidated her image and hatred of Gerald as a bully ('She alone understood him perfectly, in opposition'), for Gudrun the experience passes understanding, she sees fully and 'cannot know anymore'. As a pure violent spectacle this exceeds conventional sexual knowledge – it takes place in an economy other than that of ordinary contact and touch.

In both passages, then, vision stands in for a range of other senses, and it takes the place of other sensory ways of knowing a man: what Gudrun sees is 'like an aroma', it 'touched her with an ecstasy.' This is not simple synaesthesia, more like the appropriation of other senses into the terms and sway of vison. Gerald is *so* visually powerful that the sight of him can only be described and felt with reference to other senses. Gudrun is both visually aware and *active* – desiring or choosing to look, not touch – and she is also completely overloaded by the fullness of what she sees, so visually powerful is the spectacle of Gerald. Whilst as a visual phenomenon he is 'essentially present' – perfect even, needing to imprint himself on no other senses to make his presence felt – nevertheless it is as if the language of vision remains inadequate to the representation of him. Gudrun looks so intensely that to simply *say* that she looks is not enough. And although we are undoubtedly 'looking' at Gerald with Gudrun (readers would have to work hard to resist identification with Gudrun's experience of being visually overpowered by him) the passage pushes beyond the experience and metaphorics of sight. It is not just that Gudrun cannot believe her eyes; rather, visual possession is so overwhelming that the language of vision becomes inadequate. Or perhaps Lawrence still disapproves so strongly of the impact that vision can have upon a subject that these moments of slippage are in fact the clearest points of disavowal.

Nevertheless, whilst Gudrun might constantly translate the things she sees into the metaphorics of feeling and smell, her primary experience is that of being transfixed by the sight of Gerald. Here 'only want[ing] to see him' is directly connected with 'feel[ing] his essential presence' – Gerald is someone who can be 'had' through a woman's look, and all Gudrun must do is open herself (her eyes) to him in order that she might connect with and bask in his presence. Whilst this passage might be primarily important as an example of how 'Gudrun loved to look', here it demonstrates the complimentary truth of how 'Gerald loved to be looked at'. Despite the larger fact that *Women in Love* plays out the tragic failure in Gerald and Gudrun's relationship, from this point of view theirs is a marriage made in heaven, if not in Hollywood. It is a heaven in which the exhibitionist finds his voyeur, and touch becomes a metaphor for sight, the primary sense of desire.

The passage acts as one side of a frame, connecting with a similar section some pages later. In between, Gerald dives into the lake on which they are boating, in an abortive attempt to save his drowning sister. This whole section of *Women in Love* (the doomed party, which also largely lays out the terms of Gudrun's relationship with Gerald, and Ursula's relationship with Birkin) is charged with deathly eroticism. Gerald disappears into the black of the water, and Gudrun's 'terrible sense of fatality', of a world of absence, 'large and vacuous', corresponds directly to 'his absence' in going out of sight. In connecting with him visually she is able to connect with external reality even if it is at a distance, and so when he disappears under the surface of the water he takes Gudrun's visual anchor with him. When Gerald dives in a second time Gudrun is left 'suspended upon the surface of the insidious reality until such time as she should disappear beneath it' (249). Here we see most clearly that Gudrun's whole sense of psychic reality is fixed upon her ability to see the object of her desire: when he is gone she is gone, since his disappearance is a premonition and a foretaste of her own. Whilst a simple feminist reading of Gudrun's despair here would argue for her false consciousness, her total existential indebtedness to her man's presence worked through in visual terms – 'I *see him* therefore I am' – Lawrence's point is for once not immediately sexual–political, although it is true that what Gudrun goes through here can only be experienced by a woman in Lawrence's work. Here is an inversion, and an adult version, of the small child's game in which the child believes it is hidden from the other's sight as long as its *own* eyes are closed. For Gudrun, it is when *the other* disappears or can no longer be seen that *she* is 'hidden', and this brief experience of hiddenness ('suspended upon the surface . . . until such a time as she should disappear beneath it') instigates a crisis of subjectivity. The other side of the sadistic woman's gaze offers women no hope when they are not looking. If women are corruptly powerful when they visually fixate, they are hopelessly lost when their vision is gone. Gudrun, now, has no sight and thus no self: 'I do not see, therefore I cannot be.'

Yet on the other side of Gerald's disappearance lies another passage in which he transfixes Gudrun's gaze. Gudrun is able to swing from visual certainly to quite literally blind despair with remarkable alacrity, and as soon as Gerald pulls himself wet from the water Gudrun's thoughts turn instantly from the tragedy and return to an intense visual apprehension of him:

> Then he clambered into the boat. Oh, and the beauty of the subjection of his loins, white and dimly luminous as he climbed over the side of the boat, made her want to die, to die. The beauty of his dim and luminous loins as he climbed into the boat, his back rounded and soft – ah, this was too much for her, too final a vision. She knew it, and it was fatal. . . .

He was not like a man to her, he was an incarnation, a great phase of life.
. . . And she knew it was all no good, and that she would never go beyond
him, he was the final approximation of life to her.

'Put the lights out, we shall see better,' came his voice, sudden and
mechanical and belonging to the world of man. (WL, 248–9)

What is curious about this passage is the apparent lack of communication
between Gudrun and Gerald. Clearly, this is a culminative moment in her
realisation of her love for him, and yet quite reasonably Gerald is more
concerned with saving his sister than anything else. The fact that they are
not meeting is significant, however. Gudrun simply wants to look, and the
voyeur conventionally does not require or desire the returned gaze of the
other. Once more, for Gudrun's voyeurism to meet its match her gaze must
be precisely *not* met by his. Thus 'she saw him . . .', and she felt him to
belong 'to the world of man', and she is free to look on without the
responsibility of having her gaze returned.

As I have said, this chapter is more concerned with the experience of
being seen than with the voyeuristic gaze, but it is once more clear that
voyeurism and exhibitionism are always interdependent, just like their
more violent relations, sadism and masochism. The apparition of Gerald
is characteristic; Lawrence is never afraid to call a man beautiful, or to
use his female characters to apprehend as much on his behalf ('"You are
so *beautiful*," she murmered in her throat' (WL, 416)). Whilst I stress
again that we are still dealing with a written text, the spell which it casts
and the philosophy of sexualised vision that it weaves takes readers
directly into the domain of visual realisation and recognition. The
'meaning' of this passage is as a visual event, and even if the reader
responds on the level of character identification, she is forced to
comprehend it as a series of acts of looking, through which one character
indulges in the visual beauty of another. As with many narrative films,
identification takes place through the eyes of a subject, or through the way
that the narrative and camera construct a focal subject as one who looks.
Similarly, Lawrence forces his reader (of whatever sex) to see through the
eyes of Gudrun. In this way the reader is feminised by the visual desire
which focuses on and from the spectator-in-the-text.

The narcissistic body

But what of Gerald? He exists in a half-world, illuminated enough to be
seen, but slipping ever nearer into a darkness which, even though he is
anything but a conventional Lawrentian hero, marks him out as finally
desirable. Given the constant emphasis of *Women in Love* on Gerald's
light, Nordic qualities, this is striking. In the passage above his face is

'a piece of twilight', 'pure shadow' or 'like crystal shadow' (whatever that is), but it is lit enough to be seen by Gudrun. His loins are 'white and dimly lumimous', and it is this which makes the sight of him 'too final a vision'. Gerald manages to combine the seeable with the unseen, dim enough to be aligned with darkness, yet luminous enough to be visible to Gudrun and the implied reader who is looking over her shoulder. Thus he is cut perfectly to the warps of Lawrentian desire: slipping into the dark, his masculinity is not in doubt, yet since all of Lawrence's men must be viewed through women's eyes, he must also be visible enough to attract the female gaze.

Here, then, light is a quality of Gerald's desirability, but throughout the novel his whiteness is the hallmark of his obstinate perfection, his seamless wilfulness, his inability to love or 'only connect' (to use E.M. Forster's term). He is clothed in a dazzling Scandinavian purity, and this marks him out as the inevitable sacrificial object to his own narcissism – narcissism, that is, understood not only as pleasure in the self but as an inability to connect with the other as love object. Gerald's death in the snow is the narcissistic culmination of this. Never risking himself, he evades the violations and damage which other characters experience. Never fully consummating his relationship with Gudrun-the-castrating-woman, he escapes the threat of fundamental sexual damage, turning in on himself in an act of inward sealing off. To return to Stephen Neale on masculinity as spectacle, the parallels between my reading of Lawrence and Neal's reading of Sam Peckinpah might seem strained, but it is not only Kris Kristofferson's Billy the Kid who is 'spared any bloody and splintered death, . . . his body show[ing] no sign either of wounds or blood'. As images of narcissistic 'happy endings', in which the male body returns to itself and finds itself intact, uncastrated, the two figures are close: for Gerald too is a spectacle of 'narcissism transfigured (rather than destroyed) by death'.

A similar body presents itself in the much earlier short story 'Odour of Chrysanthemums' (1909), in which a man manages to be prime spectacle even though he is *dead* – indeed, in this story he has never been alive, and so he is another instance of man presented only through the eyes of women. The intense laying-out scene is central, in which wife and mother of the dead man enact the preparation of his body through a ritual of alternate looking and acting – undressing, washing, drying, embracing, punctuated by the women standing back to realise the visual fact of the corpse. Again the body is unmarked; despite the violence of mining work, the man is narcissistically intact, having suffocated. '"White as milk he is, clear as a twelve-month baby"' says his mother: '"Not a mark on him, clear and clean and white, beautiful as ever a child was made."'[26] And crucially the wife realises through looking at him that the reality of their marriage was never carried out through looking at all:

And her soul died in her for fear: she knew she had never seen him, and he had never seen her, they had met in the dark and had fought in the dark, not knowing whom they met nor whom they fought. And now she saw, and turned silent in seeing. . . . She looked at his face, and she turned her own face to the wall. For his look was other than hers, his way was not her way. She had denied him what he was – she saw it now. . . . She was grateful to death, which restored the truth. (Prussian, 223)

The 'truth' is then of a body returned to its primal perfection whilst the woman is shut out, yet forced to gaze on at its supreme indifference ('When they arose, saw him lying in the naive dignity of death, the women stood arrested in fear and respect. . . . Elizabeth felt countermanded. She saw him, how utterly inviolable he lay in himself. She had nothing to do with him' (Prussian, 221)). In a macabre way, the man epitomises masculine spectacle; he has no responsibility to give anything back, he is self-sufficient, empowered by the fixity of death. Death has renewed the man's dispassionate machismo: he has returned to a primitive wholeness, and, like the trees in the forest of Lawrence's *Fantasia*, relationships of looking have been rendered entirely irrelevant.

In the final chapter of *Women In Love* Birkin similarly meditates over a dead body, 'the frozen dead body that had been Gerald', and the scene is characterised by Birkin's feeling that there is no longer a way in to Gerald: he is sealed off, perfected, still available to be looked at (as Birkin is doing), but aggressively enclosed: 'Again he touched the sharp, almost glittering fair hair of the frozen body. It was icy-cold, hair icy-cold, almost venomous' (WL, 579). Meditating on ways in which Gerald might have escaped death and found a route through the snow to safety, he concludes: 'The south? Italy? What then? Was it a way out? It was only a way in again' (WL, 579–80). Gerald, then, is an apocalyptic symptom, his narcissism the individual working-through of humanity running 'into a cul-de-sac, and expend[ing] itself' (WL, 580): his perfect death the only way on – the last way in.

Gudrun is also excluded, but as both voyeur and sadist this is attractive: the voyeur does not want to be let in, the sadist does not want a willing victim. Every writer on spectacle in the cinema since Metz makes this point, and Stephen Neale is no exception. He writes: 'Voyeuristic looking is marked by the extent to which there is a distance between spectator and spectacle, a gulf between the seer and the seen. The structure is one which allows the spectator a degree of power over what is seen.'[27] For Gudrun the power is less straightforward, her femininity confusing the issue as much as it forces it. However, Gerald is still 'the exquisite adventure, the desirable unknown to her':

She looked up, and in the darkness saw his face above her, his shapely, male face. There seemed a faint white light emitted from him, a white aura, as if he were a visitor from the unseen. She reached up, like Eve reaching to the apples on the tree of knowledge, and she kissed him, though her passion was a transcendent fear of the thing he was. . . . He was so firm and shapely, with such satisfying, inconceivable shapeliness, strange yet unutterably clear. He was such an unutterable enemy, yet glistening with uncanny white fire. She wanted to touch him and touch him and touch him, till she had him all in her hands, till she strained him into her knowledge. (WL, 416).

Considering that Gerald here is the prime embodiment of plenitude, there are a remarkable number of negatives in this description. He is the desirable *un*known, he visits from the *un*seen, what she does see as his '*in*conceivable shapeliness' is still unspeakable, unthinkable – it is *so* visible as to be '*unutterably* clear', vision here superseding expression. Gerald has become so visibly manifest that he passes beyond Gudrun's understanding; even his characteristic 'white fire' is 'uncanny'. This is visual representation outdoing itself – it is blindingly spectacular. In showing us the beauty of a man, Lawrence needs to show us also the spectacle of a woman overwhelmed by its near impossibility. Visual superlatives are inadequate, only terms which will cancel out any hope we might have of understanding what is going on will do. If Lawrence is going to display a man purely as visual representation, he is equally going to disrupt that process of envisioning. Gudrun is blinded by the light – ecstatically, orgasmically so, it is true – but still her vision will not meet the language by which it is conventionally represented.

Bathing beauties

One of the most startling moments in all three versions of *Lady Chatterley's Lover* is the account of Connie's first glance of lust at the Mellors figure, washing himself in the back yard as she looks on unnoticed. Many men have baths in Lawrence's work; the domestic ritual on the living-room floor at the end of the miner's day crops up several times. One of the most intriguing accounts of this scene, pitched uneasily across the boundary of public and private acts, comes in the short story 'Jimmy and the Desperate Woman' (1924). Here Jimmy, the outsider, an urbane, up-market magazine editor in seach of a 'real woman', is forced to watch such a female bathing her husband in front of the fire:

his wife brought a bowl, and with a soapy flannel silently washed his back, right down to the loins, where the trousers were rolled back. The man was entirely oblivious of the stranger – this washing was part of the collier's ritual, and nobody existed for the moment. . . . It was a new experience for him to sit completely and brutally excluded from a personal ritual. (WRA, 118).

Although it is a man who is watching the scene here (this is uncharacteristic in Lawrence[28]) his voyeurism is no less active, and the question needs to be raised as to how this act of voyeurism sexes him. Men are not such easy voyeurs as women, so does the very act of looking feminise the subject for Lawrence? There seems to be little pleasure for Jimmy in this, and yet Lawrence goes on to emphasise the beauty of the miner's body, detailing its animal perfection, its muscle tone, and the glow of the skin in the firelight. He is particularly fond, as we shall see, of that detail of the trousers rolled down to betray the tops of a man's hips, 'right down to the loins.' The same detail is thrown in towardss the end of the 'Coal-Dust' chapter in *Women in Love*, when Ursula and Gudrun pass through the blocks of miners' dwellings and 'a miner could be seen washing himself in the open on this hot evening, naked down to the loins, his great trousers of moleskin slipping almost away' (WL, 174). This act of revealing obviously has special sexual significance, since it is what Connie's eyes alight on as well, and in every scene the women's gaze goes unnoticed. Like Richard Meyer's pin-up, the miner's eyes betray no awareness despite his central position as spectacle:

> He still squatted with his hands on his knees, gazing abstractedly, blankly into the fire. . . . But his hot blue eyes stared hot and vague into the red coals, while the red glare of the coal fell on his breast and naked body. . . . he seemed like some pure-moulded engine that sleeps between its motions, with incomprehensible eyes of dark iron-blue. (WRA, 119).

This is a scene, in itself slight, which acts as a pivot for the story. Whilst this man's narrative function is crucial, his role in the drama itself is limited, yet still he stands out as the central image of the story. In this sense he is like the miner of 'Odour of Chrysanthemums' who has a body which manages to be central even though it is dead.

Which brings me to the bathing men of the *Lady Chatterley* texts. The Mellors-figure (called Parkin in *The First Lady Chatterley* and *John Thomas and Lady Jane*), though very much alive, is a stranger in the narrative when he is stumbled upon, not yet a central character, and yet his effect on Connie is immense. In all three versions of the encounter, Connie, needing to deliver a message to the gamekeeper's cottage, finds it empty, and so she walks around to the back yard to discover a man washing himself in the open air, self-absorbed and oblivious of the fact that he is being watched. What Lawrence concentrates upon in all three versions is the primary image of the man itself, Connie's shock, and her surreptitious voyeurism. Whilst the first account is relatively short, it gets longer as Lawrence rewrites the novel, so that in the final version what Lawrence calls this 'shock of vision'[29] details every contour of the man's unknowing body. From Connie's first 'peep through the window' in which she sees 'the little dark room, with its almost sinister privacy, not wanting to be invaded', she is established as the intruding gaze on the man's self-sufficient domain; turning the corner to the yard, she finds herself fully situated as the classic female seer, 'stumbl[ing] on vulgar privacies'. Mellors is seen, but only because Lawrence has given us a pair of female eyes through which to see him:

> In the little yard two paces beyond her [at this point *John Thomas* reads, 'He was so near, Constance could have touched him'], the man was washing himself, utterly unaware. He was naked to the hips, his velveteen breeches slipped down over his slender loins. And his white, slim back was curved over a big bowl of soapy water, in which he ducked his head, shaking his head with a queer, quick little motion, lifting his slender white arms, and pressing the soapy water from his ears, quick, subtle as a weasel playing with water, and utterly alone. Connie backed away round the corner of the house, and hurried away to the wood. In spite of herself, she had had a shock.

Having seen once, we then see again; Connie sits in the wood coping with the shock and replays the scene as if in flashback. Indeed, in *The First Lady Chatterley* the flashback is longer than the original image as, 'trembl[ing] uncontrollably' (FLC, 27), she replays and 'narrates' the vision back to herself. This aftershock, an echo of afterimages, is most elaborately replayed in *John Thomas*. The original experience hits Connie so that 'there she stopped as if she had been shot' (JTLJ, 50), but the aftereffect keeps coming back like the compulsive repetition of the shell-shocked, those war-traumatised patients of Freud's who cannot help but keep replaying to themselves the image of their horror. Lawrence does not shrink from the violence of this: 'his body in itself was divine, *cleaving* through the gloom like a revelation'; later the same body is described as 'splitting the gloom' (FLC, 27), like gunshot. For all the sublime pseudo-mysticism of this ('That body was of the world of the gods . . . The sudden sense of pure beauty . . . had put worship in her heart again' (51)), what Connie keeps coming back to is the white fact of his flesh, its 'purity' and disconnectedness mirroring the narcissistic completion of Gerald and the miner in death. Lawrence may be suspicious of visual experience, but to emphasise the power of the man's flesh he makes Connie 'see' not once but twice. If you missed anything the first time, you get another chance to look; here it is in flashback:

> She saw the clumsy breeches slipping down over the pure, delicate, white loins, the bones showing a little, and the sense of aloneness, of a creature purely alone, overwhelmed her. Perfect, white, solitary nudity of a creature that lives alone, and inwardly alone. . . . Not the stuff of beauty, not even the body of beauty, but a lambency, the warm, white flame of a single life, revealing itself in contours that one might touch: a body!

Lawrence here wants to have his cake and eat it. Arguing for the pleasures of real flesh 'that one might touch' (that one must *only* touch, according to the darker discourse), he still enjoys the pleasures of flesh that one must *see*. Whilst Connie here *does not* touch the body, *it* touches *her*, through her eyes. So Lawrence tries to collapse a purely visual experience into one of 'real sex', although the whole can never be anything but a vision. And if Connie's imaginary action replay isn't 'sex in the head', then what is?

This is certainly visionary, but here, unlike the passage from *Women in Love* I looked at earlier, its movement is not its primary quality. For Deleuze cinematic images exist only within the dimension of time, they must move or cease to be cinematic.[30] No cinematic image can exist in still form – there can be no 'unique moments'. The 'privileged instants' of cinema are moving shots between cuts, slices of movement, rather than still images. In Lawrence, for the most part, the unique moment is primary. Despite his vilification of a femininity which enjoys looking in mirrors, much of Lawrence's discourse of masculine essentialism is about this – if not striking the poses of still images, then erecting and directing 'scenes' within which the male body is primary spectacle which invites the fetishistic gaze. In these scenes – Gerald Crich whipping his horse, or walking off to die, Don Ramón simply drinking his tea, Mellors washing himself – movement acts as an hypnotic invitation to the anxious or desirous gaze of the intra-diegetic women or the extra-diegetic reader. And whilst the moment of essential dark connection might be blind for its subject, the narrator enjoys it as a still spectacle. The key Lawrentian experiences are all fixed moments of Being, epiphanal poses which complete the male figure in his metaphysical landscape. It is this which makes Lawrence finally anti-cinematic, rather than his conscious polemics against the institution of cinema and its democratising power. It is also this which undermines any statements he makes celebrating becoming, flux or flow – he is finally a philosopher of Being. If masculinity appears to move, it is often through the juxtaposition of exposures or snapshots; a stilted effect of movement is created when the reader is bombarded by enough slightly different 'privileged instants' in a given scene. But more important than this is the fact of a woman's eyes, used to convey the primary pleasure in the image of a man's flesh. But this is not the only way of seeing in Lawrence, as the texts so often slip into vision-in-movement, the literary representation of moving images tearing themselves away from preferred still spectacles.

On cross-gazing: seeing as a woman

When these women 'stumble on vulgar privacies' they do more than nefariously enjoy a prohibited spectacle. These are visions, had by women, of men's bodies; microcosms of whole novels within which the world (but particularly the men in it) is seen through a woman's eyes. 'It was the vision she cherished, because it had touched her soul' (JTLJ, 51); 'it was a visionary experience; it had hit her in the middle of the body' (Lady, 111–12). So the whole novel follows the experience of its heroine, and it follows in particular detail her experience of her lover's body. When Connie says in simple justification, 'I liked your body' (Lady, 176), she isn't just speaking for herself. Women are the alibi Lawrence the gay-gazer was looking for: with Connie positioned as she is, he can claim: *I* wasn't standing there, *she* was – I was over here writing, simply *imagining* what it must be like to be a woman in the act of looking at a man. This split gaze – split perfectly along permissible gender lines – has to be bound back to itself, however. What is really at stake in making these men the most beautiful thing in the book? As Miriam Hansen asks of the Valentino phenomenon, 'If a man is made to occupy the place of erotic object, how does this affect the organization of vision?'[31] If Lawrence cannot bring himself to look at men with the eyes of a man, then he has to plead a heterosexual defence: 'Not me, but her: she looked – I only *saw* her looking.' The narrative's identification with the female gaze is, however, too close for comfort. This is what Angela Carter calls Lawrence's desire 'to be a woman so that he could achieve the supreme if schizophrenic pleasure of fucking himself'.[32] What I hope to have made clear is that this identification must by now be reread in an altogether simpler way. Here is the fantasist of Freud's 'A Child is Being Beaten', who sees, does and feels the beating all at the same time.[33] The male spectacle is central, but the female gaze is formative. Perhaps this is Lawrence-the-arch-MCP's Achilles' Heel: to say that he is both (at least) he *and* she at the same time is surely to fundamentally disturb those who believe that the sexes are essentially and eternally separate.

I began this chapter by invoking Luce Irigaray's work on women as mediators of male homosexual transactions, as a way of setting up the position of the woman's eyes in relation to Lawrence's male spectacles. In Irigaray's model, however, woman's role as mediator is essentially impotent: they are the transparent junctions through which male desire flows, passages of transaction rather than transforming agents in relationships in their own right. Certainly, Lawrence's women act as conductors in the flow of male desire, facilitating his enjoyment in, and disavowal of, the desired male spectacle. Certainly their role is to urge and allow the flow of the narrative gaze towards the prime object of beefcake. But in her very role as the agent of disavowal, the woman *has to* fit the mask of heterosexual desire. Even if the ultimate, unacknowledged *raison d'être* of beefcake is the satisfaction of the narrator's same-sex desire, its immediate justification has to be its service to a plausible heterosexual female gaze. The male writer of *The Plumed Serpent* may desire Ramón most, but it is Kate's gaze which allows this, and therefore it is Kate's gaze which we must first be able to believe in and identify with. Lawrence is desperate to assert a predominant heterosexual preference. But can we finally be sure of what heterosexuality *is*?

The implications of this are important, not just for an understanding of gay male desire as written by one of our century's prime voices of heterosexuality, but for the ease with which women are made able to channel a desire which we can so readily call 'gay', a desire which seems not to originate with these women. Are these fictions within which Lawrence's women 'feel' a desire for their men which is actually homoerotic? If so, this muddies the waters not only for our understanding of heterosexuality (which evidently can so easily slip into its other, a heterosexual view facilitating homoerotic images), it also questions the 'intrinsic' gender qualities of *any* desire. Perhaps Kate Millett's point, that Kate in *The Plumed Serpent* is only 'a female impersonator', comes near to the truth, and all we are ever dealing with in Lawrence is the male desire for men, slightly varied every now and then when the wolf dons the sheep's clothing.

I do not think so. Lawrence writes as convincingly of a desire which can begin in one form, and then can mutate by the vision of a character's sexuality into something else (the male writer showing lust for a man equally plausibly through a woman's eyes) as he does any more 'straightforward' relation. But in the warps of this channelling, neither heterosexuality nor homosexuality emerge as pure forms of desire. It may be that this analysis forces us to abandon all ideas of essentially characteristic currents of desire – those most familiarly argued for being male or female, gay or straight – and that we must question again what heterosexuality is if it can so easily become the mask for a masquerading homosexuality desperate to disavow itself. For all his mythical sexism, in this analysis Lawrence has caused us to challenge those cherished notions of male and female desire as distinguishable and essentially different things – an idea propounded by misogynists (like Lawrence) and radical feminists (like Irigaray) alike. The questions which need to be raised in this context might begin with one not only for Irigaray, but for any sexual-political movement (such as the dominant form of cultural feminism developed in the United States since the mid-1970s) which subscribes to a doctrine of essential sexual difference: If women are so radically different (as Irigaray argues), then how can they mediate male desire so effectively (as she also argues)? If male sexuality is so radically other, then how can it be channelled through female fantasies? If women can mediate male desire, then what makes it male? If gay pleasure can be had through the heterosexual eyes of character or camera – the gay use of hetero porn springs to mind here, as well as the male objects of desire in Lawrence's fiction – then what does this do to the boundaries of our cherished straight domain?

Chapter Four

◆

The pornographic gaze

and the case of Lady Chatterley

Obscene means today that the policeman thinks he has a right to arrest you, nothing else. (Px, 302)

From male beauty we move to obscene secrets. '[A] true thought', writes Lawrence in his introduction to *Pansies*, 'comes as much from the heart and the genitals as from the head.' In *Lady Chatterley's Lover* Connie's attractiveness lies not in her conventional beauty but in her corporeal, corpulent body: 'An' if tha shits an' if tha pisses, I'm glad', says Mellors (Lady, 232). Bottoms are at the bottom of things – one of the primary roots of the Lawrentian life force. In both *Lady Chatterley's Lover* and *Women in Love*, anal sexuality touches a more fundamental core than 'straighter' sex ('what one supremely wanted was this piercing, consuming, rather awful sensuality' (Lady, 258)). In *Women in Love* Ursula finally reaches 'the quick of the mystery of darkness that was bodily him' only through sodomy: this is a 'marvellous fullness of immediate gratification, overwhelming, outflooding from the source of the deepest life-force, the darkest, deepest, strangest life-source of the human body, at the back and base of the loins' (WL, 396). It is in the *Pansies* essay, however, that Lawrence's anti-metaphysical belief in the 'obscene' as the root of dark knowledge is articulated most clearly. The 'exposure' of this 'truth' requires a challenge to the terms of taste and obscenity law even sixty years later, and although Lawrence was not writing within the bounds of such specifically Draconian legislation as Section 28[1] (when he wrote that idealised image of male love in *The White Peacock* for example[2]), the pre-1959 obscenity law which prevented *Lady Chatterley's Lover* from coming into print was hardly amenable to representations of anally and genitally based 'beauty and truth'. An early reviewer of *Women in Love* wrote:

The main episode of the novel deals with the relations of two men, Gerald and Birkin, and is nothing more or less than a shameful glorification of that state of mind which in practice, as every student of crime is aware, leads to conduct which is condemned by the criminal law.[3]

The fact that visual representations of anal sexuality are still severely circumscribed by obscenity law in Britain, as gay pornographers, photographers and Safe Sex campaigners have discovered, is an index of the extremity of Lawrence's (albeit heterosexual and verbal) anal images in 1928. In present-day visual pornography, sodomy is something which even today mainstream heterosexual pornographers such as Paul Raymond (publisher of magazines including *Men Only*, *Club* and *Escort*) are careful to avoid representing: Raymond generally evades the implementation of the Obscene Publications Act by not showing actual sex or representing illegal sexual acts. Bryan Derbyshire, Britain's foremost gay magazine publisher, has been imprisoned for publishing images of penises which *might* be erect; Safe Sex Campaigners in Britain have been prevented by the same law that prosecuted Derbyshire for photographing erections even to advertise the use of condoms; and Robert Mapplethorpe's work has been at the centre of controversy in America about national funding for gay photography, as Joseph Bristow has discussed.[4] Lawrence, of course, *writes* of heterosexual sodomy, and neither *Lady Chatterley's Lover* nor *Women in Love* are picture-books. Lawrence's paintings were, however, seized under the instructions of the Home Secretary in 1929. Nevertheless, by the 1990s it has become commonplace to emphasise the tameness of Lawrence's once racy and banable works, and it is this which I want to challenge in this chapter, alongside an analysis of Lawrence's anti-metaphysic, which reads the ideal as rooted in the corruption of 'the back and base of the loins'. Jonathan Dollimore's brilliant but brief analysis of the astonishing perversity and slippery positioning of Lawrence on homosexuality and anality is underlined by an awareness of the historical and cultural risks he then took, as is Jeffrey Meyers' chapter on Lawrence in *Homosexuality and Literature 1890–1930*.[5] This sense of going beyond, going too far, saying too much, has been celebrated counter-culturally as part of a self-conscious project to get to the bottom of reality.[6] In the first part of this chapter I want to think further about sexual spectacle, and about how the notions of visual sex and sex in the head connect with Lawrence's theorisation of pornography and obscenity, words which are perhaps even more slippery now. If there is a still-contemporary truth in Lawrence's work on this matter, it is that of my epigraph: obscenity is only the thing you can be arrested for.

Lawrence and the law

Lawrence might be called a doubly transgressive writer. He is known, indeed, as the twentieth century's exemplary writer of classy 'dirty books', and although the word 'dirty' remains a dirty word in his own vocabulary (the Lawrentian sin being the masturbatory 'dirty little secret'), the primary concern of his late works is to render the unspeakable spoken, to bring into the public realm the private, secret, the taboo: the 'secret entrances', as he calls them in *Lady Chatterley's Lover*, 'in between, folded in the secret warmth' (Lady, 232). Although Lawrence has been traditionally condemned by self-appointed moral guardians as a pornographer, this is still a term which he himself would use to condemn others. Indeed, the question of looking is brought into sharp focus by his response to pornography. For Lawrence, the pornographic is the mental in sexuality, or the mental imposed upon sexuality:

> The word arse is clean enough. Even the part of the body it refers to is just as much me as my hand and my brain are me. It is not for me to quarrel with my own natural make-up. If I am, I am all that I am. But the impudent and dirty little mind wont have it. It hates certain parts of the body, and makes words representing those parts scapegoats. (Px, 303)

Lawrence's contradictory project is to cleanse language of dirty implications, whilst still condemning 'genuine pornography' which he would 'censor . . . rigorously'. Ironically sounding like a radical feminist campaigner such as Andrea Dworkin or even Millett, he calls this pornography an 'insult to the human body, . . . to a vital human relationship!.' Of Joyce's *Ulysses* Lawrence wrote to Frieda, 'the last part of it is the dirtiest, most indecent, obscene thing ever written'.[7] People in glasshouses should probably not throw stones; nevertheless, this outburst conforms with the arguments against pornography which Lawrence makes in 'Pornography and Obscenity', where it is defined as 'the attempt to insult sex, to do dirt on it' (Px, 312). It is in this piece that he coins the term 'dirty little secret'[8] to describe the sex of the reading and cinemagoing public, who want only the 'sneaking secrecy' of cheap thrills, the quick aphrodisiac of popular culture: 'One might easily say that half the love novels and half the love films today depend entirely for their success on the secret rubbing of the dirty little secret' (Px, 315). In the two or three pages which follow this, Lawrence sets out a prognosis for our culture: film-watching (in the dark, on your own) is a secret affair, leading to the secrecy of masturbation, which itself leads to despair. The result is an argument *for* censorship, even though Lawrence's own texts were, of course, heavily censored upon original publication (which he took as an injury to his own body: 'I might as well try to clip my own nose into shape with scissors. The book bleeds' (Px, 329)). Lawrence wants to turn the tables on his accusers, vindicating his texts as entirely 'honest, healthy . . . necessary for us today' (Px, 329), whilst denigrating all else (save Boccaccio) as the real filth: 'The insult to the human body, the insult to a vital human relationship! Ugly and cheap they make the human nudity, ugly and degraded they make the sexual act, trivial and cheap and nasty' (Px, 312).

Inevitably, the 'very lowest instance' he can give of the insult to sex is of (Hermione's) visual sex. ' "[Y]ou want to have everything in your own volition, your deliberate voluntary consciousness"', says Birkin of Hermione, prescribing the cure for sex in the head as having ' "that loathsome little skull . . . cracked like a nut. For you'll be the same till it is cracked, like an insect in its skin"'. He then counters Hermione's pornographic sexuality with a 'real' alternative:

> 'If one cracked your skull perhaps one might get a spontaneous, passionate woman out of you, with real sensuality. As it is, what you want is pornography – looking at yourself in mirrors, . . . so that you can have it all in your consciousness, make it all mental.' (WL, 92)

This will do as much as any other statement in Lawrence's work as a definition of pornography, pornography made flesh not in images and pictures but in the brain of a woman. Hermione's sex is intrinsically pornographic. Her narcissism, unlike Ramón's, is crystallised in vision, and the evil of onanism realised through the visual vice of mirrored self-regard doubles the sin.[9] It is also true that this form of behaviour and sexual preference (having it all in one's consciousness, making it all mental) is the more widespread phenomenon of 'sex in the head'; the problem is not simply that of an individual female character. One of Lawrence's clearest definitions of pornography also, then, turns out to be one of his strongest statements against aberrant femininity. Indeed, on the issue of Hermione, the two are the same.

There are several knots here which need to be unpicked. Lawrence is, paradoxically, a writer of 'puritanical' dirty books (Frieda Lawrence calls *Lady Chatterley's Lover* 'the last word in Puritanism' (FLC, 9)). He painted scandalous paintings, and much of his work was suppressed or only struggled into print because of its unacceptability, and it is still pursued by a feminism which would deem his work 'obscene' on political grounds.[10] What Lawrence, on the one hand, sets up as obscene (etymologically, 'off stage', that which isn't visually present or represented) and what he, on the other hand, 'exposes' and stages (explicit written images of bodies, sexual acts, 'scenes' which challenge contemporary taboos), does not necessarily correspond consistently to any set of rules – not those of the statute books, of feminism, or the rules of D.H. Lawrence himself. This is an issue within Lawrence's corpus (which itself constantly theorises what is acceptable) and for the history of reading him and his publications, but it is also an issue which focuses on how we read him. He writes about what should and should not be written, but his terms are also turned back on him by a feminism which finds him obscene for political reasons. These are some of the paradoxes which still lie at the heart of our reception of his work: Lawrence, impossibly, not only epitomises certain sexist positions on knowing women, he is also taken to be *the* writer of classic dirty books, as well as (for traditional Lawrence scholarship) an exemplary voice against perversion, fragmented sex, and the sexually inauthentic – all this, despite his notoriety and supposedly sexual radicalism established in the 1960s by the so-called 'Trial of Lady Chatterley'. In his polemical essays he establishes an uneasy alliance with certain feminisms, and even with the so-called 'Whitehouse lobby' of contemporary pro-censorship right-wingers. Where, then, does he stand?

Believing passionately in speaking for the primacy of the dark self *against* mental 'dirtiness', as well as opposing the law of what can and cannot be printed, Lawrence also broke faith with himself in *enjoying* the delights of mentality – sex in the head as well as in the 'secret places'. Not only did he transgress the law and public morality, he transgressed his own law and his own stringent heterosexist sense of the decent and healthy. He writes in '*A Propos* of *Lady Chatterley's Lover*' that 'the essential blood-contact is between man and woman, always has been so, always will be', and in *Fantasia of the Unconscious* he also writes, 'all life works up to the one supreme moment of coition' (F, 18). Yet he explores and keeps returning to an intense homoeroticism, which begins with *The White Peacock*, and can be traced right through the writing of *Women in Love, Aaron's Rod, The Plumed Serpent*, as well as poems such as 'Eloi, Eloi, Lama Sabachthani', written from the point of view of a male soldier in the act of killing another man:

> And I knew he wanted it.
> Like a bride he took my bayonet, wanting it,
> Like a virgin the blade of my bayonet, wanting it,
> And it sank to rest from me in him,
> And I, the lover, am consummate,
> And he is the bride, I have sown him with the seed
> And planted and fertilised him.
>   (Poems, 742)

Lawrence asserts the primacy of 'normal' wholesome sex, yet it is anal ecstasy which finally burns Connie's soul 'to tinder', which connects Birkin and Ursula with 'the source of the deepest life-force'. Publishers of pornographic magazines in Britain who hope to evade prosecution under the Obscene Publications Act avoid any suggestion of sodomy in their images – mid-range 'soft' porn never represents couples having actual sex anyway, and it is only recently that videos which do so have been granted certification by the British Board of Film Classification, although explicit representations of it remain firmly off the list of acceptable acts. Consequently, in the late 1920s Lawrence's central, if artistically evasive, representations of anality were way beyond what public morality expected and the law allowed, but also transgressive of his otherwise straight position on affirmable heterosexual acts.

By the late 1950s, Lawrence the (hetero)sexual dissident had a mixed profile. On the one hand he was thrillingly 'outside', because the *Lady Chatterley* texts could still not be easily or legally bought (unless you were an intellectual with connections, nefariously obtaining your continentally printed or pirated plain-wrapper copy[11]). Yet simultaneously he was culturally central for the highbrow because, backed and championed by F.R. Leavis and Cambridge criticism, he was fast being established as the still small voice of a budding discourse of psychosexual 'maturity'. Lawrence-the-literary-outlaw's mainstream vindication after the success of Penguin in 1960 is, then, preceded by the Eng. Lit. deification of him as the voice of the Authentic. 'Here was a man with the clairvoyance and honesty of genius whose living was an assertion of what the modern world had lost', wrote F.R. Leavis in 1932,[12] a position repeated in a number of ways by the defence witnesses at the trial twenty-eight years later, who had never had any difficulty getting hold of the book anyway.[13] In the eyes of the law up to the late 1950s it was enough to write explicit sex scenes to provoke the charge of obscenity; in the eyes of Cambridge criticism it was enough to grant him the status of, in David J. Gordon's utterly unironic phrase, 'inexplicable personal genius'.[14]

This much is well documented, but Lawrence's own more 'secret' places are not. As Jeffrey Meyers puts it,

> The equation of the anus with the life source is such an obscene and outrageous idea that some of the most perceptive critics have either ignored it entirely or else refused to face the full implications of Lawrence's homosexuality.[15]

The point has often been made that the prosecution would have won in the trial of *Lady Chatterley's Lover* if they had noted and argued that one of the key scenes in the novel depicts sodomy, an act illegal even between consenting heterosexual couples. *Lady Chatterley's Lover* is nothing if not a gateway text; the history of British publication in the last thirty years would have been very different if the act had been noted, but the prosecution's loss is the publisher's gain, and the trial was the test case which then allowed so much else to come into print. But Lawrence's reputation would also have been radically different if his more conventionally obscene exploration of sodomy had received as much publicity as the 'normal' intercourse of John Thomas and Lady Jane (for all the writer's celebrated openness, whilst penises and vaginas have nicknames in Lawrence, anuses cannot even be spoken of in coy euphemism). Lawrence the sodomite, the closet queen, the anally excited, the playful sado-masochist, is not the Lawrence many 'A' Level students are brought up on, but it is this Lawrence, who writes and fantasises against the grain of sexual propriety and gender-roles, whose work in its public and legal scandalousness is finally most notoriously provocative. Lawrence is both pornographer (in the sense of one who writes sexually against the grain of public morality and sometimes legality) and puritan (in his own castigation of conventional morality's own 'dirty little secret' in its visual and cerebral guise). It is on the site of obscenity that the battle against sex in the head is most clearly fought, and it is also here that Lawrence and (certain) feminism(s) finally agree. Under what circumstances, then, is Lawrence able to affirm that which he has already deemed 'dirty'?

The public and the pubic

Known during the period of his notoriety as an explicit writer, what Lawrence is explicit *about* is the material root of all cerebral and gazing activity: truth and beauty are not Platonic ideals but the mutant offspring of forces below. His desire is to cut to the foundation of metaphysical ideals and to show the insect beneath the wings, the earth beneath the blossom, but his discussion of shit, of the genital–anal root of supposed purity, is not wilful transgression fuelled by the need to shock. As a part-time anti-metaphysician, Lawrence's world-turned-upside-down shows truth to be really bottom-side-up. In both the *Pansies* Introduction and in the *Lady Chatterlies* Lawrence connects thought and beauty (the appeal of the eye), both activities of the 'upper consciousness', back to the same 'lower' roots. Beauty – both male and female – is based in the 'base' self. Thus the mental primacy of the Cocksure Woman is challenged: it is Connie's bottom, not her will or wisdom, which 'could hold the world up':

> '. . . An' ivery bit of it is woman, woman sure as nuts. Tha'rt not one of
> them button-arsed lasses as should be lads, are ter! Tha's got a real soft
> sloping bottom on thee, as a man loves in 'is guts.' . . .
>   All the while he spoke he exquisitely stroked the rounded tail, till it seemed
> as if a slippery sort of fire came from it into his hands. And his finger-tips
> touched the two secret openings to her body, time after time, with a soft
> little brush of fire. (Lady, 232).

The sexual cross-overs here are multiple: Connie's femininity rests on the uneasy assertion (uneasy, anyway, to anyone familiar with the term 'nuts' as a vulgar alternative to testicles) that her arse is 'woman sure as nuts.' Other lasses are still lasses even if, by virtue of their 'button-arses', they should be lads. It is Connie's arse here, not her cunt, which emits a hot lubricant – this is not a dry and painfully penetrated place, but an inviting and not necessarily female hole which responds to touch against the grain of the Lady's own propriety ('Connie could not help a sudden snort of astonished laughter'). The arse responds and the girl can't help it.[16]

Mellors' declaration, clarifying the notion of thought founded in sex and beauty founded in shit, is prelude to the famous scene in which he threads flowers in Connie's pubic hair. Read alongside Lawrence's discussion of the earthy roots of flowers in the *Pansies* Introduction, the significance of the threading is clear:

> The fairest thing in nature, a flower, still has its roots in earth and manure; and in the perfume there hovers still the faint strange scent of earth, the under-earth in all its heavy humidity and darkness. (Px, 302).

> With quiet fingers he threaded a few forget-me-not flowers in the fine brown fleece of the mound of Venus.
> 'There!' he said. 'There's forget-me-nots in the right place!' She looked down at the milky odd little flowers amongst the brown maiden-hair at the lower tip of her body. (Lady, 233).

The 'right place' is in the earth: Connie's brown pubic hair will do as well as the real 'under-earth in all its heavy humidity and darkness'; the difference between the 'lower tip of her body' and the flowers' 'roots in earth and manure' is not so great. In what has been taken as one of the most shocking moments of the long-banned text, one strong suggestion is the link between shit and beauty: below the 'big, wondering eyes' of Connie-the-aristocrat lurks the secret place which is more root than flower – a *common* place. When, in Chapter 7, the un-sexually-awakened Connie looks hopelessly in her mirror at her naked body it is only her buttocks ('the most beautiful part of her') which hold any promise of renewal: 'Here the life still lingered hoping. But here too she was thinner, and going unripe, astringent' (Lady, 74).

But health requires a material fuel to keep it going. Not 'the mental life' which, Connie reflects, had swindled her out of her inner self, but a sexual affirmation of one's connection with 'the below'. Moses, Mellors tells us in the forget-me-not scene, comes from the bullrushes; consciousness is rooted in a darkness which here is not mystified, but materialises in its grossest form. In the ideal upper self is written the life of the buttocks – or, written more strongly, shit is the condition of consciousness. Blue eyes have base roots ('mingled with the blue of the morning the black of the corrosive humus' (Px, 302)), just as a flower has its roots in the earth, and a dream image is the fruiting body of a network of micelium threaded through the unconscious. Even poetry, Lawrence writes elsewhere, 'ask[s] for the whiteness which is the seethe of mud' (Essays, 288).

So the head – and its perverse sex – is subordinated to the more fundamental power of Lawrence's 'lower body': this Lawrence affirms in his guise of part-time materialist. What is perhaps more interesting is the way in which, in these riskier passages, the experience of the arse and cunt takes precedence over that of the primary Lawrentian organ, the penis. The phallus may come first (as it were) on the conscious level of the sexual philosophy of *Lady Chatterley*, but in its 'secret places' the narrative affirms and enjoys submission to penetration, rather than erection and active insertion. The sodomy scene, for instance, is wholly narrated from Connie's point of view, and her experience throughout is far more important to the text than Mellors'.[17] In these few brief, risky pages a more general truth is revealed: what interests Lawrence far more than 'the Phallic hunt' is the experience of being hunted out and caught, exposed, invaded.

This emphasis on the feminine position destabilises the fixed gender positions which we might assume are operating here. Certainly Connie 'had to be a passive, consenting thing, like a slave, a physical slave', but femininity here is more like an *effect* of passivity, of the fact of being 'done to', than an instrinsic or essential quality which Connie brings to the scene. The act itself re-feminises her, as her narrative repeatedly tells us. Here Connie's gender is initially immaterial; it is the *process* of 'feminisation' which she undergoes which is important. In a sense, *any* passive partner, put into Connie's position of being hunted out by the narrative, would be feminised by virtue of this act of submission. As many S & M and Bondage and Domination practitioners know, the process of feminisation does not depend upon the presence of an anatomical woman; as Judge Schreber also knew, to be penetrated, in our culture, is to *become* a woman.[18] Lawrence sets up an experience of submission which will make a woman of you whether you are one or not.

Sodomy, then, does not 'unwoman' her – making her less of a cunt, less of a 'Lady', and more of a hole which could equally be male. Quite the opposite: 'She would have thought a woman would have died of shame. Instead of which, the shame died' (Lady, 258). The act makes her more 'openly' a woman: it renews and revives her sexual identity, it 'made a very different woman of her'. To paraphrase Carol J. Clover, whose brilliant discussion of gender roles in horror films has enormous purchase in this discussion, Connie is not passive because she is a woman, she is a woman because she 'acts' the role of passivity.[19] The arse which Mellors fucks is, then, not quite that of a 'woman sure as nuts'. This is not to say that the sex of a sodomised arse is immaterial because the act of penetration feminises it anyway, or that Mellors would be happy if Connie were less of a 'real woman' to him. *As* he fucks her, the woman comes into being. This is still a specifically feminine pleasure which Connie experiences, but Lawrence stages the coming-into-being of her womanhood *through* her passivity, and it is this sense of process, of nothing being fixed, of the doors of gender swinging open, which allows us (and Lawrence) to take part in the scene *with* Connie too. Submission and becoming-woman thus collapse into each other: not only does Lawrence use women's eyes to see masculine beauty, he uses their imaginary bodies to be on the receiving end of his own phallic hunting-out. Kate Millett's argument that 'it is through a feminine consciousness that his masculine message is conveyed'[20] needs radical reworking in terms of these sexual challenges, so that it becomes more like 'It is through a female body that his homoeroticism is enjoyed'. Mellors' pleasure is curiously absent – it is Connie the sodomised submissive who has all the fun. Here, then, phallic pleasure is subordinated to the exquisite 'sensuality sharp and searing as fire', as the text finds a way of sodomising itself, and of making a woman of itself.

This anti-metaphysic is, of course, reflected in the title of the poetry collection with which I began this discussion. Lawrence prefers pansies to *pensées*, earthed organisms to the metaphysical ether, blossoms with bottoms rather than rootless fragments of thought.[21] Arses are our versions of roots, and, as the Introduction to *Pansies* explores at length, the word 'arse' deserves its place alongside the word 'God'. Lawrence's point is that just as we have repressed the 'soil' in which we are rooted, so we have repressed the 'old words that belong to the body below the navel'. If Jonathan Swift verbally gagged at the thought that his otherwise exquisite heroine 'Celia shits', Lawrence's response is to reassure her that the act is one necessary to *his* heroines. And so the flowering of intellect needs to be reconnected with the 'lower self': 'We have roots, and our roots are in the sensual, instinctive and intuitive body, and it is here we need fresh air of open consciousness' (Px, 302).

With this imperative comes the claim that this reconnection, of word, thought and thing, takes place at several points in Lawrence's later works. In the light of this we also need to return to the question of just *what* Lawrence himself deemed 'obscene', and how he negotiated those nefarious pleasures which he also deemed taboo. If he had no truck with *that* word ('obscene' means, remember, only that the police can arrest you), if he saw his mission as reinscribing language with the repressed power of taboo words, he was nevertheless certainly not shy about using the word 'pornographic' in its most derogatory sense. The dialectic of assertion and condemnation which has characterised the public life of Lawrence's work (dark sex is textually asserted and then publicly censored), is nothing compared to the exchange of assertion and denial, the exposure and quick silencing which occurs within his work itself. I want now to look again at the sexual and visual disavowal which occurs in Lawrence's work in the context of his public image and persona: the nefarious enjoyment and circulation of transgressive pleasure which has accompanied the banning of his books. Exposing the obscene always takes place within an economy of covering, clothing, censorship and moral prescription.

The fear of the eye

> It is known that civilized man is characterized by an often inexplicable acuity of horror. The fear of insects is no doubt one of the most singular and most developed of these horrors as is, one is surprised to note, the fear of the eye. It seems impossible, in fact, to judge the eye using any word other than *seductive*, since nothing is more attractive in the bodies of animals and men. But extreme seductiveness is probably at the boundary of horror.[22]

Already we might seem as far from the eye and its look as the body will allow. Eyes are the organs of transcendence, windows to the soul; to the naïve their steady gaze guarantees sincerity. So how does this dirty work on sodomy and soil connect with the visual concerns of this book? Most obviously, there is the issue of scrutiny, of 'exposing' secret places in print, of the narrative scandalously *showing* us those experiences which should remain covered. Whilst Lawrence's literary obscenities (obscene because they are, by his own definition, policed by the law) do not immediately appeal to the eye, as would magazines or movies; these are moments which are clearly subject to the perception of our spectator-in-the-text. Connie is the hunted-out submissive, but she is also our visual focus – bearer of the passive orifices of sex and the active orifice of sight.

Secondly, eyes also have a squeamish, obscene life which has been the staple diet of horror films (also eminently censorable) at least since Buñuel's *Un Chien Andalou*. Eyes are both disgusting and desirable, the focus of feelings of abjection *and* of extreme experiences of beauty. They are the windows to the soul and, like no other part of the body, the source of squeamishness and repulsion. When Maurice in 'The Blind Man' forces Bertie to touch his damaged eyes, the scene reverberates with a power of horror entirely out of proportion to the events described:

> 'Touch my eyes, will you? – touch my scar.'
> Now Bertie quivered with revulsion. Yet he was under the power of the blind man, as if hypnotised. He lifted his hand, and laid the fingers on the scar, on the scarred eyes. Maurice suddenly covered them with his own hand,

pressed the fingers of the other man upon his disfigured eye-sockets, trembling in every fibre, and rocking slightly, slowly, from side to side. He remained thus for a minute or more, whilst Bertie stood as if in a swoon, unconscious, imprisoned. (EME, 73)

Clearly something more is going on here than an encounter over Maurice's scars. The injured eye is not the channel of disembodied images but a material socket. It has become a macabre new form of orifice, taking in not just light but fingers. Bertie, 'gazing mute and terror-struck' at the spectacle of his own fingers pressing on the blind sockets, feels trapped with 'an unreasonable fear'.

The encounter connects with a variety of wider fears about eye violence and scopic penetration. Simply the *idea* of a violent injury to the eye, which locks into a range of anxieties which I can only briefly discuss here, provokes an extreme response in both men and women. Eyes have a power of horror which other organs – even the organs of life such as the heart, the brain, the liver – entirely lack. The fear of and for the eye vastly exceeds its organic importance. Popular horror plays on this fear in an apparently inexhaustible variety of ways, and there is currently a magazine in circulation in Britain called *Eyeball* (obviously those marketing it felt that this simple bald word is suggestive enough to act as an umbrella for a variety of horrors). The reluctance of relatives of the recently dead to agree to cornea donations is well known. Whilst unseen inner organs (kidneys particularly) may be extracted with ready consent, few feel happy with their loved ones' eyes being violated, however much it will restore another's sight and however dead the original owner might be. Eyes are the gaps through which love also leaks, perhaps the most personal feature of a loved one's body. As Diane Ackerman notes of the iris, 'the pattern of colour, starbursts, spots and other features is so highly individual that law-enforcement people have considered using iris patterns in addition to fingerprints'.[23] Destroy the eye and you risk destroying both the legal and the lovable subject.

Georges Bataille's marvellously bizarre essay 'Eye' (from which my epigraph is taken), written soon after the making of *Un Chien Andalou*, claims that the notorious eye-slitting scene in that film goes so far beyond the limit of what is acceptable that after it – cinematically and experientially – anything is possible. He writes of the opening of the film:

Several very explicit facts appear in successive order, without logical connection it is true, but penetrating so far into horror that the spectators are caught up as directly as they are in adventure films. Caught up and even precisely caught by the throat, and without artifice; do these spectators know, in fact, where they – the authors of this film, or people like them – will stop? If Buñuel himself, after the filming of the slit-open eye, remained sick for a week . . . how then can one not see to what extent horror becomes fascinating, and how it alone is brutal enough to break everything that stifles?[24]

Perhaps this claim that the graphic violation of an eye on the screen is so shocking that it threatens a revolution of the given order will seem somewhat far-fetched to viewers of more recent examples of the eye violation motif in mainstream (often morally and sexually conservative) horror films. The repetition of eye-violence is by now such a familiar horror feature that the sense in which it can be termed obscene needs to be reassessed. The ghoulish cult pleasures of this spectacle might even suggest a new currency for that phrase Lawrence used to express extreme popular-cultural pleasure in *The Lost Girl*: surely the horror fan is more than anyone else 'in his eye-holes' (LG, 132, see my discussion of this in the introduction, above).

The BBFC is reluctant to allow images of the *process* of eye violence to be shown uncut (as it were) in Britain. Special effects in film produce images which technically surpass anything which could be plausibly done on stage to, say, Gloucester's eyes in *King Lear*, but precisely because of this close-up, gross potential in cinema, little can be *actually* shown in Britain. Consequently, even though we have the technology, the actual act of injury to an eye is rarely seen, but often implied. Buñuel's film is one exception, certificated whole because of its art-house status; mainstream horror is judged by a different standard, and we generally only see the *effects* of the violence, or the act obscured or at a distance. Certainly, however, violated eyes are commonplace, frequently shown after-the-fact, which is often bad enough – if anything in horror is *on* stage, it is this. Eyes are pecked out in Hitchcock's *The Birds*, mirror shards are wedged into them in Michael Mann's *Manhunter*; the pupil is penetrated with (what look like) hatpins in Dario Argento's *Suspiria*, by a splinter of wood in Fulci's *Zombie Flesh Eaters*, or it is sliced by a knife in *The New York Ripper*. Perhaps most famously, in a harrowing marriage of voyeurism and violence, a woman's eye is shot as it looks at a gun through a keyhole in Argento's *Opera*. All of these examples are subject to various levels of censorship, whether in production or later by the BBFC. We arrive *after* the birds have pecked, we find those eyes in *Manhunter* and in *Suspiria already* violated. *Opera* cuts away from the intense close-up of the bullet passing through the keyhole to show us the whole injury *from a distance*, and *The New York Ripper* cannot be seen in Britain at all. The act of violation *might* be allowed if the subject isn't technically human, as with that moment when the Terminator gouges his cybernetic eye in the film of that name, an act which would be heavily censored if Schwarzenegger were playing a 'real' person rather than a robot.

This might serve as popular-cultural support for Bataille's basic point that the eye, perhaps more than any other part of the body including the genitals, is the primary focus of taboo. His obsession with breaking down repressive structures through his writing, by exposing the eye as a key object of pornographic fixation, is well known, and so the novel *Story of the Eye* sees a range of indignities done to eyes, and to their surreal stand-ins (eggs and bull's testicles in particular). If images of extreme horror can provoke a viewing experience which 'alone is brutal enough to break everything that stifles', then eye horror must be expressed. But what characterises Bataille's work most strongly for the purposes of this argument is the way in which it marks out eyes as objects, orbs of flesh which can be degraded as effectively as the more obvious sexual organs. In a key violation of the metaphysic which posits the eye as a divine window, an interface between mind and body, Bataille follows Buñuel in asserting its gross materiality. What repels is not simply the image of a knife cutting flesh, but the simple idea that the eye, long-protected by the visor of spirituality, is just another part of the body, perhaps the most tangibly material part of all. This is the conclusion of Bataille's claim about the implications of Buñuel's scene: in breaking the taboo and making the eye violable, in showing it to be corpulent, *Un Chien Andalou* profoundly threatens the world-view of the integrated, spiritual subject who holds the eye as the symbol of sincerity and a representation or guarantee of the afterlife.

There is, of course, another dimension of violation which the Buñuel scene (and its cinematic offspring) brings into being. Eyes are not simply the source of the sadistic or desiring gaze, they are also objects of that gaze. They are organs which look and are looked at at the same time. When the object of the gaze – of author or viewer – is the eye itself, when what we are looking at is the horror which can be done to our eyes themselves, the knot of self-reference and identification tightens. How, then, can we characterise the uneasy relationship between the eye which is sliced on the screen and the eye which watches this from the auditorium?

A similar relationship exists between the reader of *Story of the Eye* and the narrative events of that text, but obviously, when the subject is eyes, the cinematic situation presents a more graphic scene of visual self-referentiality and violation. What is being violated on the screen is the organ through which we watch the violation; as Carol Clover discusses, the act of looking in such situations has to be read masochistically rather than sadistically: 'it is not the eye that kills, but the eye that is "killed"'. Lawrence too is interested in what Clover calls 'hurtable vision, vision on the defense'.[25] When the gaze rests on an image of its own injury, its (traditionally understood) masculine power is problematised. However, in reading *Story of the Eye* (or one of the Lawrence texts under discussion here) the reader witnesses the textual events as part of a written narrative, and any identification between the gaze which is destroyed in the text and the organs which are scanning the page can only take place in a displaced way. The significance of the painful jump from 'graphic' eye violence or gaze violence (enacted in ink) to visual eye violence (enacted on celluloid) is evidenced by the problems which Michael Powell experienced when bringing *Peeping Tom* (1960) to the screen. As the then head of the BBFC John Trevelyan has written, Powell first showed the script of *Peeping Tom* to the censors before shooting, who thought as a result that the film would be a positive contribution to the study of mental illness. However, when the BBFC came to see those *written* visual violences translated into *cinematic* ones, they were so shocked as to demand a series of cuts.[26] Since the film investigates the relationship between the eye (of viewer and protagonist–killer) and the camera, and of both as a weapon, it forces the viewer into visual identification with the killer and the act of killing (at the moment of death the victim is forced to watch a mirror-image of herself dying, and in watching her we are aligned with the killer).[27] The implications of Trevelyan's altered perspective on the script and the film are interesting, for the violence of and to the gaze which *Peeping Tom* explores could only really come to life once it was transformed from screenplay to visual action. Although *Peeping Tom* explores murderous gazes rather than physically violated eyes, nevertheless this instance of the qualitative difference between the violent screen gaze and its earlier written 'shadow' is telling. Clover discusses the experiential violation of eyes as they are forced to witness painful scenes. When horror cinema forces its audience to actually *look* at the violation of an eye, it subjects viewers to a doubly masochistic experience in a way which a written text on the same subject cannot. If written violences to eyes, or condemnations of the gaze, cannot challenge our view as effectively as Lawrence would like, where can he next turn?

Dilation and darkness

We have seen how men and women's various relationships to the gaze define and test their sexual and existential positions in Lawrence. But eyes themselves – the material organs which have such a hard time in horror – also stand in for a range of psychosexual and racial positions. As Lawrence writes in *The Plumed Serpent*,

> the power of the world, which [Kate] had known until now only in the eyes of blue-eyed men, who made queens of their women – even if they hated them for it in the end – was now fading in the blue eyes, and dawning in the black. (PS, 415)

Black eyes come as near to a guarantee of phallic potency as is possible:

> In his black, glinting eyes the power was limitless, and it was as if, from him,
> from his body of blood could rise up that pillar of cloud which swayed and
> swung, like a rearing serpent or a rising tree, till it swept the zenith, and all
> the earth below was dark and prone, and consummated. (PS, 324).

Goodness! – and all because his eyes were the right colour? The motif of
eye colour is so recurrent as to stand as a hallmark of personality type.
There are few blue-eyed boys in Lawrence – it is the black- and brown-
eyed males who are his heroes, identified with an authentic and idealised
image of Indian sexuality and sensibility, whilst the villains are
predominantly blue-eyed females, often American women, modern
flappers or suffragettes. The 'blue-eyed, dazed' woman who rode away
dies for being a 'quivering, nervous conscious . . . highly-bred white
woman', whilst Pauline Attenborough in 'The Lovely Lady' (1927) has
prominent grey eyes with heavy 'bluish lids', burdened by the weight of
her conscious femininity and connected by 'a little invisible wire' to her
narcissistic willpower: conventional loveliness can only be skin deep for
the blue-eyed bitch, and Pauline collapses into a malevolent suicidal
'insanity of discordance'. A similar fate had already befallen Mrs Crich in
the earlier *Women in Love*, whose encroaching madness and unwhole-
someness is characterised by her 'heavy-seeing blue eyes' (WL, 72), into
which Birkin is afraid to look, as if mental degeneration or eye colour were
contagious. Lawrence's obsession with blue as the colour of intellect and
inauthenticity is perhaps most clearly seen in the rather nasty little story
of 1926, 'Two Blue Birds', but readers are soon to pick up the significance
of forget-me-not eyes in many of his fictions. To be sure, men can also be
cursed with this pigment, the external sign that the subject's sex lies behind
the eyes (in the head) rather than below them. Clifford Chatterley is
destined for a sterile life when we are told on the second page that his eyes
are 'pale-blue, challenging [and] bright'; Gerald Crich's northern
complexion marks out his fate (like mother like son), and as both he and
Gudrun rush towards their sado-masochistic nemesis the connection and
meeting of eye colour is resonant of a whole moral judgement:

> Her dark blue eyes, in their wetness of tears, dilated as if she was startled in
> her very soul. They looked at him through their tears in terror and a little
> horror. His light blue eyes were keen, small-pupilled and unnatural in their
> vision. (WL, 493)

Daphne in *The Ladybird* has 'nerve-worn' green-blue eyes, again
burdened with 'heavy-veined lids' and 'reddened rims', another instance
of how the flesh must revolt under the pressure of feminine gazing. Despite
this, she is destined to be saved by a man who is able to dilate her pupils,
thus turning her eyes from blue to black with the power of desire.

But Lawrence's concern with the physicality of eyes runs deeper than this. They also have a darker metaphorical life in the nether world which this chapter opened up into, and I now want to explore this through a closer reading of *The Ladybird*. What I want to suggest is that there is a point at which eyes symbolically become Lawrence's 'lower' orifices. Below the bluest eye is a sexual self, repressed and atrophied or awaiting release: Lawrentian men *do not* prefer blondes, but if a white (read 'blue-eyed') woman *is* to reach sexual authenticity she must open herself to dark truths, as Connie does. In *The Ladybird* this means that her eyes must dilate so that their pale pigment is entirely obliterated by the opening dark interior. Thus the 'real' beauty of Daphne is apprehended by the dark Count Dionys as that which prowls far beneath the surface of her 'nerve-worn', green-blue eyes:

> 'You, and your beauty – that is only the inside-out of you. The real you is the wild-cat invisible in the night, with red fire perhaps coming out of its wide, dark eyes. Your beauty is your white sepulchre.'[28]

Daphne finds the power to dilate her daylight eyes, enacting her own salvation in allowing the darkness through, in the process also saving her dark self from becoming a 'white sepulchre', the 'red fire' betrays a wild inside, just as Connie's formerly 'unripe, astringent' buttocks leaked 'a slippery sort of fire'. Risking herself 'pornographically' and narcissistically by indulging in a moment of mirror-gazing, Daphne breaks beyond sex in the head: her salvation, that which makes her resolutely *not* Hermione, is her realisation that beneath the 'iris drawn tight like a screen' (TN, 37) lurks a wildcat. Here, again, the (cinema) screen is evoked not as a window into a world of difference but the closed surface which flatly prevents entry, a blue shield contracted tight on a bright day.

What is important, however, isn't the nature of the beast which is kept down or out or finally let loose. It is the action of the eye in the process of release. Eyes dilate, like vaginas and anuses: they invite a relationship, they dilate as a *sign* of relationship, of desire or arousal taking place, and this is why they are associated with beauty. Thus Dionys 'wanted them to dilate and become all black pupil, like a cat's at night'. The panicked intensity of Daphne's response indicates that either eyes are standing in for something else here, or she is reacting entirely out of proportion. Dilation turns into relaxing and unfolding: 'Supposing it should relax. Supposing it should unfold, and open out the dark depths, the dark, dilated pupil!' Eyes and anuses are not simply connected negatively, with the one standing as the underbelly, base and material condition of the other in Lawrence's metaphysic; here the pupil stands in for the dilation of earthier orifaces. Lawrence uses one of the most transcendent images in our cultural armoury – that image of the window to the soul – to speak the possibilities and dangers of other bodily openings.

Thus, what is beneath or below, comes out on top; it may spring, leak or flood out from our orifices but the point is that Lawrence's daylight selves are probably not as in control as his polemic against them would indicate. Daphne's fearful, excited astonishment at the power her opening has to dilate beyond her will ('Supposing it should relax') is important. We are clearly not concerned with the natural action of a pupil, reacting to the coming and going of light here. Yet neither is this Bataille's solid, testicular eye, disturbing because it is so tangibly vile and substantial – as Stephen King puts it, 'We all understand that eyes are the most vulnerable of our sensory organs, the most vulnerable of our facial accessories, and they are (ick!) *soft*. Maybe that's the worst.'[29]

More disturbing, perhaps, than even Bataille's gross organ is the notion that the eye is an uncontrolled opening with a life of its own and the power to invite. Certainly there is something fundamentally obscene about graphic eye violence, but this is of a different order to the idea that one's eye can open (slash) itself and let the violence in. Eyes have their own violation programmed into them, fixed in the relationship between desire and muscular control. This connection, which makes the pupil dilate when you want something, whether you wish to betray this or not, means that an eye can be 'opened up' by a desire which is internal (sexually betraying) as well as external (sadistically violent). Daphne's disturbance does not result from a violation *done to her* from the *outside*, but from her own 'relaxation' of defences. This, indeed, is sex in the head – in the anatomy of the eye itself. Whether the cat jumps out or the man comes in (in the form of Dionys' image or Bertie's fingers), what matters is that the orifice asked for it all by itself. Eyes, then, are not disturbing simply because they can be *externally* violated with the slash of a knife like Buñuel's orb in *Un Chien Andalou*, but because their opening is bodily and disturbingly uncontrollable. The eye can slash itself open without one even knowing it. It doesn't need the violence of an external agent to demonstrate its vulnerability. The eye is a way *in* as well as a way *out*. It is this disturbance of boundaries – when muscles respond to desire and override moral purpose, when the outside slips in because the walls have relaxed and dissolved – which accounts for the vulnerability and power of the eye, and in this context I would suggest that ocular squeamishness is less the result of castration anxiety than a super-sensitive fear of and for one's own penetrability. This fear for and of one's openings needs to be analysed in greater detail relative to the anxiety of lack which is currently mapped onto ocular horror.

Sodomy and heterosexuality

I have looked at two overreactions to eyes which have changed physically. Daphne's pupils dilate, Maurice's damaged eyes have become only sockets. Daphne is aghast at her own penetrability, but Bertie's panic is of a different order. Desperate to run away once the encounter has taken place, in being made to penetrate the sockets his body has been violated by an unwelcome intimacy 'which had been thrust upon him'. Maurice possesses him with hungry fingers ('He seemed to take him, in the soft, travelling grasp' (EME, 73)), and Bertie's panic, that some threshold has been transgressed, could be easily decoded in homophobic terms. These are overreactions which connect directly with the story's sense of going too far, the point of dark connection being also the point at which rules are broken. Bertie's rules of separation have been transgressed, whilst Daphne fears she will give too much away. At both moments Lawrence slides between representing the eye as vulnerable and self-betraying, but also as an organ eclipsed at moments of dark connection – Daphne's eyes dilate so much that they become pure channels, whilst Maurice's unseeing eyes signify their own materiality as well as their impotence in relation to darkness, an impotence Maurice himself has transcended.

Eyes in Lawrence are disturbing not just because of what they do but because of what they are. However, this discussion of the obscene does not rest simply on the fact of their grotesque materiality. The eye, in its relationship to the outside world, may muscularly resemble other orifices, it might stand in for alternative forms of penetration than that of the image of the other imposed on the retina. But the focus of the narrative eye on objects – and not only men's bodies – can tell us more of desires which work outside of the jurisdiction of the moral or polemical voice of the text. In the next chapter I will develop this question in relation to clothes fetishism in Lawrence; for now I want to return to the question of sodomy and sexual identity.

The sexual positions of both Daphne and Maurice are unfixed. Maurice forces his eyes to be penetrated, Daphne the blue-eyed girl loses sexual control *through* the organ which otherwise controls. The sodomy scene from *Lady Chatterley's Lover* also goes 'too far' in the sense that it challenged at least two rules of contemporary public morality: the outlawing of heterosexual sodomy and its representation in print. It is also a scene which figures characters who, for all its obvious phallic potency, cannot be fixed as active or passive, penetrated or penetrating beings. Lawrence engages in a public transgression which also needs to be read as a self-transgression, given that the rules he so often claims to play by are those of fixed gender difference. He may write in *Fantasia* that 'the great thing is to keep the sexes pure' and yet the combined connections across and between the sexes which are played out in his writing demonstrate a number of other possibilities. This is a purity which is being constantly defiled; masculinity is so often represented through the eyes of femininity, and men and woman sexually identify with each other in a number of complex ways. One prominent example of this, which will form a key component of the next chapter, is Lawrence's relishing of women's clothing. As Angela Carter puts it, 'Lawrence clearly enjoyed being a girl', so how can the sexes be pure?

Bertie's fear gives a lot away. It is the fear of 'going too far', of being *made* to penetrate another man. Daphne fears the power of her gaze in quite other terms than those which ascribe sadistic power to looking. Meanwhile, simple heterosexuality remains an elusive thing, even for a writer known for his explicit representations of the straight idyll: Connie and Mellors burn out 'the shames, the deepest, oldest shames, in the most secret places' (Lady, 257), and whilst this is still one man and one woman, we are hardly in the same straight ballpark. For Jonathan Dollimore this is not the writing of a heterosexual sodomite *or* a repressed homosexual:

> let us say rather that what is most significant about such passages is the way so much is fantasized from the position of the woman (including anal ecstasy and, elsewhere, Lawrence's almost as notorious worship of the phallus), and in a voice which is at once *blindingly heterosexist and desperately homoerotic.*[30]

Although Lawrence was banned not for his explicit homoeroticism (which also went unnoticed at the trial – no mention is made of those scenes from *The White Peacock* or *Aaron's Rod* which represent an ideal sexual contact between men), but for his representations of straight sex, the double-voice which Dollimore identifies is what interests me. With one voice he speaks an explicit (or 'blinding') heterosexism which gets him into trouble first with the law and then with feminism, whilst with the other he explores (the novel itself calls this a 'phallic hunting out') an experience of anal desire and submission which is 'desperately homoerotic'. I hesitate to order these as text and subtext: here anality is not 'below' straight sex, and the homoerotic is not baser or deeper than the hetero, and the failure of readers and prosecuters to notice the 'perverse' power of passages such as that in which Connie is sodomised does not relegate it to an unconscious figure in the carpet. Lawrence's self-transgressions are as primary as his assertion of the law, even if and as they are disavowed: he wants to, but quite explicitly *does not*, keep the sexes pure. Sex in the head, in and through the eyes, is enjoyed but disavowed; male beauty is indulged with the alibi of a female screen. These self-transgressions need to be read in the context of Lawrence's more public transgression of printing convention. The knot which results is far more telling than any assertion of clear purpose.

I am not as interested in those overt descriptions of homoeroticism (such as Birkin's fantasy gallery of policemen and soldiers who have 'intoxicated his blood' in the 'Prologue' to *Women in Love*[31]) as I am in the rather more confused way in which Lawrence slides from one kind of sexual relation to another. It is perhaps easy enough for the most part to argue for clear sexual identities in texts, and then have done with it – Lawrence as either Jeffrey Meyers' struggling gay or Carole Dix's 'Real Man'.[32] More disturbing perhaps (to his own way of thinking) is the sexual mobility, the sliding between identities and identifications, which is exposed at certain moments. When men sodomise women in Lawrence, just as when women look at men, the differences of desire which usually characterise gender become blurred. It is *Ursula* not Birkin who acts to establish 'a new current of passional electricity', who looks and traces 'the line of his loins and thighs, at the back', and who, like a sexual coloniser, hunts out the unknown thing 'more wonderful than life itself' which lay hidden at 'the back of his thighs.' In a world (Lawrence's) in which straight penetration is elsewhere so rigidly circumscribed as the prime authentic act, heterosexual sodomy is a moment of exquisite anxiety. Bertie may fear the awful intimacy of being taken by Maurice's seeing fingers, and of having to respond, but perhaps something even more confused is going on in scenes such as those from *Women in Love* and *Lady Chatterley's Lover*. This is not because there is anything essentially transgressive about it, but because of the transgression of the rules of sexual propriety which Lawrence has himself already laid down and policed. Here, sexuality is made malleable. In the *Chatterley* version, Connie, our key visual focus, gives us the eyes through which we dwell on the body of the man who then takes her to a fulfilment which is not the characteristic happy ending of heterosexual romance. If the narrative sets up the woman's gaze as the means through which the spectacle of masculinity is enjoyed, then what is our pleasure when she is phallically hunted-out? Whilst men and women's desires are supposed to be essentially different, still those differences can easily be elided when a woman's gaze acts as the channel for homoerotic desire, or when a woman's body gets the phallic hunting out which may be also being enjoyed by or meant for someone who is not a woman. Indeed, it is a man who is writing all this in the first place. If Lawrence is Mellors the phallic hunter, he is also Connie the sodomised prey.

Chapter Five

◆

On being a girl

Lawrence-against-himself

To begin with, what is the sex of D.H. Lawrence? (anonymous reviewer of *The White Peacock*, Feb. 1911).

Lawrence clearly enjoys being a girl. (Angela Carter)[1]

'Which brings me to the strange case of D.H. Lawrence', wrote Angela Carter, 'and the truism that those who preach phallic superiority usually have an enormous dildo tucked away somewhere in their psychic impedimenta.'[2] Carter's Lawrence protests too much – he is all talk and no action, a visible surface with nothing underneath. The Lawrence which I wish to discuss here is also one who is all writing and therefore very little actual dark consummation, one whose ways of seeing are at odds with his philosophy of darkness. If, for Carter, the phallic swaggering covers and clothes a deficiency, the dark protestations also accompany a desperate adherence to the conscious and the visual. Lawrence's women figure centrally in this paradox, as the embodiment and guilty subject of the gaze, the pretext for pleasures against which the text also protests, as well as that which often disrupts the smooth relationship between eye and object. In Chapter 4 I analysed how the eye betrays its 'unwholesome' desires both by its dilation and by its fixation. In the first part of this chapter I want to look more closely at the text's sartorial fixation, before moving on to discuss its final failure to come to rest.

Lawrence may have clearly enjoyed being a girl, but he also wrote an essay called 'On Being a Man'. Here, despite the strong title, being a man 'is double'; he is caught in the clash between those old dualisms: mind and body, light and darkness, purpose and helplessness, and the only thing he can finally do is know that he '*can't* know [him]self', and stop trying to illuminate the unknown. Lawrence finds himself caught in a number of ways, bound by the polarities he has set for himself and often unable to choose one over the other. He cannot 'be', or know that he is, a man, and this is not only because he has a body, but also because he might have *a woman's* body, for so the text is embodied. He cannot *only* be a man because he *also* enjoys being a girl, whether the girl is one of the sadistic seers we have already encountered or one of the female masochists whom feminism has preferred to analyse in Lawrence's work. He cannot close the eyes of our culture because the pleasures of looking are so tempting. Finally, caught in the paradox of a writer polemicising against writing through writing, he can only disavow language, and argue for silence, through writing itself.

The closet queen and the invisible man

For Lawrence, we are all essentially Invisible Men, made visible by the inauthenticity of clothing, gestures, the intrusion of public lighting:

> In the tram, in the train, [Ursula] felt the same. The lights, the civic uniform was a trick played, the people as they moved or sat were only dummies exposed. She could see, beneath their pale, wooden pretence of composure and civic purposefulness, the dark stream that contained them all. . . . all their talk and all their behaviour was a sham, they were dressed-up creatures. She was reminded of the Invisible Man, who was a piece of darkness made visible only by his clothes. (R, 448)

Clothes are a way of pinning down the dark self – they define and shape that which should go unseen in the darkness. People are 'beast[s] in sheep's clothing'; they 'assume selves as they assume suits of clothing'.[3] Clothes are surfaces for light to bounce off, they are the only way that one might know that a person is there, since, for the most part, people fail to have the courage of their dark convictions which might make them 'present' in other ways.[4] Lawrence has challenged the hallmarks of visible beauty: the pretty faces or white skin or rosy breasts of Chapter 1, the face of Valentino in Chapter 3, whilst in Chapter 4 we found the beauty of flowers rooted in manure. In *The Rainbow* Lawrence challenges the whole notion of a visible self, seen by virtue of clothing, defined by its draperies.

The issue at stake here is not that of *how* one can *know* that the dark self is there if one cannot see it, although the fact that Ursula does, after all, still '*see* . . . the dark stream that contained them all' underneath their clothing begs the question. That she still has to see, even when it is darkness which she is making visible, emphasises the necessity of sight to Lawrence despite his urging us to close our eyes. What is more interesting is the implicit idea that dark selves are like disembodied ideas. Just as Lawrence's people are not given a social shape until clothes are put on them, so ideas have no social meaning until they are dragged kicking and screaming into language. Both notions rely on the assumption that essential selves, and ideal thoughts, pre-exist the form they take in the world. People compromise themselves in becoming sartorially identifiable, just as dark thoughts are given shape by language but should rightly remain unformed, unsaid, un'known'. Clothes, and words, pin down those entities which Lawrence would have silently invisible; the only thing he can do is write novels which 'walk away with the nail'. Dark selves are pre-subjects, just as dark thoughts are pre-linguistic, and just *saying* them destroys them. In writing at all, Lawrence has submitted to a state antipathetic to him; the embodiment and incorporation of the act contradicts the 'message'. In his 1924 'Introduction to *A Bibliography of D.H. Lawrence*' Lawrence writes, 'one submits to the process of publication as to a necessary evil: as souls are said to submit to the necessary evil of being born into the flesh' (Px, 28). A curious analogy for Lawrence the celebrant of the flesh, but consistent with his contradictory celebration of the invisible man. In Chapter 2 we saw how cocksure women do not lay 'eggs' – the fecund, authentic produce of female nature, instead they lay 'a vote, or an empty ink-bottle, or some other absolutely unhatchable object, which means nothing to them' (Essays, 33). In the process of writing this, however, Lawrence is also producing an empty ink-bottle: the words are spent on the page, and books do not hatch, as Lawrence the anti-intellectual knows full well. Books, then, must always be an unproductive, inauthentic substitute for the 'real', fertile, fluid expenditure of phallic consciousness. Fertility is replaced by 'fecund' writing, or a prolific authorial career. The paradox here is this: Lawrence *writes*, and in writing it is *he* who makes (what he considers to be) the pre-linguistic ether of dark knowledge 'fall' into language. He may want his novels to walk away with the nail, but by his own definition it is the act of writing which does the nailing in the first place.

The same is true of clothing. We may all be invisible men, but a lot of pleasure is to be had in Lawrence's texts from sartorial inauthenticity. Frills might only dress up the dark creature underneath, but he enjoys this 'trick' of civic uniform. According to Angela Carter, Lawrence is seriously into women's clothing, since this is one of the things his texts most repeatedly fix upon. Despite his macho polemics, what he really likes is to catalogue 'his heroine's wardrobes with the loving care of a ladies' maid':

> If we do not trust the teller but the tale, then the tale positively revels in lace and feathers, bags, beads, blouses and hats. It is always touching to see a man quite as seduced by the cultural apparatus of femininity as Lawrence was, the whole gamut, from feathers to self-abnegation.[5]

All this, Carter argues, is clothed in a despicable, sexist disingenuousness.

In keeping with the author's own anti-authorial protestations (the novelist as 'a dribbling liar' (Px, 174), the one part of Lawrence's philosophy which we are charged to believe), we must trust the lacy evidence against the grain of the macho polemic. Lawrence, then, punishes women for indulging the vice which *is his* primary pleasure. And just as dark knowledge is only ever knowable once it has come to rest on the illuminated page, so Lawrence's women, far from being essentially invisible, are often nothing but their wardrobes: they are born into cloth, and *have* no identity underneath the petticoats. To say that they do (Carter suggests this when she writes that 'Lawrence probes as deeply into a woman's heart as the bottom of a hat-box') is to ask a form of the 'How many children has Lady Macbeth?' question. Since Lawrence's women – particularly the ones he most dislikes – seldom get the chance to be 'invisible', asking what their 'true' identity might be is a bit like asking what dark knowledge is before it enters discourse. This, finally, is Lawrence's failing for Carter; that perhaps 'for Lawrence, [women's] appearance alone constitutes their sexuality'.[6] Women's hearts, dark truths: these may exist beyond the words and hat boxes, but often all we have is texts full of clothes and words, instead of Real Women and indefinite sex. An odd result, since Lawrence is so keen to prioritise the latter and criticise the former.

Lawrence, then, is using women's apparent love of clothing to clothe his own love of clothing. It is not really Lawrence's women who love stockings, but the author himself. Consequently, his disapproval of their clothing-delight has to be read as a self-criticism. When Gudrun and Ursula parade in front of the miners in Chapter 1 of *Women in Love*, it is *Lawrence's* exhibitionism which is indulged, but the girls who have to endure the ridicule of the mob. Carter's point is a simple one: Lawrence is a sneaky old queen but not man enough, for all that, to admit to it, and so he uses women to indulge his nefarious pleasures. Lawrence,

> is attempting to put down the women he has created in his own image for their excessive reaction to the stockings to which he himself has a very excessive reaction indeed, the deep-down queenly, monstrous old hypocrite that he is.[7]

Hermione has a 'love of beautiful, extravagant dress' which the novel indulges as much as it criticises her; Gudrun's stockings are a focus and motif for the book, relished as their owner becomes more repellant. The two are intimately bound up with each other, the pleasures of feminine trappings being enjoyed as much as the fact of feminine intellect is degraded. Lawrence details the spectacle of many a woman, not as pure flesh akin to his naked male beefcake, but with an eye, instead, on their love of the dressing-up box. There is something desperately excessive about the resulting tableaux, and also a strange sense that Lawrence is already scripting the costume changes for when his novels hit the screen.[8]

What is primarily interesting for Carter, however, isn't the unconscious femininity which this clothes cultivation might betray. The display is pure transvestism, and it is transvestism rather than latent femininity which manifests itself as a desire to wrap his text in feminine fripperies. In characterising women and in showing the world through their eyes, he betrays his own desire, to paraphrase Ursula's thought in *The Rainbow*, to 'assume the self of femininity as he assumes its suits of clothing'. Lawrence *becomes* a woman in writing and dressing them, but still, for Carter, he remains essentially a *masculine* 'beast in sheep's clothing'. Even though Lawrence clearly enjoyed being a girl, he enjoyed being a female impersonator even more, and the two are not the same. Thus it is textual transvestism rather than textual femininity which leaks through and betrays itself, an argument which finally supports an idea of essential gender beneath-the-stockings: '[T]he nature of female impersonation in art is a complex business and the man who sets out to do it must be careful not to let his own transvestite slip show, especially if he does not like women much.'[9] If Carter's Lawrence is a transvestite, he can never really be a girl. Like Tristessa in her novel *Passion of New Eve*, Lawrence is *so* good at female impersonation that he *has* to be a man: only a man can conceive the image of perfect femininity so immaculately.

Lest all this gender-bending and all these layers of visible cloth and essential darkness are getting confusing, let me recap. According to Ursula, people are (or ought to be) invisible; clothing drags them into the light. But we also have ample evidence of a narrative focus which keeps compulsively dragging, not just people into clothes, but male desire into drag. Lawrence represents people who are really invisible running away from the fact of their invisibility by getting dressed, in the process giving him the secret opportunity of indulging his own clothes fetishism on the side. Gudrun is ultimately punished, whilst she acts as a prime focus for the text's nefarious sartorial delight. People are and should be invisible, but that doesn't stop Lawrence from offering us the pleasures of their flamboyant visibility. This is a bodily and scopic version of the paradox of Lawrence's formal situation: words uneasily clothe dark thoughts, just as dark selves are inauthentically dressed. As we saw in Chapter 1, darkness and silence, invisibility and abstention from speech, amount to an ideal. In terms of his own philosophical polemic, Lawrence should neither finally try to know and speak nor try to see. In fact not only does he do both, he enjoys doing them too.

Landscape and lingerie

If Lawrence represents spectacular men in a state which is as near to invisibility as possible, he does the opposite with women. For Carter, this finally signifies a disavowed transvestism. But another possibility presents itself in her short paper, which is that of fetishism, a model for male responses to the trappings of femininity which deserves fuller treatment. Before discussing this I want to clarify my differences with Carter: I am far more interested in exploring the fact of narrative pleasure in the disavowed, rather than in exposing the disingenuousness of the act itself. The pleasure in the spectacle of clothing is finally more revealing of other currents at work in the text than Carter's blank statement of Lawrence's contradictions. Concentrating more on moral censure, on the evasion rather than the fact of pleasure in Lawrence, she misses the very point which she herself makes, and then drops: 'Lawrence clearly enjoys being a girl.' Carter prefers to see him first as a closet queen (pretending to be a woman but then standing by his own manhood), then as a fetishist (only interested in women's clothing because he cannot assimilate his vision of the real women underneath). Despite her title Lawrence's queenliness is not as important to her argument as his hypocrisy.

For Freud, however, the fetishist and the transvestite are two quite different animals, and the one does not slip into the other quite so smoothly. Freud's classic fetishist is the man who is so disturbed by the sight of the 'castrated' female genitals that he fixates on the next and nearest visual thing available, which becomes his fetish-object, standing in for a feminine sexuality which cannot be spoken. Freud rationalises fetishism in these terms:

> Thus the foot or shoe owes its preference as a fetish – or a part of it – to the circumstance that the inquisitive boy peered at the woman's genitals from below, from her legs up; fur and velvet – as has long been suspected – are a fixation of the sight of the pubic hair, which should have been followed by the longed-for sight of the female member; pieces of underclothing, which are so often chosen as a fetish, crystallise the moment of undressing, the last moment in which the woman could still be regarded as phallic.[10]

The evidence of this in Lawrence's corpus is manifold. We are shown stockings but not the legs underneath, and so vibrant are they that we even forget that there *are* legs underneath. As Philippa Tristram writes: 'one might also observe that the loins, which figure so insistently in the prose, are always male. His women do not have them. They have stockings.'[11] Whilst men's clothes are taken off in the sight of women, women's clothes are piled *on* in the sight of everyone, even (or perhaps especially) on the most sexually potent female figures, so that 'it is like strip-tease in reverse;

the more clothes he piles on her, the more desirable she becomes, because the less real'.[12]

But for Freud's model to work, all this has to come about in response to a textual moment of anxiety. If, for Carter and Tristram, the woman's body cannot be seen in its place for all the folds of lace and bright stockings, it can at times in Lawrence's corpus be seen everywhere else. In *Mr Noon* even Lawrence's beloved landscape takes on the ominous curves of the female form, and pursues him as a psychotic distortion of the 'natural', as the landscape is distorted into ravenous (here, ravine-ous) femininity writ large, capable of repelling if not raping the masculine:

> The valley began to depress him. The great slopes shelving upwards, far overhead: the sudden dark, hairy ravines in which he was trapped: all made him feel he was caught, shut in down below there. He felt tiny, like a dwarf among the great thighs and ravines of the mountains. There is a Baudelaire poem which tells of Nature, like a vast woman lying spread, and man, a tiny insect, creeping between her knees and under her thighs, fascinated. Gilbert felt a powerful revulsion against the great slopes and particularly against the tree-dark, hairy ravines in which he was caught. (Noon, 251)[13]

Both 'ravine' and 'ravenous' are etymologically linked to 'rapine', seizing and taking away by force: they are also linked both to rape and to rapture. Gilbert's fascination with both Johanna and the landscape in which they meet continually slips into a 'rapturous' account of her ability to sweep him off his feet, to annihilate him, to subjugate him as victim. His desire and his repulsion are thus bound in the battle in which Johanna's appetite threatens to destroy him, or at least to 'use' him and render him useless. The above passage from *Mr Noon* is closely followed by an account of Everard's words to Johanna, in which his love is declared to be his willingness, or desire, to be 'cut to pieces for' her (Noon, 253). This is clearly a scenic version of the sadistic actions of the female gaze which we encountered in Chapter 2.

In *The Plumed Serpent* this problem of sexual terrain is tackled with a full battery of machismo. As Alistair Niven points out, Lawrence 'often describes Mexico in harsh images of male sexuality: phallic cacti and sperm-like water',[14] as a counter to this European landscape which is, by turns, a fearfully engulfing female body, or else enclosed by industrial, wilful (by association *feminine*) mentality, like the hedged-and-fenced English landscape of *St Mawr*. The Mexican countryside is consequently masculinised: the fruit on the 'ponderous mango-trees' are, for instance, 'like the testes of bulls' (PS, 422). This is a clear form of geographical retribution, but the answers elsewhere are not so straight. The rampant Bertha of *John Thomas and Lady Jane* frightens the boy Parkin with the sight of her 'absence' so much that when they grow up and marry, he can only make love to her if he shaves her first. In Hilary Simpson's reading, this makes Bertha 'castrated', but I am more interested in the fetishistic move which takes place here: Parkin only remembers the vision as shock at the 'presence' of female pubic hair which is already standing in for another thing he cannot speak ('"Black hair! An' I don't know why, it upset me an' made me hate the thoughts of women from that day"'[15]).

Feminist criticism has often celebrated the points at which a feminine threat like that of Bertha or the landscape seems momentarily to be dominant, but I prefer to show the ambiguities of response to that threat. Whilst Kate Millett's objective was to attribute all possible flows of desire in the text to its univocal misogyny, more recent writers have characteristically attributed Lawrence's vitriol against women wholly to his ultimate fear of them. For instance, Sheila MacLeod writes that 'Lawrence's outbursts of misogyny spring from . . . [an] unshakeable belief in the frailty of the male and the comparative unquenchable strength of the female'.[16] Carol Dix repeatedly sides with both 'poor Lawrence' and 'poor Mellors', who have, apparently, been pathetically exhausted and sexually abused by women – Parkin's pubic misfortune and the female gang-rape of 'Tickets, Please' are cited in evidence. Dix's hope is to prove that Lawrence The Man was originally intimidated by that femininity he sought to intimidate by vilifying it in writing. Offering a twist to Freud's account of fetishism, MacLeod writes that it is men not women who embody a lack: ' The women's secret is menstruation, but the men's secret – which no woman must ever be allowed to discover – is that there is no men's secret.'[17] Gilbert Noon notices this same deficiency at one point where he yearns for male company: 'He knew what [men] were. He knew that they had no wonderful secret – none: rather a wonderful lack of secret' (Noon, 228). MacLeod reaches her conclusion through an analysis of Lawrence's need to veil his own personal heart of darkness. Darkness is lack, but all the hapless man can do is to deify that absence in a kind of literary dance of the seven veils. Similarly, Hilary Simpson connects this in Lawrence with Otto Weininger's identification of masculine fear: 'the deepest fear of man; the fear of the woman, which is the fear of unconsciousness, the alluring abyss of annihilation'.[18]

This is where Freud's model of fetishism is perhaps most useful. The reader of Freud could not fail to see the man in the landscape of *Mr Noon* as the little boy in the essay on 'Fetishism' (1927), climbing up inside the woman's skirt where he will impossibly *see* an absence, an all-too-present *lack* of a penis. Gilbert is equally appalled, offering a literary case history of that Freudian point of trauma, following which the traumatised male builds himself constructions – fetishes – with which to fill the impossible ravine. It might be said that Gilbert's experience is that moment of shock before the absence is reified into the tangible fetishised object, before he, in Freud's words, disavows 'his perception of the woman's lack of a penis'.[19]

For the purposes of making sense of this, of the senselessness of what Lawrence finds under a woman's skirt, we need to read further into *Mr Noon*, right to the end, in fact. We have seen the moment of appalled horror, but not the organisation of a substitute. If the sight of a woman's body laid bare across the hills is too much for Lawrence, then something must be constructed, as with the fetishist, to fill in the gap, to obliterate the image of absence or castration. In *Mr Noon*, the characteristically open way which Lawrence has of closing his texts is loosened even more. In a novel where the 'vulgarity' of the female absence is actually acknowledged, the literally unfinished text still 'closes' with the hope that perhaps it didn't happen after all, perhaps it can be un-seen. This is why we are left at the close with a wistful catalogue of female clothing. The book ends, eerily 'beholding',

> an enormous black hat of chiffon velvet and black plumes – huge: a smaller hat of silky woven staw, very soft: a complicated Paquin dress of frail, dark-blue, stone-blue silky velvet and purplish heavy embroidery, for evening wear: a complicated whitey-blue petticoat of very soft silk: a voluminous dressing-gown wrap of thin silk and endless lace: a chemise of more lace than linen: two pairs of high laced shoes, of greeny grey thin kid with black patent golosh: (Noon, 292)

And then what? The colon is all: this is the end of the novel, and we shall never know. What comes after this endless lace, the sighting of these marvellously fetishistic shoes, is, indeed, unspeakable. Unnervingly endless, drifting off into nothing as concrete as a closure, this box of tricks is the other, more comfortable thing which Lawrence's 'tiny insect, creeping between her knees and under her thighs, fascinated' substitutes and then finds.

Had *Mr Noon* been published when Carter wrote her article, no doubt she would have had a field day with it, but in concentrating on *Women in Love* she also misses the various women in police uniform who crop up as evidence in Lawrence's castigation of the cocksure woman. In *Apocalypse* Lawrence looks for the phallic in the modern, knowing woman and, on seeing that it is not there, places 'some sort of bludgeon – or is it called a baton! – up her sleeve.' Up her sleeve? Or is it under her 'fluffy white' skirt, where he manages to imagine a 'stiffness'? It is clearly impossible that the woman who knows could also 'contain' Johanna's enrapturing absence; under our knowing and seeing woman's skirts he doesn't find the absence characteristic of the castrated chasm, but instead the rod of the Logos which returns her to the phallic: 'Let her dress up fluffy as she likes, or white and virginal, still underneath it all you can see the stiff folds of the modern policewoman, doing her best, her level best.'[20] The fantasy here isn't so much the straightforward one of women-in-uniform, it is a woman who can be defined and pinned down to the law,

reassuringly identified as phallic (and cocksure) through her adherence to
the baton. Thus any vision of an impossible femininity is fended off before
it can disturb. The woman is nothing but a layering of uniforms, the virgin
on top and the policewoman underneath, with the baton standing in for
her power. This neat identification or rounding-up of all the unwieldy
aspects of femininity is also present in the short story of 1910, 'The White
Stocking', in which the stocking stands in for the secret desires of its
(female) owner. Here Lawrence plays with a woman's relationship to the
stocking, which acts as screen and trigger for her desires, so that her
identity gradually collapses into the fabric of the stocking. Consequently,
when a man picks up the stocking which has spilled from her pocket he
possesses it as if it were actually her:[21] ' "That'll do for me," he whispered
– seeming to take possession of her. And he stuffed the stocking into his
trousers pocket, and quickly offered her his handkerchief' (Prussian, 177).

In Freud's essay, clothes and objects stand in for a feminine sexuality
which cannot be spoken. Lawrence's observations of opulent physical
detail, framing and isolating sexually charged fragments, tell a bigger
story, not just of a femininity which disturbs but of a textual gaze which
breaks the rules. Turning Lawrence's own theories of obscenity back onto
the text at these moments, the nefarious pornographic gaze may be
punished in the end (as is the owner of the white stocking), but it is given
ample room for indulgence before this ever occurs. Lawrence isn't simply
a textual fetishist; rather, fetishism stands as another scopophilic position
which is criticised but simultaneously enjoyed; it is part of the process of
disavowal which allows him to say one thing (theoretically and
philosophically) and enjoy another (fetishism and voyeurism between the
lines). This anxious oscillation is characteristic: preaching the discourse
of the invisible man, he still puts on the stockings.

I began by looking at Ursula's image of invisible men, essentially 'dark'
people who 'fall' into clothing, or ideal bodies which are falsified by
clothes. This discussion of fetishism has traced through one possibility of
the gaze in the text, but a question is raised by the various other gazes
which also take place. The fetishist does not fixate on objects as coverings
for dark bodies, but as concealments of an absent penis. So is the
relationship of narrative voice to represented (and dressed up) woman that
of desire, but a desire which can only be triggered once their absence (the
fact of castration) is concealed? Or is the narrative gaze closer than this,
since it is a gaze which – remember – so often slides from a representation
of the woman to a representation of the world through her eyes? Is gazing
at the female body fetishistic or identificatory? The difference could not
be greater: if Lawrence's dressed-up women are fetishistic, they display
themselves concealed as a channel for heterosexual desire and male
anxiety. If they are displaced indulgences in transvestism, they figure as

images of identification for Lawrence, weaving very different fantasies and constructing images as substitutes for himself. As vessels for the desire of the cross-dresser their role is twisted: Lawrence's clothed women are impersonations of his own female impersonation, channelling a desire which is both homoerotic and narcissistic.

Both possibilities figure elsewhere in Lawrence's work. It is not only Gudrun and Ursula who 'get the greatest joy out of really lovely stockings' (WL, 532); Paul Morel in the new *Sons and Lovers* does too. The now-uncensored hero had to wait until 1992 before he could put on Clara's stockings in print, but now he does so in an ecstasy of self-division, or more accurately self-multiplication, for Paul's pleasures here are many. Committed alone, the act manages to suggest narcissism, masturbation *and* straightforward heterosexual intercourse (Paul inserts himself into the stockings, which stand in for the absent Clara), whilst still being the clearest example of actual transvestism in Lawrence's work. Paul is both his own masturbatory self as well as 'being' the sexiest part of Clara, but his masculinity is also debased by this unwholesome proximity to the trappings of womanhood.[22]

All of the above examples challenge what is at stake in the gaze, its mutable function, its mutation under the influence of desire. In Chapter 3 I argued that Lawrence has to write himself into a position of cross-gazing (a visual version of cross-dressing) in order to enjoy the spectacle of his own sex. By now that suggestion, and that gaze, has been developed in a number of directions. The look, like sexual identity itself, can be twisted to the demands of desire. Far from establishing or founding sexual difference, the look challenges it, encourages the malleability of difference. Back and forth, the look – of desire, of men and women – subverts the fixed place of the seer. The look in Lawrence demonstrates that gender difference is, to appropriate a quotation from Carol J. Clover, 'less a wall than a permeable membrane'.[23] Women may look, but they see men on behalf of other men: your desire might be channelled through the eyes of one (a camera, perhaps, or – at its simplest – a character) who is not you. Identity depends upon position: we do not see fixedly, and mobility changes our emphasis and our view. That sadistically gazing woman might at first define difference quite neatly (she looks and he is looked at; she illuminates and he is dark), but her role also mutates to facilitate other ways of seeing. A woman in Lawrence's writing might look with the eyes of male gay desire, or the status of her body as object might shift. The field of vision, and its consequences for our certainty of sexual difference, is disrupted.

Fantasy and multiple subjectivity

I want to avoid a reading of Lawrence which allows each of these different pleasures to collapse into and signify the other. The point is not that Lawrence's writing manifests a homogenous polymorphous perversity, but that it explores a range of different and contradictory desires dividing it against itself. In particular I want to avoid sexist celebrations of genius such as, say, Carol Dix's or Norman Mailer's (but there are numerous examples), which argue for Lawrence's ability to imaginatively *be* another sex in all his misogyny. Dix's Lawrence is 'a woman in a man's skin'; Mailer's is 'a prematurely ageing writer with the soul of a beautiful woman'.[24] For both, Lawrence ostensibly closed the gender gap to the extent that he understood women better than they did. This is, at the same time, a Lawrence who argues that men and women are essentially different, and failing to mark the difference or to close that gap is blasphemy. What, then, is at stake in these cross-identifications, in the gaze facilitating contradictory desires?

The desire at work in Lawrence's texts is (at least) a double one, but the way in which that doubleness operates is not, at first, clear. Peter Widdowson uses Gămini Salgădo's phrase 'radical indeterminacy' to characterise a doubleness in Lawrence, but the two sides Widdowson identifies do not implode or clash, engendering a crisis in the sovereign masculinity of the text. Instead they are positioned as happily coexistent sides of a dialectic or choice (to be made by the reader), or a series of rich possibilities which justify Lawrence's status as an 'endless' cultural object of fascination. Widdowson's question – 'Can there really be, simultaneously, the phallocrat/misogynist *and* the liberating writer of the phallic imagination?'[25] – not only slides over the obvious feminist point that phallic liberation is already misogynistic, it gives no sense that doubleness or contradiction might gouge a gap, might signal a blind spot in the text and its sex. For Salgădo, *Women in Love* '*accommodates* contradictory readings' so strongly that this open liberalism becomes 'the novel's intention'.[26] Contradiction does not provoke any form of crisis; rather, it is characteristic of the novel's happy multiplicity. It is recent feminist work on the female spectator which might, at this turn, be most pertinent, particularly reformulated versions of Mulvey's problematic female viewer as one who is, in Tania Modleski's words, '*both* passive and active, homosexual and heterosexual'.[27]

I want to develop this discussion of contradictory and split desires in Lawrence through some psychoanalytic perspectives on fantasy. Elizabeth Cowie calls fantasy 'the *mise-en-scène* of desire',[28] and Lawrence's visual set-pieces can be understood as fantasies in this cinematic sense. Much recent feminist film theory has worked with the psychoanalytic notion of the multiple subject of fantasy, a subject which has been better understood by film theorists than by literary critics (despite Freud's point that creative writing is the exemplary form of fantasy[29]). I will briefly outline some positions which Freud set out in ' "A Child is Being Beaten" ', which have been enormously influential.

In *The Rainbow* Lawrence writes of 'the man who reviles his mistress, yet who is in love with her' (R, 350), as an illustration of a double position, reviling 'the monstrous state and yet adher[ing] to it'. This love/hate, and sometimes masochistic, dichotomy is ever-present in Lawrence's work, but the fantastic subject pushes the contradiction further. In fantasy it is possible to be many different things at once. Because of this the subject of fantasy can only problematically be termed 'one': the fantasist is able to look and be looked at simultaneously, she can be the subject of domination whilst she also dominates, and she can orchestrate a situation within which she submits and oversees. In the world of sado-masochistic practices the ambivalence which characterises the seat of power in Hegel's 'Master–Slave' dialectic is lived, exploited and enjoyed; just *who* is in control in a voluntary domination scenario is not obvious.[30] Freud's theoretical discussion of fantasy supports the lived practice of S & M, but Freud's work also demonstrated that the occupation or construction of a multiple position in fantasy is not simply the prerogative of those who consciously act out scenes of domination in which the controller and object are unfixed. Everyone does it:

> Actually, we can never give anything up; we only exchange one thing for another. . . . the growing child, when he stops playing, gives up nothing but the link with real objects; instead of *playing*, he now *phantasies*. He builds castles in the air and creates what are called *day-dreams*. I believe that most people construct phantasies at times in their lives. This is a fact which has been long overlooked.[31]

But in fantasising, what is it that everyone does? In ' "A Child is Being Beaten" ' – a key discussion of fantasy and subjectivity – the fantasist is able to occupy several positions – subject/seer, object/seen, or identification with the whole scene. Freud guides us through the implications of a fantasy which has no single, fixed, subjective centre. He constructs a narrative by working from the enigmatic statement 'A Child is Being Beaten' which is so nebulous that it is 'impossible at first even to decide whether the pleasure attaching to the beating-phantasy was to be described as sadistic or masochistic'.[32] It is an experienced 'event' – culminating in masturbation – but the position of identification of the author of the fantasy is not straightforward. The map which is eventually drawn is of a multiple self which experiences the fantasy of the beating from a variety of angles – the fantasist emerges as a fragmented self which occupies a range of positions within and around the fantasy of the title. At the moment of crisis the fantasist cannot choose which position to occupy – master, slave, voyeur and more, the effect is that of doubling and division, like that described in Freud's later essay 'Splitting of the Ego in the Process of Defence', when the subject experiences a conflict between instinct and reality: 'the child takes neither course, or rather he takes both simultaneously, which comes to the same thing. He replies to the conflict with two contrary reactions, both of which are valid and effective.'[33]

That a fantasy can have no origin or centrally directed subject is at first difficult to comprehend, especially since, as Freud points out, this is an explicitly masturbatory fantasy, and stories constructed (consciously or not) for the purposes of masturbation are often, in our culture, notoriously monotonous and centred on a fairly clear-cut set of subject positions and narrative moves. Who is doing what to whom could not be clearer in mainstream pornography. Here, however, the fantasy of Freud's patients is much more fragmented, but he at least begins with the conviction that somewhere within the scene a discussion of masochism will emerge. Only the fantasy itself is given at first, without origin, owner or object:

> Who was the child that was being beaten? The one who was himself producing the phantasy or another? Was it always the same child or as often as not a different one? Who was it that was beating the child? A grown-up person? And if so, who? Or did the child imagine that he himself was beating another one? Nothing could be ascertained that threw any light upon all these questions – only the hesitant reply: 'I know nothing more about it: a child is being beaten.'[34]

When forced to be clearer, the (female) fantasist clarifies the actors in her scene in three stages: first, the fantasy is 'My father is beating the child'. Then it becomes 'I am being beaten by my father'. And finally, 'I am probably looking on'. At this final moment of feminine voyeurism, the victim is male, there is a crowd of other onlookers, and Freud's question has to be: 'By what path has the phantasy of strange and unknown boys being beaten . . . found its way into the permanent possession of the little girl's libidinal trends?'[35] Who, then, is the fantasist – what is her desire, and can these twists be reduced to a key moment of identification which predominates? Is she finally sadistically voyeuristic, or this mixed with the earlier and quite different positions? It seems that this fantasy satisfies a multiple subject which is simultaneously the sadistic viewer and the masochistic object of both beating and gaze.

In her introduction to *Feminism and Film Theory* Constance Penley offers '"A Child is Being Beaten"' as a text which could break the impasse in current feminist theory, in that it fundamentally challenges the 'male gaze' position on women and cinema. She writes:

> As a model for understanding identification in relation to sexual difference, the feminist interest in this structure of fantasy lies in the fact that such a model does not dictate in advance what 'masculine' or 'feminine'

identification would be or how an actual spectator might take up any of the possible positions. Several new questions can be raised by acknowledging the complexity of the process of identification for both men and women. What, for example, would feminine voyeurism or fetishism be? What is the role of masochism in the male spectator's relation to the film?[36]

I want to argue that Lawrence-as-fantasist (Freud's exemplary fantasist, the creative writer, and the focus of split and apparently contradictory subject positions) offers a site upon which Penley's questions are worked through: the role of feminine voyeurism and fetishism, the uneasy male gaze forced to focus on images it reviles, a narrative gaze which interrogates the world from a number of antagonistic positions. Above all, Lawrence's texts are fantasies not as fixed *objects* but scenes within which the subject shifts and splits, in the sense developed by Laplanche and Pontalis in their important essay, 'Fantasy and the Origins of Sexuality':

> Fantasy . . . is not the object of desire, but its setting. In fantasy the subject does not pursue the object or its sign: he appears caught up himself in the sequence of images. He forms no representation of the desired object, but is himself represented as participating in the scene, although, in the earliest forms of fantasy, he cannot be assigned any fixed place in it.[37]

In *Twilight in Italy* this possibility of fantasy is explicitly played out through an ironic discussion of the male manipulation and creation of female images which will then, in Virginia Woolf's words, act 'as looking-glasses reflecting men at twice their natural size.' Here, however, men can fantasise being any size at all, or many sizes at once. Of the theatrical spectacle of female victimage Lawrence asks,

> Why are women so bad a playing this part in real life, this Ophelia–Gretchen role? Why are they so unwilling to go mad and die for our sakes? They do it regularly on the stage.
> But perhaps, after all, we write the plays. (Italy, 72)

Having set up the masochistic female spectacle in a way which marks the discrepancy between real female resistance and ideal roles in a world in which the pen was overwhelmingly in men's hands (demonstrating a self-deprecating irony for which he is seldom credited), Lawrence explores the implications of this for the male viewer. This is where he most lucidly acknowledges that in his identifications and relationships with the women he sees on stage, the subject of fantasy – here the theatrical spectator – can be truly multiple, and *anything* '*but* a dull and law-abiding citizen' (Italy, 72). Lawrence can be both the 'black-browed, passionate, ruthless, masculine villain' *and* the 'hero, . . . fount of chivalrous generosity and faith', accessing a double self; by then in aligning himself with the (male) writer of the piece, he finds a third position. 'We' write the plays, and then we watch them: 'Dear Heaven, how Adelaida wept, her voice plashing like violin music, at my ruthless, masculine cruelty. Dear heart, how she sighed to rest on my sheltering bosom! And how I enjoyed my dual nature! How I admired myself!'

Finally there is pleasure, and self-regard – the gaze comes home. Just as so often the woman's eyes mediate the gaze of man to man, directing his disavowed look onto his glistening body, so here the actress can take up the words of men and activate them, becoming a screen against which all their contradictory self-images can bounce. Lawrence speaks as writer and reader, as director and audience, as villain and hero, but here it is woman who is situated as spectacle, the blank screen upon which the multiple possibilities of these roles are played out. It is interesting that the view of art which Lawrence's response to this spectacle of women uncovers is one in which the reading or viewing subject is split, made multiple by its contradictory reactions to what it sees. I now want to turn to a specific example of a shifting gaze which accompanies a process of subjective splitting: a series of moments which are explored towards the end of *The Rainbow*, during which Ursula not only enjoys the disavowed, but slides from one side of the camera to the other.

The travelling gaze

The gaze in Lawrence's writing is a shifting or travelling one, and 'it' is more than double. Despite his protestations for an essential difference between the sexes, the shifting focus of desire in Lawrence's fantasy texts betrays the fact that identity is not so fixed or divisible. Lawrence contradicts himself, and the novels contradict the theories. But not only does he demonstrate an excitement in relation to the feminine gaze which cuts against this castigation of it, he also shows its focus in the process of travelling. On the question of the gaze Lawrence's text is in constant movement, and three moments scattered across a few pages towards the end of *The Rainbow* demonstrate this amply. In the passages at which I want to look here, Lawrence can be seen to be still in the process of *gathering* a yet-to-be-stabilised perspective on vision. In the first passage, Ursula is proposed to by the earthy gardener Anthony, whose 'golden-brown eyes . . . gleam[ed] like the eyes of a satyr as they watched her' (R, 413). Her confusion and her refusal of this prototype of ideal Lawrentian masculinity are much more interesting than the acceptance and submission of Lawrence's later women, since the series of positions on vision suggested here cannot easily be resolved. In turning from the organic English Anthony to the European, cosmopolitan but less idealised Anton, Ursula the 'traveller' not only marks herself out as a modern and modernist subject, moving uneasily between love-objects rather than resting in one as 'home' (as her Brangwen ancestors had done), she refuses to take up a single position in relation to the gaze. She is inconsistent, nomadic, moving across contradictory positions regarding both vision and men.[38]

Tony Pinkney's brilliant discussion of Lawrence's work as the literary realisation of the architecture of modernism touches on the role of nomadism in a variety of modern aesthetics. Ursula's travelling gaze is an important articulation of opposition to the vision of Englishness which Pinkney discusses.[39] Ursula, like Lawrence, is 'a traveller on the face of the earth, and [Anthony] was an isolated creature living in the fulfilment of his own senses' (R, 417). One might think that this latter fulfilment is something of a Lawrentian ideal, but at this point it is exactly what Ursula is moving away from:

> She turned away, she turned round from him, and saw the east flushed strangely rose, the moon coming yellow and lovely upon a rosy sky, above the darkening, bluish snow. . . . He did not see it. He was one with it. But she saw it, and was one with it. *Her seeing separated them infinitely.* (R, 416–17, my emphasis)

Here, then, the child Ursula which we met in Chapter 1, who sees things because she is separate from them, has grown up; still her father's daughter, she must reject the more unconscious, unseeing man – the man who is *at home*, who knows his place. But by the next chapter something has shifted: inauthentic vision and dark knowledge begin to come apart in her experience, and with this Ursula's (and Lawrence's) identification with the latter is crystallised.

I want to explore how Lawrence connects vision with sexual identity, specifically in terms of the frames or limits he erects, by looking at the way that Lawrence plays with the visual frame which constitutes the subject's field of experience, as well as the astonishing imagery which accompanies this uneasy philosophical shift, from light to darkness. If Lawrence condemns women for looking and for dressing up, he still indulges them in the act, and shows the pleasurable consequences of visual limits. If Ursula is to turn from light to darkness, she can only do so with reference to vision, not simply as the oppositional term to be dialectically negated, but in the terms of the visual as a pleasure and a rich metaphorical source which will not so easily be cancelled out or switched off. Lawrence cannot speak Ursula's dawning conversion to the discourse of darkness without deploying a dazzling range of images. Her shift *towards* darkness is paradoxically accompanied by an intense, luminous series of 'visions', as darkness is gradually teased from the fabulous, flickering confusion of blindingly visual experience. Indeed, for the older Ursula of the end of *The*

Rainbow, the world of Marsh Farm has already become a magic-lantern show, the pre-cinematic – by now archaic – series of frozen images animated only if the viewer's perspective brings them emotionally to life: 'She wished [her past] could be gone forever, like a lantern-slide that was broken.'

The first vision emerges from her growing disillusionment with conventional knowledge:

> At the Anglo-Saxon lecture in the afternoon, she sat looking down, out of the window, hearing no word, of Beowulf or of anything else. Down below, in the street, the sunny grey pavement went beside the palisade. A woman in a pink frock, with a scarlet sunshade, crossed the road, a little white dog running like a fleck of light about her. The woman with the scarlet sunshade came over the road, a lilt in her walk, a little shadow attending her. Ursula watched spellbound. The woman with the scarlet sunshade and the flickering terrier was gone – and whither? Whither?
>
> In what world of reality was the woman in the pink dress walking? (R, 435)

This is an image which is playing with the visions, or visual possibilities, of modernism. It is certainly epiphanal, its physical quality resonating with a transcendent significance for Ursula which is more than the sum of its parts. In many senses this is an image honed according to the gospel of imagism:[40] sharp, devoid of superfluous emotional content, it serves Ursula's adolescent nihilistic questioning only after the fact. Tony Pinkney calls *Sons and Lovers* 'the first Imagist novel',[41] and if this is the case *The Rainbow* might be the second (although Pinkney argues for its Gothic modernism). Pound's 'Hard light, clear edges' are here *in* the frame, but the primary sharp edge is the frame itself. The woman comes and then is gone: there is no before or after, no narrative causes or consequences, rather like the contextless, enigmatic fantasies of Freud. Here is a visual version of the claim Lawrence was later to make for free verse: 'in free verse we look for the insurgent naked throb of the instant moment. . . . It does not want to get anywhere. It just takes place' ('Preface to New Poems', *Essays*, 290).

With these ideas Lawrence is theoretically situated within a philosophy of presence, arguing for a writing which has no history, and a 'moment' which can be felt in full, sensual immediacy. Despite this, there are many more material precedents for such an immediacy scattered across his work. In trying to make this a 'nakedly throbbing' 'instant moment', Lawrence has first to limit his field; offering Ursula simply looking at another woman's brief life entirely defined by a pool of light. Whilst Ursula's adolescent questions wholesomely address the meaning of life, women look at women in Lawrence and the significance of sex must hover somewhere over the encounter. The scene is bathed in the intensity of one of Freud's primal scenes, in which sexual identification and difference are etched out of a visual shock and enabled by anxious voyeurism. A woman walks on screen and then off again. Ursula's vision is defined and limited – edited and chosen – by the window frame itself. It is the process of framing which makes this such a classic modernist epiphany. Just like the voyeur–hero of Hitchcock's *Rear Window*, Ursula's perspective is limited and intensified by her immobility. She is subject to what Christian Metz calls the regime 'of the primal scene and the keyhole': framing the scene denies the answers which might be revealed in off-screen space, and here, as in Metz's cinema, the denials which the frame offers 'gamble simultaneously on the excitation of desire and its non-fulfilment'.[42] Lawrence may sometimes say too much, but he also knows how to say not enough. This is the modernism which believes that 'less is more', Pound's championed brevity and lack of superfluity. The intensity of Ursula's vision confirms that Lawrence knows the pleasures of the keyhole, deploying, again in Metz's terms, 'the *boundary* that bars the look, that puts an end to the "seen", that inaugurates the downward (or upward) tilt into the dark, towards the unseen, the guessed-at'.[43]

Kaja Silverman has read cinematic pleasure and involvement as partly bound up with a replay of Freud's fort/da game, or the moment in the subject's development when she or he learns to cope with loss: a thing (the mother) is *there* and then it is *gone*. This is one way of reading the spectator's response to the cinematic termination of an image when the shot is cut; the spectator indulges in the full image and then its loss, 'a constant fluctuation between the imaginary plenitude of the shot, and the loss of that plenitude through the agency of the cut'.[44] The limit or loss of the image as Ursula experiences it could equally be read as a playing-out of the fort/da game, but the framing of a shot, the immobility of the camera eye here, also produces other effects. The image is there, and then it is gone, but the binocular vision Ursula is fixed into by the window frame offers spatiality as a more profound limit than the time dimension within which editing works. The woman is lost as she goes out of range; she is not just lost as time (the frenetic quality of editing) moves her on or juxtaposes her with what comes next. And the spatial limitation of frame or screen has consequences for the subjective quality of the image itself.

For all Lawrence's diatribes against secret scopophilia, he displays lots of people secretly looking at each other across his work, fantasies of voyeurism which initially fix the illicit viewer on the outside. The first four chapters of *Aaron's Rod* are particularly striking for this, all taking place at night, with those on the inside defined by the light which shuts others out. Aaron is an habitual, if accidental voyeur, and his family are singularly lax at closing the curtains. The opening three pages of Chapter 4 are extraordinary for this sense of the outsider peering into a world which excludes but still excites him. Lawrence may champion darkness, but he can still arrange a seductive literary encounter with voyeurism:

> So he saw a curious succession of lighted windows. . . .
> And thus the whole private life of the street was threaded in lights. There was a sense of indecent exposure. . . . He felt himself almost in physical contact with the contiguous stretch of back premises. (AR, 51–2)

Looking in at the back, or 'through the wrong end of a telescope', his visual field is distorted, but defined. A similar image is used in *Women in Love* in an exchange between Ursula and Hermione on Gudrun's artistic vision, when it is said that 'She likes to look through the wrong end of the opera-glasses, and see the world that way' (WL, 88). Telescopes and opera glasses magnify specific areas if used properly, or else they diminish that limited area if used backwards, but in both cases they enforce a blinkered but intensified view. The object is augmented by its limits. Window frames make voyeurs of us all, whether we are looking out or looking in: Aaron on one side, Ursula on the other, Gudrun on both, these are visual experiences intensified by limits imposed upon the field of vision.

So we have a steady frame, and the intensity of the moment, but in Ursula's vision we also have movement 'on screen'. For all the blindingly bright post-impressionist qualities of the woman with her dog crossing the street, this is another of Deleuze's movement-images, a scene in transit. Ursula sits, and the world moves dazzlingly before her. The camera is fixed, but the viewer is transfixed by the scene she witnesses. This is a 'short', an early cinematic narrative which ends before the audience's questions are answered. Yet another window frame in Lawrence acts as the screen for a brief moving image upon which the eyes of the narrative rest, eyes which are both transfixed by the stunning vision, and yet which voyeuristically lack all control over the thing witnessed, which inevitably shifts beyond the scenes. Yet again 'the world of reality' is condensed to a vision-in-movement in a way which is briefly but finally more culturally significant than Lawrence's favoured stasis of darkness.

The image is resonant of the examples of primitive cinema which form the subject of Noel Burch's film and accompanying pamphlet *Correction Please*, which Judith Mayne also discusses in *The Woman at the Keyhole*. These are films which play out the voyeurism of later cinema in both narrative and framing devices; in Mayne's words, primitive cinema 'is made to the measure of male desire'.[45] But this desire is voyeuristic, and the 'making' is itself modernistically self-referential. Burch in particular highlights,

> the plethora of 'voyeur films' that developed at that time, with a husband (or peeper) spying on a bride (or show-girl, model, etc.) from behind boudoir curtains or screen, or else with a chambermaid, bathing attendant or other peeper peering through a keyhole with his or her back to the camera.[46]

An example is the 1900 short, *As Seen Through a Telescope*, which consists of two shots of a man with a telescope interspersed with an irised shot of his view through the telescope of a woman and a man fumbling with her petticoats. The man with the telescope becomes our literal spectator-in-the-text, and our complicity in his voyeurism is foregrounded by the identification of camera view with telescope view. The 1902 film *Peeping Tom* also foregrounds the apparatus of cinematic voyeurism in its through-the-keyhole indulgence, alongside the male spectator, of a scene of a woman undressing. A less salacious example is G.A. Smith's *Grandma's Reading Glass* (1900), noted for its interpolated close-ups of the objects (a watch, a canary) seen through the glass, as well as Grandma's eye itself. Each of these images is 'framed by a circular black mask, representing the field of vision of the reading-glass . . . [a] frame-within-a-frame'.[47]

Whilst these subjects might easily have contributed to Lawrence's view that cinema encourages the 'dirty little secret', the point this serves here is more formal. The typical 'primitive' cinematic scene involves no camera movement at all, and events unfold at a fixed distance of medium long-shot. Ursula's vision is acted out within these strict formal possibilities. When the woman moves into off-screen space the questions of afterlife certainly begin, but the point is that she *lives* only in the spotlight of Ursula's perception, her life only has reality as a moving, visual thing. How she is realised as a primitive movement-image resonates with the visual preoccupations of Lawrence's cultural moment far more than where she goes when she disappears. As she struts her hour across the stage she is primarily a shifting of colours, bathed in light, her shadow her servant and her dog, flickering both with Lawrentian life and perhaps with the instability of an early cinematic image, shudders into 'a fleck of light.' Were this moving vision the only visual realisation in Lawrence's work, it would amply counter the heavy barrage of desperate dark prescription which weighs down his more polemical texts.

The frame of vision

But, as this book demonstrates, it is not. Lawrence is as visually obsessed as any of his modernist contemporaries, and as keen to present – against himself – the power of images as resonant as this one. Yet what continues to characterise his encounters with vision, both in *The Rainbow* and in his corpus as a whole, is the act of framing itself. The frame – the limit, horizon, boundary of light or knowledge, within which one sees and knows as a gendered being, outside of which is darkness – appears in a number of places and guises. Jacqueline Rose discusses the relationship between visual representation, the act of seeing, and the construction of sexual subjectivity in 'Sexuality in the Field of Vision'.[48] Lawrence cannot think sexual identity or achievement without connecting it to a discourse of visual range – the visible challenged or constructed in terms of the sexual. This shakes down into an emphasis on the masculinising power of identification with the darkness – that which lies beyond the horizons – and the feminising power of identification with the light. In making the boundary between light and dark this simple, Lawrence hopes that sexual identity will become this simple and clear-cut too. Femininity, Lawrence might argue, is fit subject for the through-the-keyhole voyeurism of primitive film, since femininity is constructed in, and consciously identifies with, the field of the visible. In leaving the screen, the woman in Ursula's vision enters masculine territory, a sexuality ideally *outside* of the field of vision, entering the unknown. In questioning her disappearance ('Whither?'), and in rejecting (as she had earlier in the chapter) a positivism which argues that 'There *is* no darkness', Ursula aligns herself not with cocksure mentality but with that darkness, which 'wheeled round about, with grey shadow-shapes of wild-beasts, and also with dark shadow-shapes of the angels, whom the light fenced out, as it fenced out the more familiar beasts of darkness' (R, 438).

There is no visual, or sexual, twilight zone here; sexual difference is demarcated by the fence of light, and one chooses one's visual options as and when one chooses one's authentic or fallen identity. Lawrence's ideal subject should not be able to slide from looking to looked at to viewing the whole scene (like Freud's fantasist). In rejecting the straight, visibly self-evident answers of positivism, Ursula also pushes towards the dark. Assuming that it is *possible* for us to escape the visual and our sexual definition and mutation within it and of it, Lawrence marks out a set of choices as clear as those offered to the sheep and the goats. Inauthentic sexuality *does* reside in the field of vision, whilst darkness somehow escapes: choose one or the other, but not both. Unfortunately, fantasies are not so simple.

A little later in *The Rainbow*, Ursula looks into her microscope, and what she sees is a clearing in the forest. What is important here is the way that Ursula's sense of identity begins to glue itself together only very uneasily in response to the 'field of light' which the microscope defines:

> She looked still at the unicellular shadow that lay within the field of light, under her microscope. It was alive. She saw it move – she saw the bright mist of its ciliary activity, she saw the gleam of its nucleus, as it slid across the plane of light. . . . Suddenly in her mind the world gleamed strangely, with an intense light, like the nucleus of a creature under the microscope. Suddenly she had passed away into an intensely-gleaming light of knowledge. (R, 441)

Here Ursula is on both sides of the window: seeing but bathed in light, subject and object of understanding. Whilst wanting to give us an experience of consummate connection, what we get is a partial identification with both sides of the slide. A vitalist gloss bathes Ursula's fractured relationship with the field of light, but still her revelation – a significant shift in her move towards dark maturity – is the 'light of knowledge'. Passing away from consciousness, one nevertheless 'gleams.' We have moved into the territory of visual metaphorics here, and however hard Lawrence-the-dark might try to cleanse language of photons, it is steeped in them. The dominance of visible imagery is one thing, but how subjects behave in relation to it is quite another. In her double identification Ursula jumps from seer to seen, from positivism to an epiphanal passing away, which is also a sliding in subjection to the light. The text is clearly astonished by both possibilities of seeing, neither of them constituting the ideal self in all its dark authenticity, both perhaps more intriguing for all that. If earlier Ursula had preferred the dark continent beyond the borders of the microscope light, here she is both positivist gaze and organic object, but somehow also sliding across and blurring the difference between these positions.

Elsewhere in Lawrence's work and related texts, this clear desire to mark a difference and to identify with one side or the other is combined with a sense that each side is constantly vulnerable to subversion from the other. 'I cannot be bullied back into the appearance of love' he writes in 'Know Deeply, Know Thyself More Deeply', one of the *Pansies* poems, 'any more than August can be bullied to look like March' (Poems, 477– 8). With such assertions he resists reversing the teleological development which sweeps us from that early moment of coming to the light back towards the 'mature' embrace of darkness. In practice, however, the visible and viewing self is only uneasily gathered together, and always under siege of night raiders from the forest. Or to put it another way, the dark self cannot leave vision alone. The whole metaphorics of the light of reason and the darkness of the unconscious is implicated in this model: Freud's image of the 'darkest' recesses of the psyche, for instance, is the 'navel of the dream, the place where it straddles the unknown'. This place can only be accessed through the interpretation of its fungal fruit, the symptoms which poke through from the forest into the light: 'Out of one of the denser places in this meshwork, the dream-wish rises like a mushroom out of its mycelium.'[49] Elsewhere, Lawrence had prescribed a form of psycho-analysis to catch what he calls his 'serpent of secret and shameful desire': 'Let me bring it to the fire to see what it is.'[50] This is our culture's familar notion of the light of reason eclipsing and scrutinising darkness; in Schopenhauer's words, 'the light of knowledge penetrates into the workshop of the blindly operating will, and illuminates the vegetative functions of the human organism.'[51] Lawrence also uses a geographical horizon as the frame of one's visual field in *Studies in Classic American Literature*. Against James Fenimore Cooper's mythical American frontier, he posits a beyond 'within' which the dark body can run free:

> Who knows what will come out of the soul of man?
> The soul of man is a dark vast forest, with wild
>   life in it.
>
> (Studies, 17).

Later he continues:

> This is what I believe:
> *'That I am I.'*
> *'That my soul is a dark forest.'*
> *'That my known self will never be more than a little*
>   *clearing in the forest.'*
> *'That gods, strange gods, come forth from the forest*
>   *into the clearing of my known self, and then go back.'*
>
> (Studies, 22, Lawrence's italics)

Like Nietzsche's understanding of the ego as a clearing ('an *apparent* unity that encloses everything like a horizon',[52] having the power to define only the field of vision and of grammatical sense, and nothing beyond), Lawrence's egoistic statement 'I am I' can only make sense up to the edge of the clearing. Where the forest starts dark faith must begin, and knowledge cannot penetrate.

If the infant moment of visual awakening in Ursula's childhood which I discussed earlier sets her seeing self in motion, then these later points, scattered across the cusp of adulthood, reverse the process. If the child is set rolling into a seeing, conscious future by her father's desire, then the grown, sexualised Ursula touches the invisible and so begins to travel *back* to another kind of 'dark' future through her final meeting with Anton. Visual development is positively arrested, as Ursula reverses her earlier moment of patriarchal release. The 'normal' track of growing up into vision is reversed. In a few brief turns, Ursula realises herself as a seer (the culmination of her childhood sense), turns back in criticism of enlightened knowledge, has a religious experience of life which is powerfully visual (through the microscope), and finally embraces Anton in some of the darkest moments of Lawrence's writing. What happens between these points is not consistent: Ursula looks at herself, changes her mind, looks again, and finally leaves off looking, but the final moment does not override the preceding equivocations. These positions on sexuality and difference are situated as disturbances or shifts in her relationship to vision.

This series of moments at the end of *The Rainbow* struggle through the problem of becoming-visual as a negotiation of sexuality. But they also show sexuality, in its visual connection, as an area of difficulty. Overtly, visual sexuality is disrupted, *not* in order to rupture oppressive structures of difference *per se*, but as a way *back* to even more archaic, previsual, essentially delineated forms of difference. The female gaze ('naturally' and materially in Kate's fish-hook eyes) fundamentally establishes sexual difference for Lawrence. Women look, men are dark: this is modern gender. If the woman fails to see, if her vision is troubled or pleasurably misdirected, difference is also troubled, and its neat demarcation is messed up. The sexual scene, or rather the seen of sex in the head, emanates from her desire to look. Similarly, its other, the dark unseen, can only be conceived in Lawrence's corpus as the space outside, the dark continent or Utopian moment of escape. Its existence is also troubled by her failure to look, or by her look offering narrative pleasures with which the darkness cannot compete. Trusting too much in the mechanics of perception as an index of visual power and visibility, Lawrence assumes that darkness signals the limit of the eye's empire, that a sexuality given free reign beyond the borders will escape the terms of difference and visibility. But Lawrence's masculine Dark Continent is no freer of the judgements of his female fantasies than Freud's feminine Dark Continent was able to escape the imperialism of psychological territorialisation. As long as darkness and the forest are characterised as 'beyond', the relationship of need between these realms and the woman of the clearing will remain. However, Lawrence's fields of vision and unvision are not so pure. If he would inhabit the darkness, he can't help but make the occasional dawn raid to enjoy the pleasures of the light. I am reminded of Nietzsche's abyss-seer. Lawrence looks long into the abyss of the looker, and finds that he has become one himself. Fighting the monsters of vision, he becomes one.

Vision is central to the organisation of sexuality and subjectivity: within 'the field of vision', argues Lacan, 'the original subjectifying relation' takes place.[53] But sexuality also disrupts the easy relationship between the eye and the perceived, between the seeing other and the seen self: 'If one does not stress the dialectic of desire one does not understand why the gaze of others should disorganise the field of perception.'[54] The sexuality of Lawrence's texts is not straightforward. Men look at men, or they use women's eyes to look at men. Women look at everything. The field of vision which dominates Lawrence's texts is never disallowed, even if the act of vision is disavowed. Lawrence is not simply a writer of sexuality because of the element in his work which provoked his notorious clashes with censorship law. He is a writer of sexuality in and through his struggle with the gaze, its history and its cultural objects. What you see may contribute to and construct your sexuality (as Freud's many instances of the crucial 'scenes' of individual history show[54]), but vision is itself already disturbed *by* sexuality. Sexuality challenges the subject–object relationship of any act of looking, the self-evidence of perception which finally, in Lawrence, cannot exist. A woman may look at a man, in an act which can be violently mapped onto the pattern and fantasy of a sadistic female visually hounding the passive male. But whether this is the only relationship at stake in the woman's look contained by a man's text is questionable. Lawrence's cocksure woman is like Hitchcock's 'woman who knew too much' (the title of Tania Modleski's book on them), and Alice Jardine's comment, which is quoted by Modleski, will do for both: 'Man's response in both private and public to a woman who *knows* (anything) has most consistently been one of paranoia.'[56] It might seem that Lawrence's paranoia goes so far that he has to look at the world through the eyes of his fear just to make sure that he knows what he is afraid of. If knowing and seeing women provoke paranoia, he will see *with* them as an act of psychic patrolling, knowing one's enemy so well that one becomes it. There is a close etymological link between paranoia and ecstasy, between erecting boundaries and doing away with them.[57] Earlier in *Gynesis* Alice Jardine gives 'hysteria (confusion of sexual boundaries)' as the other of paranoia. Without going into the relationship between hysteria and ecstasy here, there is a sense in which both states facilitate a slip from the desperate policing of sexual borders which some forms of paranoia require, into the position of the other side (that which was previously *outside* of one's paranoid constructions). Thus Lawrence slides from anger at the knowing, sadistically scopophilic woman to identification *with* her (in his role as visual writer); from fear and loathing, to identification and pleasure in the power of her look.

Visual pleasure is only one of the ways in which clear sexual difference is disrupted. It might seem odd to centre this discussion on pleasure when pleasure for *one* of Lawrence's identities provokes disturbance in the others. Modleski calls her study of Hitchcock a book 'on masculine subjectivity in crisis'.[58] This reading of Lawrence has tried to demonstrate that the crisis at the heart of his work on culture and vision seriously undermines his masculinity – a crisis which is no longer even masculine. In moving *back*, descending from a personal enlightenment back to an individual dark age, Lawrence fantasises a binary choice we would all negotiate: Heaven or Hell, Dark or Light, Masculine or Feminine, you choose. What this simple either/or option forgets – its blind spot, as it were – is that pleasure-against-the-grain and the crisis it provokes disturbs the possibility of rational choice. The text slips into indulging a number of subject positions it does not overtly approve of: men-on-men through women's eyes, the ambiguous pleasures of dress, the pleasures of ocular violation, so that even *it* cannot choose. These pleasures spoil the ballot paper.

Lorenzo is no ordinary closet queen. His case does not rest simply in the contradiction between the Real Man underneath and the female frills which clothe him, or in the male desire to see through a woman's eyes (and put on her stockings too). There is an exquisite pleasure to be had from playing with the apparently separate identities of light and darkness, the visible and the invisible. That which metaphysics has fundamentally laid asunder, Lawrence will marry and mix and subvert. If there is a radical, physical difference between light and dark, the seen and the unseeable, it is there to be transgressed, even if transgression brings with it another set of paradoxes. Lawrence plays with light, and with sexual identity, so powerfully and anxiously that the metaphysical bedrock begins to crumble. Jonathan Dollimore writes that 'Lawrence audaciously sexualises Western metaphysics', but this sexualisation is at the same time visualised. Light and darkness, identity and absence, female and male, are so intricately crossed that metaphysics becomes sexual-physics or photo-sexuality, a marriage of gender and light. So when the invisible man dresses up, the act of cross-dressing is not only reliant upon the charged mixture or contradiction of genders, but upon the ambiguity of seeing and not seeing a thing at the same time. Lawrence's books are magic lanterns, within which the dark self enjoys the brief day of visibility, without finally believing in any one thing.

Lawrence may have famously written in a letter that 'I shall always be a priest of love',[59] but the question is what kind of love and what kind of priest? What is the sexuality of this love, and is the priest one who, in writing and preaching, does little of the acting-out himself? If 'speech is the death of Pan, who can but laugh and sound the reed-flute',[60] then Lawrence the writer is less the priest of love than god's murderer. This is in keeping with many of the moments at which Lawrence writes against-himself which this book has addressed. In *Women in Love* Gerald says to Birkin 'You like the wrong things . . . things against yourself' (WL, 133). Lawrence also likes the wrong things, writing and looking against-himself.

Notes

Introduction

1. The term 'cocksure' comes from two essays by Lawrence written in 1928, 'Women Are So Cocksure' and 'Cocksure Women and Hensure Men', collected in *A Selection from Phoenix* (Harmondsworth 1979), pp. 390–2, and *Selected Essays* (Harmondsworth 1980), pp. 31–4. Lawrence's 'cocksure woman' is the woman who wears the trousers, who has her sex in her head, and whose modern mind is fixated upon the primacy of looking and knowing. Throughout Lawrence's work 'cocksure' qualities, visual obsession and mental power are conflated as the attributes of modern femininity.

2. D.H. Lawrence, *Fantasia of the Unconscious/Psychoanalysis and the Unconscious* (Harmondsworth 1978) p. 85, hereafter abbreviated as F in my text.

3. D.H. Lawrence, *The Lost Girl* (Harmondsworth 1950), p. 183, hereafter abbreviated as LG in my text. The coming of the cinema to the Potteries town of *The Lost Girl* is discussed in Chapters 6, 7 and 8 of that novel.

4. D.H. Lawrence, 'When I went to the film' in *The Complete Poems*, collected and edited with an Introduction and Notes by Vivian de Sola Pinto and F. Warren Roberts (Harmondsworth 1977), p. 443, hereafter abbreviated as Poems in my text.

5. D.H. Lawrence, *Twilight in Italy* (Harmondsworth 1977), p. 62. Hereafter this will be referred to in my text as Italy.

6. See Gilles Deleuze, *Cinema 1: The Movement-Image* (London 1986).

7. Christian Metz, *Psychoanalysis and Cinema: The Imaginary Signifier* translated by Celia Britton, Annwyl Williams, Ben Brewster and Alfred Guzzetti (Basingstoke 1982), p. 61.

8. Elizabeth Bowen, 'Why I go to the Cinema', in *Footnotes to the Film*, edited by Charles Davy (London 1938), p. 212; I am indebted to Ann Thompson for pointing me towards this rewarding essay.

9. In her book on inter-war romance, Alison Light makes the link between

popular images of 'easy' women and 'easy' culture into a point about the perception of working-class women at that time. In this context she discusses how readers and viewers were characterised as a body, 'whose individuality is effaced' as they abandon themselves to the screen or to the 'tide of cheap, easy fiction', 'waiting passively to be stimulated.' Light continues:

> What might strike the reader now examining these criticisms is how much the descriptions echo traditional views of feminine sexuality as a whole, and can be readily collapsed into a vocabulary of distaste for the lower-class woman in particular. . . . if they enjoy it, they must be, like the fictions, cheap and easy (Alison Light, *Forever England: Femininity, literature and Conservatism between the Wars* (London 1991), p. 160)

Light's quotes are from Storm Jameson's 'Novels and Novelists' and 'Apology for my Life' in *Civil Journey* (London 1939), pp. 83 and 19; later Light writes that 'Jameson (an admirer of the Leavises and an English graduate herself) lamented a fiction "infected with film technique" and feeding "herd prejudice"' (p. 161).

10. D.H. Lawrence, 'Pornography and Obscenity', in *A Selection from Phoenix* (Harmondsworth 1979), p. 315.

11. D.H. Lawrence, 'A Propos of Lady Chatterley's Lover', in *A Selection from Phoenix* (Harmondsworth 1979), p. 335. Hereafter essays from this volume will be referred to in my text under the abbreviation Px.

12. Mary Ann Caws, *The Eye in the Text: Essays on Perception, Mannerist to Modern* (New Jersey 1981), p. 4.

13. D.H. Lawrence, 'Making Pictures', in *Selected Essays* (Harmondsworth 1980), p. 301.

14. D.H. Lawrence, *Women in Love* (Harmondsworth 1989), p. 133. Hereafter referred to in my text as WL.

15. Jane Davis, 'Envoi: the genie in the second-hand shop' in *Rethinking Lawrence*, edited by Keith Brown (Milton Keynes 1990), p. 181.

16. 'Making Pictures', in *Selected Essays* (Harmondsworth 1980), p. 303. Essays from this volume will hereafter he referred to in my text as Essays.

17. D.H. Lawrence, *The Plumed Serpent* (Harmondsworth 1977) pp. 196–7. Hereafter this will be referred to in my text as PS.

18. Hilton Tims, *Emotion Pictures: The 'Women's Picture' 1930–55* (London 1987), p. 12.

19. D.H. Lawrence, 'In Love' in *The Woman Who Rode Away* (Harmondsworth 1984), p. 160. Hereafter stories from this volume will be referred to in my text as WRA.

20. Miriam Hansen, *Babel and Babylon: Spectatorship in American Silent Film* (Cambridge, Mass. and London 1991), p. 254. I am grateful to Richard Maltby for pointing me towards this text and its discussion of Valentino and his female audience.

21. D.H. Lawrence, 'Flapper Vote', in *Poems*, pp. 573–4. See also the excellent Introduction and Part One of Billie Melman's *Women and the Popular Imagination in the Twenties: Flappers and Nymphs* (Basingstoke 1988), pp. 1–37, for a discussion of this issue.

22. See Stephen Heath, 'On Screen, in Frame: Film and Ideology', in *Questions of Cinema* (Basingstoke 1981) and Virginia Woolf, 'Mr Bennett and Mrs Brown', from *The Captain's Death Bed*, collected in *Virginia Woolf: Selections from her Essays*, ed. Walter James, (London 1966), pp. 95–115.

23. Rachel Bowlby, *Just Looking: Consumer Culture in Dreiser, Gissing and Zola* (London 1985), p. 15.

24. The term is taken from the title of Alan Spiegel's *Fiction and the Camera Eye: Visual Consciousness in Film and the Modern Novel* (Charlottesville 1976).

25. Robert Richardson, *Literature and Film* (Bloomington 1969).

26. See Frank Kermode's 'apocalyptic' reading in *Lawrence* (London 1973).

27. In particular see Chapters 1 and 2 of Bowlby's *Just Looking*, pp. 1–34.

28. Q.D. Leavis, *Fiction and the Reading Public* (Harmondsworth 1979), p. 168.

29. ibid., p. 213.

30. ibid., p. 194.

31. F.R. Leavis, 'Reminiscences of D.H. Lawrence', in *Scrutiny*, vol. 1, no. 2, September 1932, p. 190.

32. Francis Mulhern, *The Moment of Scrutiny* (London 1979), p. 125.

33. See D.H. Lawrence, 'The Spirit of Place', the first essay collected in *Studies in Classic American Literature* (Harmondsworth 1977), hereafter referred to in my text as Studies.

34. D.H. Lawrence, *England, My England* (Harmondsworth 1978), p. 33. Hereafter stories collected in this volume will be referred to in my text as EME.

35. F.R. Leavis, *Mass Civilisation and Minority Culture* (Cambridge 1930), p. 10.

36. Robert W. Millett agrees with Lawrence to the extent that he can write,

> If Lawrence had been able to view many of the programs that are currently being screened on television and in theatres, one can be reasonably sure that he would have raised his voice even louder in vehement condemnation of the forces that encourage this falsity in feeling in individuals and society. (*The Vultures and the Phoenix* (London and Toronto 1983), p. 59)

37. D.H. Lawrence, *The Trespasser* (Harmondsworth 1979), pp. 30–1.

38. Virginia Woolf, 'The Cinema' (1926), collected in *Virginia Woolf: Selections from her Essays*, edited by Walter James (London 1966), pp. 172–7.

39. W.H. Mellers, 'The Hollywooden Hero', from *A Selection from Scrutiny*, compiled by F.R. Leavis, vol. 2 (Cambridge 1968), p. 90.

40. Mellers writes: 'we must remember, too, that though there is much that is deliberately vicious in glycerine tears, yet a form of art or entertainment so popular and universal cannot exist without incarnating, even fortuitously, some of the values which the people who patronise it honestly live by' (ibid., p. 90).

41. David Boadella, *The Spiral Flame* (Buffalo 1978), p. 40.

42. For an account of the development of Cambridge criticism and the influence of *Scrutiny* in the development of English studies see Mulhern's *The Moment of Scrutiny* op. cit., and Chris Baldick's *The Social Mission of English Criticism: 1848–1932* (Oxford 1983).

43. Freud uses this phrase in a footnote in *Studies on Hysteria* (1893–5) (with Joseph Breuer) (Harmondsworth 1980), p. 181.
44. Sheila MacLeod, *Lawrence's Men and Women* (London 1985), p. 170.
45. I discuss the feminist debate over Lawrence in 'The Trial of D.H. Lawrence', *Critical Survey*, Spring 1992.
46. See, for example, Michel Foucault, 'Las Meninas' in *The Order of Things* (London 1985), and 'The Eye of Power' in *Power/Knowledge* (New York 1980). For a discussion of Foucault's position and influence on this question see Martin Jay's excellent article 'In the Empire of the Gaze: Foucault and the Denigration of Vision in Twentieth-century French Thought', in *Foucault, A Critical Reader*, edited by David Couzens Hoys (London 1986).
47. *Studies*, p. 8. Lawrence also surprisingly champions an anti-humanist 'death of the author' position at other points in his writing, such as at the close of the essay 'The Novel', where he writes, 'Oh, give me the novel! Let me hear what the novel says./As for the novelist, he is usually a dribbling liar' (Px, 174).
48. Tania Modleski, *The Women Who Knew Too Much: Hitchcock and Feminist Theory* (New York and London 1988), p. 3.
49. Harold Bloom, *Kabbalah and Criticism* (New York 1975), p. 104.

Chapter 1

1. In *Beyond Good and Evil* Nietzsche writes 'Whoever fights monsters should see to it that in the process he does not become a monster. And when you look long into the abyss, the abyss also looks into you.' Translated by Walter Kaufmann (New York 1969), p. 98.
2. *Fantasia*, p. 11. This sets the tone for the book – at other times Lawrence can be found arguing, for example, 'At the lumbar ganglion I know that I am I, in distinction from a whole universe, which is not as I am' (F, 35), and 'The life of individuals depends directly upon the moon, just as the moon depends directly upon the life of individuals' (F, 179).
3. Despite this, Lawrence is still able, at other moments, to characterise femininity as a 'dark continent': 'the true polarity of consciousness in woman is downwards. Her deepest consciousness is in the loins and belly' (F, 188).
4. In *Klein* Hanna Segal writes that Melanie Klein 'considered the impulse to search for knowledge (epistemophilia) so fundamental that up till 1934 she used the term "epistemophiliac instinct"' (London 1979), p. 68. Klein herself observes that 'the epistemophilic impulse aris[es] and coexist[s] with sadism', and 'the epistemophilic instinct and the desire to take possession come quite early to be the most intimately connected with one another', pp. 72 and 98 of *The Selected Melanie Klein*, edited by Juliet Mitchell (Harmondsworth 1986). Klein also writes in *The Psychoanalysis of Children* that 'sadistic impulses . . . activate the child's instinct for knowledge' (London 1980), p. 174. Freud makes a similar connection between sadism and looking, and in Chapter 2 I will discuss this in more detail in terms of Lawrence's view of the sadism of the female gaze.

5. Catherine Clément, *The Lives and Legends of Jacques Lacan*, translated by Arthur Goldhammer (New York 1983), pp. 163–4.

6. The composite discussion of castrating women as educators which takes place across Lawrence's work will be discussed fully in Chapter 2.

7. This title echoes that of Paul de Man's seminal series of readings, *Blindness and Insight: Essays in the Rhetoric of Contemporary Criticism* (London 1983).

8. Jonathan Dollimore, *Sexual Dissidence* (Oxford 1991), p. 275, Dollimore's emphasis. This will be further discussed in Chapters 3 and 4 below.

9. G.W.F. Hegel, 'Independence and Dependence of Self-Consciousness: Lordship and Bondage' (sometimes known as the 'Master–Slave dialectic'), pp. 111–19 of *Phenomenology of Spirit*, translated by A.V. Miller (Oxford 1977).

10. For a discussion of theories of separation–individuation (particularly Margaret Mahler's analysis of the child's individuation 'from an initial symbiotic unity with the mother'), and the relationship between Winnicott and Hegel, see Jessica Benjamin, *The Bonds of Love* (London 1990. pp. 11–84.

11. Benjamin, p. 38.

12. D.H. Lawrence, *The Rainbow* (Harmondsworth 1979) p. 221. Hereafter this will be referred to in my text as R.

13. D.H. Lawrence, *Twilight in Italy* (Harmondsworth 1977), p. 81.

14. Rachel Bowlby discusses the convergence of the spectacle of the shop and the growth of cinema, and Lawrence's awareness of the relationship between Birkin's illuminated figure in the window and Ursula's position as passive spectator needs to be read in relation to this. See Bowlby, Introduction (pp. 1–17), *Just Looking* (London 1985).

15. See Tony Pinkney's excellent study of Lawrence's modernism, *D.H. Lawrence*, (Hemel Hempstead 1990).

16. For this it is applauded by Frederick Ramey in 'Words in the Service of Silence: Preverbal Language in Lawrence's *The Plumed Serpent*' in *Modern Fiction Studies*, vol. 27, Winter 1981–2, pp. 613–21.

17. D.H. Lawrence, *Mornings in Mexico/Etruscan Places* (Harmondsworth 1977), p. 45. Hereafter this will be referred to in my text as Mexico.

18. Ramón's narcissism, then, has to be understood as a kind of incest with the self. So persistent is the desire to return here that these passages could be interpreted as literary accounts of the circular movement of Freud's death drive, the drive to return to an 'original' blank obscurity, or the baseline of excitation expressed by Freud's alternative Nirvana Principle. There is also a connection here with Nietzsche's principle of the eternal recurrence. The problem with both of these analogies is that Lawrence's form of return is expressed in service of a unified notion of the self – the circle comes back on itself, the outside is closed out, and light cannot penetrate. Returning to the self in Lawrence is part of a prayer to the interior. Freud's and Nietzsche's circularities are quite different in that they are part of a larger problematisation of identity rather than a system which seeks to unify it.

Chapter 2

1. Paul Virilio, *War and Cinema: The Logistics of Perception*, translated by Patrick Camiller (London 1988) p. 3.
2. See, in particular, Linda Williams, 'When the Woman Looks', in *Re-Vision: Essays in Feminist Film Criticism*, edited by Mary Ann Doane et al. (Frederick, Md. 1984), but this is a thriving area in feminist film criticism: also see Mary Ann Doane, 'Film and the Masquerade: Theorising the Female Spectator' in *Screen* special edition on feminism and the gaze, vol. 23, no. 3–4, Sept–Oct 1982; special edition of *Camera Obscura* on 'The Spectatrix' (1989, 20–1); *Female Spectators: Looking at Film and Television* (edited by Deirdre Pribram) (London 1988); Judith Mayne's *The Woman at the Keyhole: Feminism and Women's Cinema* (Bloomington 1990); and 'The Cinema Spectator' in John Ellis's *Visible Fictions* (London 1982).
3. Diane Ackerman, *A Natural History of the Senses* (New York 1991), p. 230.
4. In *Herself Beheld: The Literature of the Looking Glass* Jenijoy La Belle writes:

   Most authors who criticise the glass do so because it is a sign of a woman's submission to masculine values. Lawrence presents just the reverse: the mirror does not make the woman a slave to the male world, but stimulates a woman's self-consciousness that inhibits her merging into the male (Ithaca and London 1988, p. 72).

5. D.H. Lawrence, 'The Wilful Woman' in *The Princess and Other Stories* (Harmondsworth 1980), p. 16. Hereafter stories from this volume will be referred to in my text as 'Princess'.
6. Mayne, op. cit., p. 17.
7. E. Ann Kaplan, 'Is the Gaze Male?' in *Desire: The Politics of Sexuality*, edited by Ann Snitow et al. (London 1983).
8. Constance Penley, 'Introduction – The Lady Doesn't Vanish: Feminism and Film Theory', in *Feminism and Film Theory*, ed. Penley (London 1988), quotation p. 7.
9. Hélène Cixous, 'Sorties', in *The Newly Born Woman* (with Catherine Clément), translated by Betsy Wing (Manchester 1986), all quotations p. 63. Graham Hough also discusses some of the binary oppositions with which Lawrence explicitly works in *The Dark Sun* (Harmondsworth 1961), p. 260.
10. Linda Williams, op. cit., p. 83.
11. J. Laplanche and J.-B. Pontalis, *The Language of Psycho-Analysis*, translated by Donald Nicholson-Smith (London 1983), p. 9.
12. Sigmund Freud, *Three Essays on the Theory of Sexuality* (1905), in Pelican Freud Library vol. 7, *On Sexuality* (Harmondsworth 1981), p. 70.
13. Freud, ibid., p. 73, Freud's italics.
14. For a fuller discussion of this, see Linda R. Williams, 'Submission and Reading: Feminine Masochism and Feminist Criticism', in *New Formations* ('Modernism/Masochism'), Spring 1989.
15. See Laura Mulvey, 'Visual Pleasure and Narrative Cinema', *Screen* 16, 1975, pp. 6–18. Key texts in the developing debate around Mulvey include Mary Ann Doane, *The Desire to Desire: The Woman's Film of the 1940s*

(Bloomington 1987); Kaja Silverman, *The Acoustic Mirror: The Female Voice in Psychoanalysis and Cinema* (Bloomington 1988); the collection of essays edited by Constance Penley, *Feminism and Film Theory*, op. cit.

16. Penley, p. 7.
17. ibid.
18. From Lorraine Gamman and Margaret Marshment, 'Introduction', in *The Female Gaze: Women as Viewers of Popular Culture*, edited by Gamman and Marshment (London 1988) p. 1.
19. Lawrence began *The Sisters*, from which both *The Rainbow* and *Women in Love* developed, when he was living in Italy in 1913; *Women in Love* was finished in October 1916 whilst he was living in Cornwall, unable to leave Britain because of the war, but frustrated at staying on since the suppression of *The Rainbow* in 1915 after which he wrote: 'I hope to be going away in about a fortnight's time: to America: . . . but nothing is settled yet. We have got passports. It is the end of my writing for England' (*The Collected Letters of D.H. Lawrence*, edited by Harry T. Moore (London 1962), p. 376).
20. D.H. Lawrence, *Sons and Lovers* (Harmondsworth 1977), p. 307, Lawrence's italics. Hereafter this will be referred to in my text as S&L.
21. Teresa de Lauretis, 'Film and the Visible', in *How Do I Look?* edited by Bad Object Choices (Seattle 1991).
22. Gertrude Koch, 'Why Women Go to Men's Films' in *Feminist Aesthetics*, edited by Gisela Ecker, translated by Harriet Anderson (London 1985), p. 109.
23. Carole J. Clover, *Men, Women and Chain Saws* (London 1992), p. 175.
24. Miriam Hansen, *Babel and Babylon: Spectatorship in American Silent Film* (Cambridge, Mass. 1991), p. 269.
25. Linda Williams, op. cit., p. 83.
26. Hansen, op. cit., p. 279.
27. Koch, loc. cit.
28. Emile Delavenay, 'D.H. Lawrence and Sacher-Masoch' in *The D.H. Lawrence Review*, Summer 1983, this and subsequent quotes, p. 122.
29. ibid., p. 123.
30. Stephen Heath, 'Difference' in *Screen*, vol. 19, no. 3, Autumn 1978, p. 92.
31. Philip Rieff, *The Triumph of the Therapeutic: The Uses of Faith after Freud* (London 1966) p. 206.
32. In this Lawrence follows Schopenhauer: 'a man inherits his moral nature, his character, his inclinations, his heart, from his father, but the degree, quality, and tendency of his intelligence from the mother' (Arthur Schopenhauer, *The World as Will and Representation*, vol. 2 (New York 1966), p. 517).
33. Scott Sanders, *D.H. Lawrence: The World of the Major Novels* (London 1973), p. 160.
34. D.H. Lawrence, *Mr Noon* (Cambridge 1984), p. 205. Hereafter this will be referred to in my text as Noon.
35. As Mabel Dodge Luhan (Lawrence's model for the Wilful Woman) writes in her *Intimate Memoirs*, 'the function of the male principle is to give impetus to the feminine life' (*European Experiences*, vol. 2 of *Intimate Memoirs*, New York 1935, quoted by Hilary Simpson, *D.H. Lawrence and Feminism* (London 1982), p. 158).

36. D.H. Lawrence, *Aaron's Rod* (Harmondsworth 1977), pp. 122–3. Hereafter this will be referred to in my text as AR.

37. D.H. Lawrence, unpublished letter to Robert Mountsier, 20 January 1917, quoted by Simpson, op. cit., pp. 66–7.

38. Delavenay, op. cit., p. 143. Delavenay's point is that Lawrence enacted a kind of textual repression in 'mutilating' his infant text. This is an image which Freud employs in 'Analysis Terminable and Interminable', when censorship in writing is used to illustrate 'actual' repression:

> if the authorities ... wanted ... to conceal any indication that the text had been mutilated [they could] ... proceed to distort the text. Single words would be left out and replaced by others, and new sentences interpolated. Best of all, the whole passage would be erased and a new one which said exactly the opposite put in its place. ... it is highly probable that the corrections had not been made in the direction of truth (*Standard Edition of the Complete Works of Sigmund Freud*, vol. XXIII (London 1953–74), p. 236. Hereafter I will refer to this as S.E.)

39. George H. Ford employs the term 'use' to naïvely argue against critical *mis*use of 'the artist' in service of the critic's ideological position:

> yet how often we encounter pages in which our attention has been shifted away from Lawrence to the critic himself, pages devoted to an airing of Dr Leavis's likes and dislikes in religion, or in academic and literary politics. In the pejorative sense of the verb (as Lawrence himself employed it) the artist in such pages is being used. (*Double Measure: A Study of the Novels and Stories of D.H. Lawrence* (New York 1965) p. 5.)

40. D.H. Lawrence, *Lady Chatterley's Lover* (Harmondsworth 1990), p. 210, Hereafter this will be referred to in my text as Lady.

41. D.H. Lawrence, *John Thomas and Lady Jane* (Harmondsworth 1977), p. 231. Hereafter this will be referred to in my text as JTLJ.

42. Simpson, op. cit., p. 147. See also Chapter 7, 'A Literary Trespasser', of *D.H. Lawrence and Feminism*, in which the question of Lawrence's plagiaristic 'trespass' upon his female friend's writings is discussed.

43. D.H. Lawrence, *Apocalypse* (Harmondsworth 1979), p. 4. Hereafter this will be referred to in my text as Apocalypse.

44. All quotations from Nick Browne, 'The Spectator-in-the-Text: The Rhetoric of *Stagecoach*', in *Narrative, Apparatus, Ideology: A Film Theory Reader*, edited by Philip Rosen (New York 1986), pp. 102–19.

45. Alison Light, 'Feminism and the Literary Critic' in *LTP*, no. 2, 1983, pp. 61–80, quotation, p. 64.

46. See George Eliot, *The Lifted Veil* (London 1985).

47. See Simone de Beauvoir, 'D.H. Lawrence or Phallic Pride' in *The Second Sex* (Harmondsworth 1981), pp. 245–54.

48. US Defense Secretary W.J. Perry, quoted by Virilio, op. cit., p. 4.

Chapter 3

1. Miriam Hansen, *Babel and Babylon: Spectatorship in American Silent Film* (Cambridge, Mass. and London 1991), p. 260.
2. See in particular, Nietzsche's *On the Genealogy of Morals*, which itself had an enormous influence on Michel Foucault's work on the punishment-spectacle in *Discipline and Punish: The Birth of the Prison*, translated by Alan Sheridan (New York 1979).
3. George H. Ford, 'Note on Lawrence's Prologue to *Women in Love*', in *The Rainbow and Women in Love* (Macmillan Casebook), edited by Colin Clarke (London 1969), p. 37 (originally published in *Texas Quarterly*, VI, Spring 1963).
4. See Jeffrey Meyers, *Homosexuality and Literature 1890–1930* (London 1977).
5. Tony Pinkney, *D.H. Lawrence* (Hemel Hempstead 1990), p. 108.
6. Luce Irigaray, 'Commodites Among Themselves', in *This Sex Which is Not One*, translated by Catherine Porter (New York 1985), p. 193.
7. Angela Carter, 'Lorenzo as Closet Queen', in *Nothing Sacred* (London 1982) pp. 161–8.
8. Roland Barthes, 'Striptease' in *Mythologies*, translated by Annette Lavers (London 1981), pp. 84–7, quotation p. 84.
9. Freud, *Three Essays on the Theory of Sexuality* (Harmondsworth 1981), pp. 69–70.
10. Stephen Neale, 'Masculinity as Spectacle: Reflections on Men and Mainstream Cinema', in *Screen*, vol. 24, no. 6, Nov–Dec 1983.
11. Sigmund Freud, 'Instincts and their Vicissitudes' (1915), in *On Metapsychology*, Pelican Freud Library Volume 11, Harmondsworth 1984. See pp. 124–5 for a discussion of this reversal.
12. See *Women in Love*, pp. 169–71. All subsequent references to this scene come from these pages.
13. See Laura Mulvey, 'Visual Pleasure and Narrative Cinema', in *Screen*, vol. 16, 1975, pp. 6–18.
14. Quoted by Billie Melman, in *Women and the Popular Imagination in the Twenties: Flappers and Nymphs* (Basingstoke 1988), p. 100.
15. ibid., p. 103.
16. Christian Metz, *Psychoanalysis and Cinema: The Imaginary Signifier* (Basingstoke 1982), p. 60.
17. ibid.
18. Richard Meyer, 'Rock Hudson's Body' in *Inside/Out: Lesbian Theories, Gay Theories*, edited by Diana Fuss (London 1991), p. 261.
19. D.H. Lawrence, from version of 'The Prologue' collected in *Women in Love* (Cambridge 1987), p. 493.
20. Meyer, op. cit., p. 262.
21. Metz, op. cit., p. 61.
22. ibid., p. 63.
23. ibid., p. 62.
24. ibid., p. 63, Metz's italics.

25. Gilles Deleuze, *Cinema 1: The Movement-Image*, translated by Hugh Tomlinson and Barbara Habberjam (London 1986), p. 2.
26. D.H. Lawrence, 'Odour of Chrysanthemums', in *The Prussian Officer* (Harmondsworth 1969), p. 222. Hereafter stories from this collection will be referred to in my text as Prussian.
27. Neale, op. cit., p. 11.
28. Another exception, in which a man gazes *directly* at men washing (as opposed to those times when the narrative uses the eyes of women to view the scene), comes in *Mornings in Mexico*, when Lawrence himself stumbles upon two men and a woman in a water-channel. Later he spies another naked man, and here the power of the physical spectacle corresponds directly to the absence of spirit:

    And I, going round the little hummock behind the wild guava tree . . . , came upon a golden-brown young man with his shirt just coming down over his head, but over no more of him. Hastily retreating, I thought again what beautiful, suave, rich skins these people have; a sort of richness of the flesh. It goes, perhaps, with the complete absence of what we call 'spirit'. (Mexico 31).

29. This scene occurs in all three versions of the novel: see Lady, pp. 68–70; JTLJ, pp. 50-2; *The First Lady Chatterley* (Harmondsworth 1978), p. 27. Hereafter *The First Lady Chatterley* will be referred to in my text as FLC.
30. Deleuze writes:

    Any other system which reproduces movement through an order of exposures (*poses*) projected in such a way that they pass into one another, or are 'transformed', is foreign to cinema. This is clear when one attempts to define the cartoon film; if it belongs fully to the cinema, this is because the drawing no longer constitutes a pose or a completed figure, but the description of a figure which is always in the process of being formed or dissolving through the movement of lines and points taken at any-instant-whatevers of their course. The cartoon film . . . does not give us a figure described in a unique moment, but the continuity of the movement which describes the figure. (p. 5)

31. Hansen, op cit., p. 252.
32. Carter, op. cit., p. 163.
33. See Sigmund Freud, ' "A Child is Being Beaten" (A Contribution to the Study of the Origin of Sexual Perversions)' (1919), in *On Psychopathology* (Harmondsworth 1981). I will discuss the importance of this essay for an understanding of multiple identification and fantasy in Chapter 5.

Chapter 4

1. Section 28 of the Local Government (Amendment) Act came into force in Britain in May 1988 (as Clause 29), with the purpose of restricting the 'promotion' or publication of homosexual material, works or any representations

which would show 'the acceptibility of homosexuality as a pretended family relationship' (quoted by Simon Watney in *Inside/Out: Lesbian Theories/Gay Theories*, edited by Diana Fuss (London 1991) p. 388).

2. See Chapter VIII, 'A Poem of Friendship', in D.H. Lawrence, *The White Peacock* (Harmondsworth 1979).

3. W.C. Pilley, in *John Bull*, 17 September 1921, in *D.H. Lawrence*, edited by H. Coombes (Harmondsworth 1973), p. 145.

4. See Joseph Bristow, 'Unsafe Sex? Eliding the Violence of Sexual Representation', paper given at the Feminist Criticism Conference, Exeter University 1992. I am grateful to Joseph Bristow for giving me access to this paper, ahead of its forthcoming publication in *Gender Studies and Feminist Criticism: New Developments*, edited by Sally Ledger, Josephine McDonagh and Jane Spencer, Harvester Wheatsheaf, forthcoming.

5. See Jonathan Dollimore, 'D.H. Lawrence and the Metaphysics of Sexual Difference', pp. 268–75 of *Sexual Dissidence: Augustine to Wilde, Freud to Foucault* (Oxford 1991), and Jeffrey Meyers, *Homosexuality and Literature 1890–1930*(London 1977).

6. The argument for Lawrence's liberationist sexuality characterises a significant slice of Lawrence criticism, for example Anaïs Nin's early celebration of Lawrence, *D.H. Lawrence: An Unprofessional Study* (London 1961), Carol Dix's simple-minded *D.H. Lawrence and Women* (London 1980), or here, Charles Rossman:

> For it is a fact that Lawrence made a substantial contribution to the sexual freedom that we presently enjoy, and to our ways of defining ourselves. His work may contain reactionary, even unpalatable, facets, but its central thrust was liberating in its day and continues to offer deep and valuable engagement to countless readers. ('"You are the Call and I am the Answer": D.H. Lawrence and Women', in *The D.H. Lawrence Review*, vol. 8, no. 3, Fall 1975, pp. 257–8)

This discourse of sexual authenticity and its relationship to the Chatterley trial is also analysed by Jonathan Dollimore in 'The Challenge of Sexuality', in *Society and Literature 1945–1970*, edited by Alan Sinfield, (London 1983), and (with reference to Lawrence's work generally) by Stephen Heath in *The Sexual Fix* (Basingstoke 1982).

7. Quoted by Declan Kiberd in *Men and Feminism in Modern Literature* (Basingstoke 1985), p. 168.

8. An example of how Lawrence can be all things to all sexual liberationists lies in the fact that he is surprisingly championed in quite different terms by Gilles Deleuze and Félix Guattari in *Anti-Oedipus*, where the 'dirty little secret' is used to describe the 'shameful' bourgeois sexuality of Freudianism:

> Let us keep D.H. Lawrence's reaction to psychoanalysis in mind, and never forget it. In Lawrence's case, at least, his reservations with regard to psychoanalysis did not stem from terror at having discovered what real sexuality was. But he had the impression – the purely instinctive impression

– that psychoanalysis was shutting sexuality up in a bizarre sort of box painted with bourgeois motifs, in a kind of rather repugnant artificial triangle, thereby stifling the whole of sexuality as production of desire so as to recast it along entirely different lines, making of it a 'dirty little secret,' the dirty little family secret, a private theatre rather than the fantastic factory of Nature and Production. (*Anti-Oedipus: Capitalism and Schizophrenia*, translated by Robert Hurley, Mark Seem and Helen R. Lane (London 1984), p. 49.)

9. For Tony Pinkney the failure of Miriam in *Sons and Lovers* is established in visual terms which are quite the opposite of this representation of Hermione. In his gothic reading of the novel, she displays a vampiric inability to relate to mirrors, but for all her sins at least this guarantees a need for connection, even if it is desperately spiritual. See Tony Pinkney, *D.H. Lawrence* (Hemel Hempstead 1990), pp. 31–7.

10. See Linda R. Williams, 'The Trial of D.H. Lawrence', *Critical Survey*, vol. 4, no. 2, 1992.

11. *The First Lady Chatterley* and *John Thomas and Lady Jane* didn't appear unexpurgated in Britain until 1972, although a very mild Frieda-authorised expurgated version of *The First Lady Chatterley* had appeared in the United States in 1932.

12. F.R. Leavis, 'Reminiscences of D.H. Lawrence', in *Scrutiny*, vol. 1, no. 2, September 1932.

13. John Sutherland writes:

One of the more surprising things to emerge at the Old Bailey trial was that all the 'experts' had apparently contrived to read the ostensibly banned novel without any difficulty at all. A perverse construction was put on this by Colin MacInnes who argued that the trial was evidently redundant. (p. 11 of *Offensive Literature: Decensorship in Britain, 1960–1982* (London 1982).)

14. David J. Gordon, *D.H. Lawrence as a Literary Critic* (London 1966), p. 22 footnote.

15. Meyers, op. cit., p. 148.

16. On this issue, Meyers notes the abysmal gap in Lawrence 'between sexual idealism and sexual reality', since 'Both doctors and homosexuals agree that the first experience of anal penetration is extremely painful' (pp. 149, 178). Against this 'tender' sodomy in *Lady Chatterley's Lover*, Tony Pinkney emphasises the Imagistic 'hardness' of anal sex in *Women in Love*:

As [Birkin] incessantly tells Ursula, he wants 'something much more impersonal and harder' . . . and this is how he gets it: her anus is 'dryer' than her vagina, 'harder' to penetrate, and 'impersonal' in that, buggering from behind, one avoids what Birkin would see as the sentimentalities of face-to-face intimacy . . . Dry, hard, impersonal, clear, cool: by now Birkin's keywords seem to come straight out of a thesaurus composed by T.E. Hulme. (Pinkney, p. 88).

17. In this respect Just Jaeckin's dreadful 1981 film of the book is accurate, since it studiously follows Connie's perspective so that the camera only fully dwells upon Mellors when Connie's eyes finally do so, in the scene when she catches him washing.

18. See D.P. Schreber, *Memoirs of my Nervous Illness* (1903), translated by I. MacAlpine and R. A. Hunter (London 1955) and Freud's analysis of this, 'Psychoanalytic Notes on an Autobiographical Account of a Case of Paranoia (Dementia Paranoides) (Schreber)', in Pelican Freud Library vol. 9, pp. 131–226.

19. Carol J. Clover writes: 'Sex, in this universe, proceeds from gender, not the other way around. A figure does not cry and cower because she is a woman; she is a woman because she cries and cowers' (*Men, Women and Chain Saws* (London 1992), p. 13). A point about identification follows from this point about gender as determined by actions: in being forced to identify with penetrability rather than 'hunting out' in this text, we are – whatever our sex – feminised in our reading, just as Connie is 'renewed' in her femininity by penetration.

20. Kate Millett, *Sexual Politics* (London 1982), p. 239.

21. Lawrence's flowers, more Georgia O'Keeffe than aesthetically disembodied English watercolours, also have erections: 'the mulleins would sway their soft, downy erections in the air' (EME, 36).

22. Georges Bataille, 'Eye', in *Visions of Excess: Selected Writings 1927–1939* translated by Allan Stoekl (Minneapolis 1985), quotes pp. 17 and 19.

23. Diane Ackerman, *Natural History of the Senses* (New York 1991), pp. 232–3.

24. Bataille, op. cit., p. 19.

25. Clover, op. cit., p. 181; p. 205.

26. See John Trevelyan, *What the Censor Saw* (London 1977) pp. 159–60.

27. Carol J. Clover brilliantly discusses this in her chapter on *Peeping Tom*, 'The Eye of Horror', pp. 166–230.

28. D.H. Lawrence, *The Ladybird* in *Three Novellas* (Harmondsworth 1978), p. 36. Hereafter this will be referred to in my text as TN.

29. Stephen King, *Danse Macabre*, quoted by Carol J. Clover (1992), p. 166.

30. Jonathan Dollimore, *Sexual Dissidence*, op. cit., pp. 274–5, Dollimore's emphasis.

31. See 'Prologue', in *Women in Love* (Cambridge 1989), quote p. 503.

32. For Meyers Lawrence's homosexuality is often characterised by hatred of women, his misogyny following from his latent sexual preference. For Dix, Lawrence-the-proto-feminist is not misogynistic, and therefore he cannot be gay; he is a Real Man who loves women (for Dix, all gay men hate women). George Donaldson negotiates the debate on Lawrence's homosexuality in a different way: 'Readers who have sought to escape what is unsatisfactorily indefinite, by supposing a homosexual implication, have some excuse for their conduct, even though there is no clear justification for it' ('Men in Love? D.H. Lawrence, Rupert Birkin and Gerald Crich' in *D.H. Lawrence: Centenary Essays*, edited by Mara Kalnins (Bristol 1986), p. 54).

Chapter 5

1. Reviewer of *The White Peacock* quoted by Declan Kiberd in *Men and Feminism in Modern Literature* (Basingstoke 1985), p. 136; Angela Carter, 'Lorenzo as Closet Queen', in *Nothing Sacred* (London 1982), p. 162.

2. Carter, op. cit., p. 162.

3. For some people, however, the clothes have stuck, and they can never become naked again. This is Lawrence on Englishmen in the *Phoenix* essay 'Love was once a Little Boy':

   > No matter how they pull their shirts off they never arrive at their own nakedness. They have none. They can only be undressed. Naked they cannot be. Without their clothes on, they are like a dismantled streetcar without its advertisements; a sort of public article that doesn't refer to anything. (See *Phoenix II*, edited by Warren Roberts and Harry T. Moore (New York 1968), p. 458.)

4. In 'Costumes of the Mind: Transvestism as Metaphor in Modern Literature' Sandra M. Gilbert discusses transvestism in a range of modern texts (including Lawrence's *The Fox*), where she juxtaposes Woolf's notion that 'costume is inseparable from identity' with Yeats's position, that 'a heart's truth ... stands apart from false costumes': 'For Woolf, we are what we wear, but for Yeats, we may, like Lear, have to undo the last button of what we wear in order to dis-cover and more truly re-cover what we are' (see *Writing and Sexual Difference*, edited by Elizabeth Abel (Hemel Hempstead 1982), pp. 193–4). Lawrence may polemically prefer the latter position, but he still manages to enjoy the former. Gilbert's further point, that the connection between costume and identity is recoined by modernism in a unique way due to the growing influence of the fashion industry, deserves further development in terms of Lawrence's anxiety about modern spectacle.

5. Carter, op. cit., pp. 162–3.

6. ibid., p. 168.

7. ibid., p. 164.

8. Shirley Russell, Ken's first wife, costume designer for both Russell's *Women in Love* and Just Jaeckin's *Lady Chatterley's Lover*, follows this opulence in detail, the latter an example of soft porn clothed by English Heritage.

9. ibid., p. 162.

10. Sigmund Freud, 'Fetishism' (1927), in volume 7 of Pelican Freud Library, *On Sexuality* (Harmondsworth 1981), pp. 354–5.

11. Philippa Tristram, 'Eros and Death (Lawrence, Freud and Women)', in *Lawrence and Women*, edited by Anne Smith (London 1978), quotation p. 143.

12. Carter, op. cit., p. 166.

13. The Cambridge edition also cites Tolstoi's similar experience of landscape in its explanatory notes: '"The old man dreamt that he was standing between the woman's legs, in front of him a deep, dark ravine, which sucked him in ..." (*Reminiscences of Tolstoi*, by Gorky, p. 31).' See *Mr Noon* p. 328. Emile Delavenay cites a similar passage from an early Lawrence short story, 'The

Shades of Spring', in support of his theory that Lawrence and Sacher-Masoch have much in common psychologically (Delavenay, 'D.H. Lawrence and Sacher-Masoch' in *D.H. Lawrence Review*, vol. 6, Summer 1973, p. 132).

14. Alistair Niven, *D.H. Lawrence: The Novels* (Cambridge 1978), p. 169.
15. JTLJ, 230; Hilary Simpson also discusses this in *D.H. Lawrence and Feminism* (London 1982).
16. Sheila MacLeod, *Lawrence's Men and Women* (London 1985), pp. 6–7.
17. ibid., p. 78.
18. From Otto Weininger, *Sex and Character* (London 1906), quoted by Simpson, op. cit., pp. 90–1.
19. Freud, 'Fetishism', op. cit., p. 352.
20. D.H. Lawrence, *Apocalypse* (Harmondsworth 1979), p. 95.
21. Whilst this interpretation, that the woman's identity collapses into the stocking itself when the man appears, is consistent with Freud's reading of male fetishism, Jenijoy La Belle emphasises the woman's relationship with her mirror, since this is a story which 'traces just how the male/female bond breaks down as the mirror/female bond becomes stronger', aligning the story more with the visual relationships explored in *Women in Love* than with the fetishism of *Mr Noon*. See *Herself Beheld: The Literature of the Looking Glass* (Ithaca and London 1988), p. 61.
22. See D.H. Lawrence, *Sons and Lovers* (Cambridge 1992), p. 381.
23. Carole J. Clover, *Men, Women and Chain Saws* (London 1992), p. 46.
24. Carol Dix, *D.H. Lawrence and Women* (London 1980), p. 13; Norman Mailer, *The Prisoner of Sex* (London 1971) pp. 151–2.
25. Peter Widdowson, 'Introduction: Post-modernising D.H. Lawrence', in *D.H. Lawrence*, edited by Peter Widdowson (London and New York 1992) p. 18.
26. Gāmini Salgādo, 'Taking a Nail for a Walk: On Reading *Women in Love*', in Widdowson, op. cit., p. 137.
27. Tania Modleski, *The Women Who Knew Too Much: Hitchcock and Feminist Theory* (New York 1988), p. 6.
28. Elizabeth Cowie, 'Fantasia', *m/f*, 9, 1984, p. 71.
29. In 'Creative Writers and Day-Dreaming' (1908 (1907)) Freud closes the gap between unconscious phantasy and conscious creativity, or rather, he explores how the writer 'does the same as the child at play'. When the writer 'undoes the contrast between play and reality' she turns her unconscious fantasies into real textual events and plays with fiction as the scenes of desire (quotations, p. 132 of Pelican Freud Library, vol. 14, *Art and Literature* (Harmondsworth 1985)). Laplanche and Pontalis develop this: 'Freud always held the model fantasy to be the reverie, that form of novelette, both stereotyped and infinitely variable, which the subject composes and relates to himself in a waking state' (Jean Laplanche and J.-B. Pontalis, 'Fantasy and the Origins of Sexuality', in *The International Journal of Psycho-analysis*, vol. 49, part 1, 1968, p. 13). Since these points emphasise the relationship between conscious and unconscious fantasy as one of continuum, I will use the term 'fantasy' (rather than 'phantasy', the conventional term for unconscious fantasies), except where the word is spelled otherwise in quotation.
30. Writers on this subject testify to the pleasures of this slippage: see in particular

the essays collected in *Leatherfolk: Radical Sex, People. Politics and Practice*, edited by Mark Thompson (Boston 1991). This is also the importance of the Master–Slave dialectic for some Marxists: the mutual need of master for slave (as founder of his position as master) and of slave for master (as controller of his labour situation).

31. Freud, 'Creative Writers and Day-Dreaming', op. cit., p. 133.
32. Sigmund Freud, '"A Child is Being Beaten" (A Contribution to the Study of the Origin of Sexual Perversions)' (1919), in Pelican Freud Library vol. 10, *On Psychopathology* (Harmondsworth 1981), p. 166.
33. Sigmund Freud, 'Splitting of the Ego in the Process of Defence' (1940 (1938)), in Pelican Freud Library vol. 11 *On Metapsychology* (Harmondsworth 1984), p. 461.
34. Freud, '"A Child is Being Beaten"', p. 165.
35. ibid., p. 171.
36. Constance Penley (ed.), *Feminism and Film Theory* (London 1988), p. 22.
37. Laplanche and Pontalis, 'Fantasy and the Origins of Sexuality', op. cit., p. 17.
38. This sense and impulse of movement is also present in 'John', the essay in *Twilight in Italy* which deals with the migrant figure impelled to move between Italy and America, 'being conveyed from one form of life to another, or like a soul in trajectory, that has not yet found a resting-place'. John's nomadism is given as a kind of fall, as he is urged by history from the unknowing to the conscious without a qualm or, indeed, a thought:

> He seemed scarcely like a person with individual choice, more like a creature under the influence of fate which was disintegrating the old life and precipitating him, a fragment inconclusive, into the new chaos. . . . Nothing was more painful than to see him standing there in his degraded, sordid American clothes, on the deck of the steamer, waving us good-bye, belonging in his final desire to our world, the world of consciousness and deliberate action. (Italy, 125–6).

39. Tony Pinkney writes of travel and movement in *Women in Love*:

> The 'crisis of war' takes place during the car drive; next we find them on top of a tram, then crossing the Channel by ship ('they went right to the bows of the softly ploughing vessel', as if they somehow seek to outpace it or urge it on), and finally hurtling across the Continent by train. All of which is a far cry from Paul Morel cycling up to Willey Farm to see Miriam. Ursula and Birkin's 'pure trajectory' (to borrow the novel's phrase) is not an accident of the relationship but rather its very stuff and substance; Ursula was 'not at ease till they were on the train again . . . So long as they were moving onwards she was satisfied'. (*D.H. Lawrence* (Hemel Hempstead 1990) p. 90).

40. See the imagism anthologies, *Des Imagistes* (1914), *Some Imagist Poets* (1915, 1916, 1917); and essays by Ezra Pound ('A Few Don'ts by an Imagiste'; 'Language') and F.S. Flint ('Imagisme.') collected in *Imagist Poetry*, edited by Peter Jones (Harmondsworth 1981).
41. Pinkney, op. cit., p. 42.

42. Christian Metz, *Psychoanalysis and Cinema: The Imaginary Signifier* (Basingstoke 1982) p. 95, p. 77.
43. ibid., p. 77, Metz's emphasis.
44. See Kaja Silverman, 'Masochism and Subjectivity', in *Framework*, no. 12 (1980), pp. 2–9.
45. Judith Mayne, *The Woman at the Keyhole: Feminism and Women's Cinema* (Bloomington 1990), p. 160.
46. Noel Burch, 'Correction Please: Or How We Got Into the Movies' in *Afterimage* no. 8/9, winter 1980, pp. 22–38, quotation p. 32.
47. Michael Channan, *The Dream that Kicks: The Prehistory and Early Years of Cinema in Britain* (London 1980), pp. 294–5. See also brief discussion of this film in Rachael Low and Roger Manvell, *The History of British Film 1896–1906* (London 1973), p. 49. I am indebted to Nigel Floyd for discussing this subject with me, and for giving me access to his dissertation on voyeurism in cinema. Judith Mayne also discusses primitive cinema in part 3 of *The Woman at the Keyhole*.
48. See Jacqueline Rose, 'Sexuality in the Field of Vision', in *Sexuality in the Field of Vision* (London 1986), pp. 225–33.
49. Sigmund Freud, *Standard Edition* vol. 5, p. 530, quoted by Samuel Weber in *The Legend of Freud* (Minneapolis 1982), p. 75.
50. D.H. Lawrence, 'The Reality of Peace' in *Phoenix: The Posthumous Papers of D.H. Lawrence*, edited by Edward D. McDonald (London 1936), pp. 677–80.
51. Arthur Schopenhauer, *The World as Will and Representation*, vol. 1 (New York 1966), p. 151.
52. Friedrich Nietzsche, *The Will to Power*, translated by Walter Kaufmann (New York 1968), p. 281, n. 518.
53. Jacques Lacan, *The Four Fundamental Concepts of Psycho-Analysis*, translated by Alan Sheridan (New York and London 1981), p. 87.
54. ibid., p. 89.
55. See Rose, op. cit., p. 227, for a discussion of this.
56. Alice Jardine quoted by Tania Modleski in *The Women Who Knew Too Much*, op. cit., p. 13.
57. See Linda R. Williams, 'Submission and Reading: Feminine Masochism and Feminist Criticism' in *New Formations* ('Modernism/Masochism'), Spring 1989.
58. Modleski, op. cit., p. 9.
59. D.H. Lawrence, *The Collected Letters of D.H. Lawrence*, edited by Harry T. Moore (London, 1962), pp. 172–3.
60. D.H. Lawrence, 'Pan in America' in *Phoenix* (1936), p. 27.

◆
Bibliography

Ackerman, Diane: *A Natural History of the Senses* (New York 1991).

Baldick, Chris: *The Social Mission of English Criticism: 1848–1932* (Oxford 1983).

Barron, Janet: 'Equality Puzzle: Lawrence and Feminism', in *Rethinking Lawrence*, edited by Keith Brown (Milton Keynes 1990).

Barthes, Roland: 'Striptease', in *Mythologies*, translated by Annette Lavers (London 1981).

Bataille, Georges: *Story of the Eye* (1928), translated by Joachim Neugroschel (Harmondsworth 1982).

Bataille, Georges: *Visions of Excess: Selected Writings 1927–1939*, translated by Allan Stoekl (Minneapolis 1985).

Beauvoir, Simone de: 'D.H. Lawrence or Phallic Pride', in *The Second Sex* (1949), (Harmondsworth 1981).

Beja, Morri: *Film and Literature: An Introduction* (New York 1979).

Benjamin, Jessica: *The Bonds of Love* (London 1990).

Bentley, Eric (ed.): *The Importance of Scrutiny: Selections from 'Scrutiny: A Quarterly Review', 1932–1948*, (New York 1964).

Berger, John: *Ways of Seeing* (London 1972).

Blanchard, Lydia: 'Love and Power: A Reconsideration of Sexual Politics in D.H. Lawrence', in *Modern Fiction Studies*, vol. 21, no. 3 1975–6.

Blanchard, Lydia: 'Women Look at Lady Chatterley: Feminine Views of the Novel', in *D.H. Lawrence Review*, vol. 11, Fall 1978

Bloom, Harold: *Kabbalah and Criticism* (New York 1975).

Boadella, David: *The Spiral Flame* (Buffalo 1978).

Bowen, Elizabeth: 'Why I go to the Cinema', in *Footnotes to the Film*, edited by Charles Davy (London 1938).

Bowlby, Rachel: *Just Looking: Consumer Culture in Dreiser, Gissing and Zola* (London 1985).

Bristow, Joseph: 'Unsafe Sex? Eliding the Violence of Sexual Representation', paper given at the Feminist Criticism Conference, Exeter University 1992.

Browne, Nick: 'The Spectator-in-the-Text: The Rhetoric of *Stagecoach*', in *Narrative, Apparatus, Ideology: A Film Theory Reader*, edited by Philip Rosen (New York 1986)

Bryson, Norman et al.: *Visual Theory: Painting and Interpretation* (Cambridge 1991).

Burch, Noel: 'Correction Please: Or How we got into the Movies', in *Afterimage*, no. 8/9, Winter 1980, pp. 22–38

Carter, Angela: 'Lorenzo as Closet Queen', in *Nothing Sacred* (London 1982), originally published in *New Society* 1978.

Caws, Mary Ann: *The Eye in the Text: Essays on Perception, Mannerist to Modern* (New Jersey 1981).

Channan, Michael: *The Dream that Kicks: The Prehistory and Early Years of Cinema in Britain* (London 1980).

Cixous, Hélène, and Clément, Catherine: *The Newly Born Woman*, translated by Betsy Wing, (Manchester 1986).

Clarke, Colin (ed.): *The Rainbow and Women in Love: A Casebook*, (London 1969).

Clément, Catherine: *The Lives and Legends of Jacques Lacan*, translated by Arthur Goldhammer (New York 1983).

Clover, Carol J.: *Men, Women and Chain Saws* (London 1992).

Cohen, Keith: *Film and Fiction/The Dynamics of Exchange* (New Haven 1979).

Coombes, H. (ed.): *D.H. Lawrence* (Harmondsworth 1973).

Cowie, Elizabeth: 'Fantasia', *m/f*, 9, 1984.

Davis, Jane: 'Envoi: The Genie in the Second-hand Shop', in *Rethinking Lawrence*, edited by Keith Brown (Milton Keynes 1990).

Delaney, Paul: *D.H. Lawrence's Nightmare: The Writer and his Circle in the Years of the Great War* (Hemel Hempstead 1979).

Delavenay, Emile: 'D.H. Lawrence and Sacher-Masoch', in *D.H. Lawrence Review*, vol. 6, Summer 1973.

Deleuze, Gilles: *Cinema 1: The Movement-Image*, translated by Hugh Tomlinson and Barbara Habberjam (London 1986).

Deleuze, Gilles and Guattari, Félix: *Anti-Oedipus: Capitalism and Schizophrenia*, translated by Robert Hurley, Mark Seem and Helen R. Lane (London 1984).

Dix, Carol: *D.H. Lawrence and Women* (London 1980).

Doane, Mary Ann: *The Desire to Desire: The Woman's Film of the 1940s* (Bloomington 1987).

Doane, Mary Ann: 'Film and the Masquerade: Theorising the Female Spectator', in *Screen*, vol. 23, no. 3–4, Sept–Oct 1982.

Dollimore, Jonathan: *Sexual Dissidence: Augustine to Wilde, Freud to Foucault* (Oxford 1991).

Dollimore, Jonathan: 'The Challenge of Sexuality', in *Society and Literature 1945–1970*, edited by Alan Sinfield, (London 1983).

Donaldson, George: 'Men in Love? D.H. Lawrence, Rupert Birkin and Gerald Crich', in *D.H. Lawrence: Centenary Essays*, edited by Mara Kalnins (Bristol 1986).

Draper, R.P.: 'The Defeat of Feminism: D.H. Lawrence's *The Fox* and "The Woman Who Rode Away"', in *Studies in Short Fiction*, vol. 3, 1966.

Dworkin, Andrea: *Pornography: Men Possessing Women* (London 1983).

Eliot, George: *The Lifted Veil* (London 1985).

Ellis, John: *Visible Fictions* (London 1982).

Ford, George H.: *Double Measure: A Study of the Novels and Stories of D.H. Lawrence* (New York 1965).

Ford, George H.: 'Note on Lawrence's Prologue to *Women in Love*', in *The Rainbow and Women in Love* (Macmillan Casebook), edited by Colin Clarke (London 1969), originally published in *Texas Quarterly*, VI, Spring 1963.

Foucault, Michel: *Discipline and Punish: The Birth of the Prison*, translated by Alan Sheridan (New York 1979).

Foucault, Michel: *The Order of Things* (London 1985).

Foucault, Michel: *Power/Knowledge* (New York 1980).

Freud, Sigmund: '"A Child is Being Beaten" (A Contribution to the Study of the Origin of Sexual Perversions)' (1919), in *On Psychopathology*, Pelican Freud Library (hereafter PF) vol. 10 (Harmondsworth 1981).

Freud, Sigmund: 'Character and Anal Eroticism' (1908), in PF vol. 7, *On Sexuality* (Harmondsworth 1981).

Freud, Sigmund: 'Creative Writers and Day-Dreaming' (1908 (1907)), in PF vol. 14, *Art and Literature* (Harmondsworth 1985).

Freud, Sigmund: 'The Economic Problem of Masochism' (1924), in PF vol. 11, *On Metapsychology* (Harmondsworth 1984).

Freud, Sigmund: 'Fetishism' (1927), in PF vol. 7, *On Sexuality* (Harmondsworth 1981).

Freud, Sigmund: 'Instincts and their Vicissitudes' (1915), in PF vol. 11, *On Metapsychology* (Harmondsworth 1984).

Freud, Sigmund: 'Negation' (1925), in PF vol. 11, *On Metapsychology* (Harmondsworth 1984).

Freud, Sigmund: 'On Narcissism: An Introduction' (1914), in PF vol. 11, *On Metapsychology* (Harmondsworth 1984).

Freud, Sigmund: 'Psychoanalytic Notes on an Autobiographical Account of a Case of Paranoia (Dementia Paranoides) (Schreber)', in PF vol. 9, pp. 131–226.

Freud, Sigmund: 'Remembering, Repeating and Working-Through (Further Recommendations on the Technique of Psycho-analysis II)' (1924 (1914)), translated by Joan Riviere, in *Standard Edition of the Complete Works of Sigmund Freud* vol. 12.

Freud, Sigmund: 'Splitting of the Ego in the Process of Defence' (1940 (1938)), in PF vol. 11, *On Metapsychology* (Harmondsworth 1984).

Freud, Sigmund: *Three Essays on the Theory of Sexuality* (1905), in PF vol. 7, *On Sexuality* (Harmondsworth 1981).

Freud, Sigmund and Breuer, Joseph: *Studies on Hysteria* (1893–5), PF vol. 3 (Harmondsworth 1980).

Gamman, Lorraine and Marshment, Margaret (eds): *The Female Gaze: Women as Viewers of Popular Culture* (London 1988).

Gilbert, Sandra M.: *Acts of Attention: The Poems of D.H. Lawrence*, (Ithaca and London 1972).

Gilbert, Sandra M.: 'Costumes of the Mind: Transvestism as Metaphor in Modern

Literature', in *Writing and Sexual Difference*, edited by Elizabeth Abel (Hemel Hempstead 1982).

Gordon, David J.: *D.H. Lawrence as a Literary Critic* (London 1966).

Hansen, Miriam: *Babel and Babylon: Spectatorship in American Silent Film* (Cambridge, Mass. 1991).

Heath, Stephen: 'Difference' in *Screen*, vol. 19, no. 3, Autumn 1978.

Heath, Stephen: 'On Screen, in Frame: Film and Ideology', in *Questions of Cinema* (Basingstoke 1981).

Heath, Stephen: *The Sexual Fix* (London and Basingstoke 1982).

Hegel, G.W.F.: *Phenomenology of Spirit*, translated by A.V. Miller (Oxford 1977).

Hough, Graham: *The Dark Sun: A Study of D.H. Lawrence* (Harmondsworth 1961).

Irigaray, Luce: *This Sex Which is Not One*, translated by Catherine Porter (New York 1985).

Jay, Martin: 'In the Empire of the Gaze: Foucault and the Denigration of Vision in Twentieth-century French Thought', in *Foucault, A Critical Reader*, edited by David Couzens Hoys (London 1986).

Jones, Peter: *Imagist Poetry*, (Harmondsworth 1981).

Kaplan, Cora: 'Radical Feminism and Literature: Rethinking Millett's *Sexual Politics*', in *Sea Changes: Culture and Feminism* (London 1986).

Kaplan, E. Ann: 'Is the Gaze Male?' in *Desire: The Politics of Sexuality*, edited by Ann Snitow, Christine Stansell and Sharon Thompson (London 1983).

Kermode, Frank: *Lawrence* (London 1973).

Kiberd, Declan: *Men and Feminism in Modern Literature* (Basingstoke 1985).

Klein, Melanie: *The Psychoanalysis of Children* (1932) (London 1980).

Klein, Melanie: *The Selected Melanie Klein*, edited by Juliet Mitchell (Harmondsworth 1986).

Koch, Gertrude: 'Why Women Go to Men's Films', in *Feminist Aesthetics*, edited by Gisela Ecker (London 1985).

Kuttner, Alfred Booth: '*Sons and Lovers*: A Freudian Appreciation' (1916), in *Sons and Lovers: A Casebook*, edited by Gāmini Salgādo (London 1975), originally published in *The Psychoanalytic Review*, July 1916.

La Belle, Jenijoy: *Herself Beheld: The Literature of the Looking Glass* (Ithaca and London 1988).

Lacan, Jacques: *The Four Fundamental Concepts of Psycho-Analysis*, translated by Alan Sheridan (New York and London 1981).

Laplanche, Jean and Pontalis, J.-B., 'Fantasy and the Origins of Sexuality', in *The International Journal of Psycho-analysis*, vol. 49, part 1, 1968.

Laplanche, Jean and Pontalis, J.-B. *The Language of Psycho-Analysis*, translated by Donald Nicholson-Smith (London 1983).

Lauretis, Teresa de: 'Film and the Visible', in *How Do I Look?* edited by Bad Object Choices (Seattle 1991).

Lawrence, D.H.: *Aaron's Rod* (Harmondsworth 1977).

Lawrence, D.H.: *Apocalypse* (Harmondsworth 1979).

Lawrence, D.H.: *The Collected Letters of D.H. Lawrence*, edited by Harry T. Moore (London 1962).

Lawrence, D.H.: *The Complete Poems of D.H. Lawrence* edited by Vivian de Sola Pinto and F. Warren Roberts (Harmondsworth 1977).

Lawrence, D.H.: *England, My England* (Harmondsworth 1978).

Lawrence, D.H.: *Fantasia of the Unconscious/Psychoanalysis and the Unconscious* (Harmondsworth 1978).

Lawrence, D.H.: *The First Lady Chatterley* (Harmondsworth 1978).

Lawrence, D.H.: *John Thomas and Lady Jane* (Harmondsworth 1977).

Lawrence, D.H.: *Lady Chatterley's Lover* (Harmondsworth 1990).

Lawrence, D.H.: *The Lost Girl* (Harmondsworth 1950).

Lawrence, D.H.: *Love Among the Haystacks and Other Stories* (Harmondsworth 1978).

Lawrence, D.H.: *Mornings in Mexico/Etruscan Places* (Harmondsworth 1977).

Lawrence, D.H.: *The Mortal Coil and Other Stories* (Harmondsworth 1977).

Lawrence, D.H.: *Mr Noon* (Cambridge 1984).

Lawrence, D.H.: *Phoenix: The Posthumous Papers of D.H. Lawrence*, edited by Edward D. McDonald (London 1936).

Lawrence, D.H.: *Phoenix II: Uncollected, Unpublished and Other Prose Works*, collected and edited with introduction and notes by Warren Roberts and Harry T. Moore (London 1968).

Lawrence, D.H.: *The Plumed Serpent* (Harmondsworth 1977).

Lawrence, D.H.: *The Princess and Other Stories* (Harmondsworth 1980).

Lawrence, D.H.: *The Prussian Officer* (Harmondsworth 1969).

Lawrence, D.H.: *The Rainbow* (Harmondsworth 1979).

Lawrence, D.H.: *Selected Essays* (Harmondsworth 1980).

Lawrence, D.H.: *A Selection from Phoenix*, edited by A.A.H. Inglis (Harmondsworth 1979).

Lawrence, D.H.: *Sons and Lovers* (Harmondsworth 1977).

Lawrence, D.H.: *Sons and Lovers*, edited by Helen Baron and Carl Baron, (Cambridge 1992).

Lawrence, D.H.: *St Mawr/The Virgin and the Gipsy* (Harmondsworth 1979).

Lawrence, D.H.: *Studies in Classic American Literature* (Harmondsworth 1977).

Lawrence, D.H.: *Three Novellas: The Ladybird/The Fox/The Captain's Doll* (Harmondsworth 1928).

Lawrence, D.H.: *The Trespasser* (Harmondsworth 1979).

Lawrence, D.H.: *Twilight in Italy* (Harmondsworth 1977).

Lawrence, D.H.: *The White Peacock* (Harmondsworth 1979).

Lawrence, D.H.: *The Woman Who Rode Away and Other Stories* (Harmondsworth 1984).

Lawrence, D.H.: *Women in Love* (Harmondsworth 1989).

Lawrence, D.H.: *Women in Love*, edited by David Farmer, Lindeth Vasey and John Worthen, (Cambridge 1987).

Leavis, F.R.: 'D.H. Lawrence and Professor Irving Babbit', in *Scrutiny*, vol. 1, no. 3, December 1932

Leavis, F.R.: *D.H. Lawrence: Novelist* (1955) (London 1967).

Leavis, F.R.: 'The Literary Mind' in *Scrutiny*, vol. 1, no. 1, May 1932.

Leavis, F.R.: *Mass Civilisation and Minority Culture* (Cambridge 1930).

Leavis, F.R.: 'Reminiscences of D.H. Lawrence', in *Scrutiny*, vol. 1, no. 2, September 1932.

Leavis, F.R.: (ed.) *A Selection from Scrutiny*, vol. 1 and 2 (Cambridge 1968).

Leavis, Q.D.: *Fiction and the Reading Public* (1932) (Harmondsworth 1979).

Light, Alison: 'Feminism and the Literary Critic', in *LTP*, no. 2, 1983.

Light, Alison: *Forever England: Femininity, literature and Conservatism between the Wars* (London 1991).

Low, Rachael and Manvell, Roger: *The History of British Film 1896–1906* (London 1973).

MacLeod, Sheila: *Lawrence's Men and Women* (London 1985).

Mailer, Norman: *The Prisoner of Sex* (London 1971).

Man, Paul de: *Blindness and Insight: Essays in the Rhetoric of Contemporary Criticism* (London 1983).

Marcuse, Herbert: *Eros and Civilisation* (London 1969).

Mayne, Judith: *The Woman at the Keyhole: Feminism and Women's Cinema* (Bloomington 1990).

Mellen, Joan: *Big Bad Wolves: Masculinity in the American Film* (New York 1977).

Mellers, W.H.: 'The Hollywooden Hero' (1939), in *A Selection from Scrutiny*, edited by F.R. Leavis, vol. 2 (Cambridge 1968).

Melman, Billie: *Women and the Popular Imagination in the Twenties: Flappers and Nymphs* (Basingstoke 1988).

Metz, Christian: *Psychoanalysis and Cinema: The Imaginary Signifier* (Basingstoke 1982).

Meyer, Richard: 'Rock Hudson's Body', in *Inside/Out: Lesbian Theories, Gay Theories*, edited by Diana Fuss (London 1991).

Meyers, Jeffrey: *Homosexuality and Literature 1890–1930* (London 1977).

Millard, Elaine: 'Feminism II: Reading as a Woman: D.H. Lawrence, *St Mawr*', in *Literary Theory at Work: Three Texts*, edited by Douglas Tallack (London 1987).

Millett, Kate: *Sexual Politics* (1970) (London 1982).

Millett, Robert W.: *The Vultures and the Phoenix: Paintings of D.H. Lawrence* (London and Toronto 1983).

Modleski, Tania: *The Women Who Knew Too Much: Hitchcock and Feminist Theory* (New York 1988).

Moore, Harry T.: 'D.H. Lawrence and the Flicks', in *Film/Literature Quarterly* (Special Edition: 'D.H. Lawrence'), vol. 1, no. 2.

Morrissette, Bruce: *Novel and Film: Essays in Two Genres* (Chicago 1985).

Mulhern, Francis: *The Moment of Scrutiny* (London 1979).

Mulvey, Laura: 'Visual Pleasure and Narrative Cinema', in *Screen*, 16, 1975.

Neale, Stephen: 'Masculinity as Spectacle: Reflections on Men and Mainstream Cinema', in *Screen*, vol. 24, no. 6, Nov–Dec 1983.

Nietzsche, Friedrich: *Beyond Good and Evil* (1886), translated by Walter Kaufmann (New York 1969).

Nietzsche, Friedrich: *On the Genealogy of Morals* (1887), translated by Walter Kaufmann (New York 1969).

Nietzsche, Friedrich: *The Will to Power* (1883–8), translated by Walter Kaufmann (New York 1968).

Nin, Anaïs: *D.H. Lawrence: An Unprofessional Study* (1932) (London 1961).

Niven, Alistair: *D.H. Lawrence: The Novels* (Cambridge 1978).

Penley, Constance (ed.): *Feminism and Film Theory* (London 1988).

Pinkney, Tony: *D.H. Lawrence* (Hemel Hempstead 1990).

Pribram, E. Deirdre (ed.): *Female Spectators: Looking at Film and Television* (London 1988).

Ramey, Frederick: 'Words in the Service of Silence: Preverbal Language in Lawrence's *The Plumed Serpent*', in *Modern Fiction Studies*, vol. 27, Winter 1981–2.

Richardson, Robert: *Literature and Film* (Bloomington 1969).

Rieff, Philip: *The Triumph of the Therapeutic: The Uses of Faith after Freud* (London 1966).

Rolph, C.H. (Pseud. of C.R. Hewitt): *The Trial of Lady Chatterley: Regina v. Penguin Books Limited* (Harmondsworth 1961).

Rose, Jacqueline: *Sexuality in the Field of Vision* (London 1986).

Rossman, Charles: 'You are the Call and I am the Answer: D.H. Lawrence and Women', in *The D.H. Lawrence Review* (Special Issue: D.H. Lawrence and Women), vol. 8, no. 3, Fall 1975.

Sagar, Keith: *D.H. Lawrence: A Calendar of his works*, (Manchester 1979).

Sagar, Keith (ed.): *A D.H. Lawrence Handbook*, (Manchester 1981).

Salgādo, Gāmini: 'Taking a Nail for a Walk: on Reading *Women in Love*', in *D.H. Lawrence*, edited by Peter Widdowson (London and New York 1992).

Sanders, Scott: *D.H. Lawrence: The World of the Major Novels* (London 1973).

Schopenhauer, Arthur: *The World as Will and Representation*, vols 1 and 2, translated by E.F.J. Payne (New York 1966).

Schreber, D.P.: *Memoirs of my Nervous Illness*, translated by I. MacAlpine and R.A. Hunter (London 1955).

Scott, James F.: 'The Emasculation of *Lady Chatterley's Lover*', in *Film/Literature Quarterly*, vol. 1, no. 2.

Sedgwick, Eve Kosofsky: *Between Men: English Literature and Male Homosocial Desire* (New York 1985).

Segal, Hanna: *Klein* (London 1979).

Silverman, Kaja: *The Acoustic Mirror: The Female Voice in Psychoanalysis and Cinema* (Bloomington 1988).

Silverman, Kaja: 'Masochism and Subjectivity', in *Framework*, no. 12 (1980).

Simpson, Hilary: *D.H. Lawrence and Feminism* (London 1982).

Smith, Anne (ed.): *D.H. Lawrence and Women* (London 1978).

Solecki, Sam: 'D.H. Lawrence's View of Film', in *Film/Literature Quarterly*, vol. 1, no. 2.

Spiegel, Alan: *Fiction and the Camera Eye: Visual Consciousness in Film and the Modern Novel* (Charlottesville 1976).

Spilka, Mark: 'On Lawrence's Hostility to Wilful Women: The Chatterley Solution', *D.H. Lawrence and Women*, edited by Anne Smith (London 1978).

Stoehr, Taylor: '"Mentalized Sex" in D.H. Lawrence', in *Novel*, no. 8, 1975.

Stubbs, Patricia: 'Mr Lawrence and Mrs Woolf', in *Women and Fiction: Feminism and the Novel 1880–1920* (Hemel Hempstead 1981).

Sutherland, John: *Offensive Literature: Decensorship in Britain, 1960–1982* (London 1982).

Tallack, Douglas (ed.): *Literary Theory at Work: Three Texts* (London 1987).

Thompson, Mark (ed.): *Leatherfolk: Radical Sex, People. Politics and Practice* (Boston 1991).

Tims, Hilton: *Emotion Pictures: The 'Women's Picture' 1930–55* (London 1987).

Trevelyan, John: *What the Censor Saw* (London 1977).

Tristram, Philippa: 'Eros and Death (Lawrence, Freud and Women)', in *Lawrence and Women*, edited by Anne Smith (London 1978).

Veitch, Douglas W.: *Lawrence, Greene and Lowry: The Fictional Landscape of Mexico* (Waterloo, Ontario 1978).

Virilio, Paul: *War and Cinema: The Logistics of Perception*, translated by Patrick Camiller (London 1988).

Watney, Simon: 'School's Out', in *Inside/Out: Lesbian Theories/Gay Theories*, edited by Diana Fuss (London 1991).

Weber, Samuel: *The Legend of Freud* (Minneapolis 1982).

Widdowson, Peter (ed.): *D.H. Lawrence* (London and New York 1992).

Williams, Linda: 'When the Woman Looks', in *Re-Vision: Essays in Feminist Film Criticism*, edited by Mary Ann Doane, Patricia Mellenkamp and Linda Williams (Frederick, Md. 1984).

Williams, Linda R.: 'Submission and Reading: Feminine Masochism and Feminist Criticism', in *New Formations* ('Modernism/Masochism'), Spring 1989.

Williams, Linda R.: 'The Trial of D.H. Lawrence', *Critical Survey*, Spring 1992.

Woolf, Virginia: 'Mr Bennett and Mrs Brown' and 'The Cinema' (1926), in *Virginia Woolf: Selections from her Essays*, edited by Walter James (London 1966).

◆
Index